Footloose Pilgrims

P
STOC

P
CITY

In Memory of
Edward Richard "Doc" Lynam
1898–1971

Library of Congress Control Number:		2014915322
ISBN:	Hardcover	978-1-4990-6601-2
	Softcover	978-1-4990-6602-9
	eBook	978-1-4990-6603-6

First Edition

This book was printed in the United States of America.

Rev. date: 08/26/2014

To order additional copies of this book, contact:
Xlibris LLC
1-888-795-4274
www.Xlibris.com
Orders@Xlibris.com
638198

Footloose Pilgrims

A Journal of Moped Travels
Through Europe

Dick Lynam
&
Bill Lynam

CONTENTS

ACKNOWLEDGMENTS

I will be forever grateful to, Maria—my dedicated and loving wife, partner, and friend, whose inexhaustible energy and enthusiasm made this project happen.

Special thanks to Neill Oswald Kuehn for translating the original typed document into digital form.

Kudos to Scott Craig for exemplary editing and editorial assistance in getting the wrinkles out of the text.

Love and appreciation to my son Ian for his incredible assistance, art direction, and technical skills that allowed this journal to reappear after being ignored for so long.

PREFACE

MY BROTHER AND I KEPT A JOURNAL of our impressions while traveling through post-war Europe in the 1950s. We saw Europe rebuilding with the aid of the Marshall Plan after the end of World War II. The Russian occupation was threatening half of Europe, and there was much concern about what this meant.

We started our journey slowly and with experience made travel mode changes and picked up a little speed. Initially, we hitchhiked and did a lot of walking in the rain in England, Ireland, and Scotland. On the continent, it was three-speed bicycles for a while, then on to mopeds—motorized bikes—so we could get up those hills and cover more distance and still stay in budget. We made this trip on a shoestring at a time when the exchange rate to the dollar was favorable.

Growing up in the U.S. Pacific northwest, Dick and I were familiar with our part of the country but were also intensely curious about all those other places we knew about but had never visited.

Our only out-of-country experience was when we went to Vancouver College, a boarding school run by the Christian Brothers of Ireland in Vancouver, British Columbia, for two years. It was the third and fourth grade for me and seventh and eighth for Dick at that school.

Returning to the United States, I went to St. Leo's Grade School, while he went to Bellarmine High in Tacoma, Washington. We both attended Seattle University.

In British Columbia, I picked up a Canadian accent and learned their way of spelling. Later, I was reminded that it was not the way "Yanks" sound or spell. In high school, we picked up the rudiments of Latin, reading Cataline, Cicero, and Virgil's *Aeneid*. In college, we picked up a little French and Spanish, four years of Aquinian philosophy, and degrees in English literature. Having been inoculated with contemporary and classical languages and Western European history, our goal for this trip was to ascend the steps of the Parthenon in Athens. We also had the desire to bust out of the cocoon of our current lives and see how the rest of the world worked and lived.

You can only read so much about foreign ports of call before they pique your curiosity to see them in person. From the seventeenth century to about 1840 and the commencement of railroad transportation, it was the English fashion of the upper class to send young men off to Europe for the Grand Tour. We'd read about this and decided to put together our own grand tour. In truth, it was a modest tour. Instead of staying for years and learning the language and mores of the Europeans, we set out to buzz through Europe, hopefully on $5 a day, and absorb as much of the scene as we could. We thought it was something like the *hajj*—the pilgrimage a Muslim must make—to travel at least once in a lifetime to Mecca in Saudi Arabia to circle the Kaaba and show solidarity with Islam.

It would take about 6,500 miles to step on the European continent. Other than curiosity about the eastern United States and Europe, we'd heard that Sir Thomas Beecham, a visiting British conductor in Seattle, stated that "Seattle was an intellectual dustbin." As natives and upholders of the local flame, we took umbrage. We vowed to overcome any provincialism we might harbor and make sure that we became world travelers, intellectually fit and not tainted with close-minded, xenophobic prejudices.

Dick graduated from Seattle University two years before our trip in 1954 and then did a six-month tour of duty as a U.S. Army liaison officer at Aberdeen Proving Grounds in Maryland to fulfill his Second Lieutenant's Reserve Officer Training Corps commission. After leaving active duty, he found his way to Galveston, Texas and worked for the *Galveston Daily News*.

I was a sophomore at Seattle University when we jointly decided to go to Europe and bicycle the continent. The plan was to search out ships going to and from Europe that would be affordable and give us sufficient travel time in between so we could see all the wonders of the "old country."

We decided to pool whatever earnings we could accumulate beforehand to afford this adventure—Dick from his newspaper earnings and myself from my boiler tender wages at Boeing, where I worked while an undergraduate.

I researched ship fares that had European destinations in *Fodor's Europe on $5 Dollars a Day*. The *Arosa Kulm*, a Panamanian registry ship that was departing New York for England, was the most promising. Its departure date of September 5, 1958 became our target date. We put a down payment on the trip, so we were committed. I also found the Compania Colonial de Navigaceo's ship, the *Santa Maria*, that would take us home again from Lisbon, Portugal, via many ports of call: Vigo, Spain; Funchal, Madeira; Tenerife, in the Canary Islands; La Guaira, Venezuela; Havana, Cuba, and Ft. Lauderdale, Florida, before going on to Brazil.

We had to round up passports, visas, yellow fever inoculation shots for South America, international driver's licenses, traveler's checks, and letters of good character from the local police, plus luggage and clothing. I quit my job at Boeing and Dick his on the Galveston newspaper. He drove up to Washington State in his 1949 canary yellow Oldsmobile, that would take us across country.

We asked Jim Baydo, our neighborhood friend, to join us, but he was just back from graduate work at the London School of Economics and working, so could only do the cross-country portion of the trip before returning to his job in Seattle.

When Dick arrived in Puyallup in August, all arrangements were made. We were ready to start our drive across the United States to New York City and find our ship, the *Arosa Kulm*, to begin our grand tour of Europe and other continents on the cheap.

Throughout our trip abroad, our dad, Ed Lynam, handed our letters home to a local columnist at the *Puyallup Valley Tribune*. They published them in our hometown newspaper, so our friends, neighbors, and the town folk knew of our travels. At the end of our adventures, Dick typed our journal—more than half a year of constant travel that changed the way two brothers viewed the world.

Bill Lynam
Prescott, Arizona

Bill Lynam, Jim Baydo, Dick Lynam in front of Dick's 1949 Oldsmobile as we are about to begin our trip to New York from Puyallup, Washington.

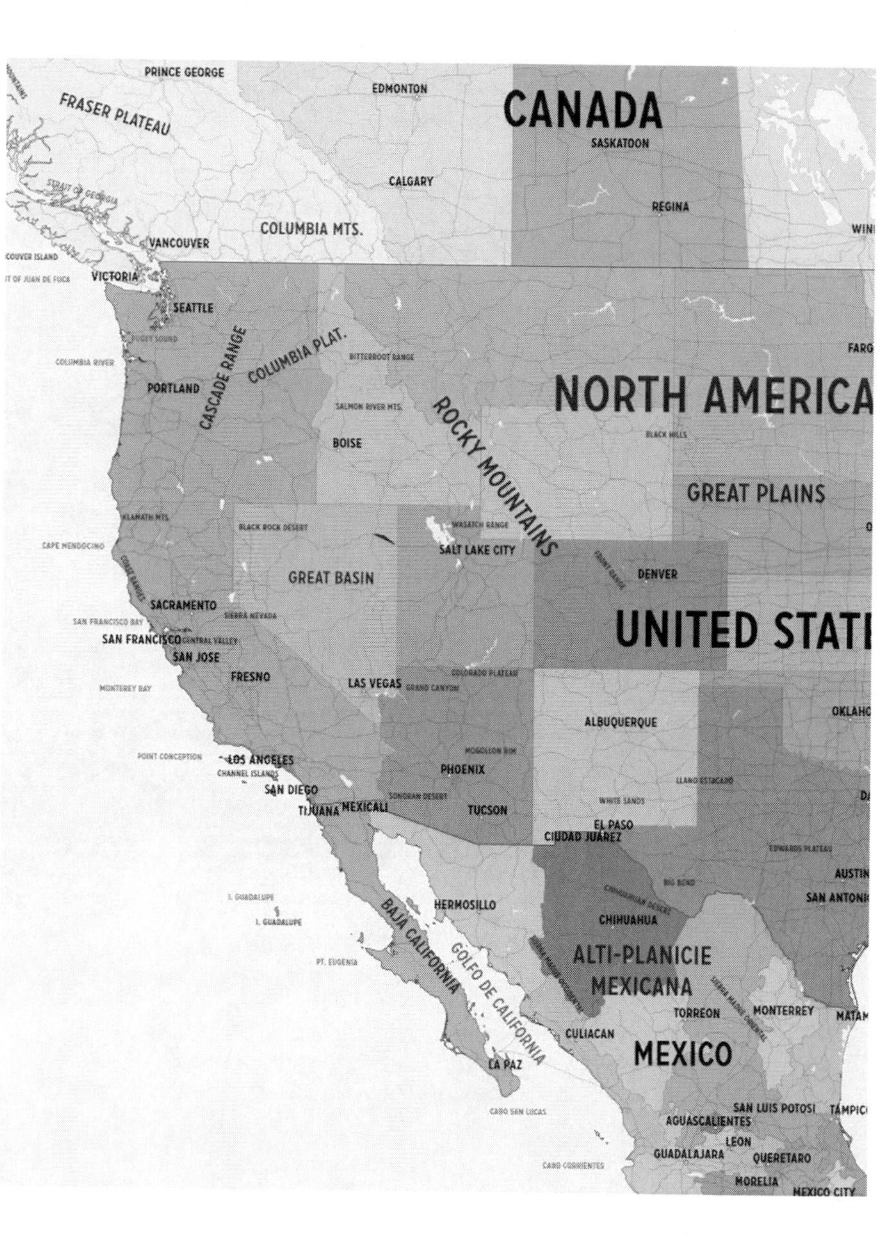
PRINCE GEORGE
EDMONTON
CANADA
FRASER PLATEAU
SASKATOON
CALGARY
REGINA
COLUMBIA MTS.
VANCOUVER
VICTORIA
SEATTLE
CASCADE RANGE
COLUMBIA PLAT.
PORTLAND
NORTH AMERICA
ROCKY MOUNTAINS
BOISE
GREAT PLAINS
SALT LAKE CITY
GREAT BASIN
DENVER
SACRAMENTO
UNITED STAT
SAN FRANCISCO
SAN JOSE
FRESNO
LAS VEGAS
ALBUQUERQUE
LOS ANGELES
PHOENIX
SAN DIEGO
TIJUANA
MEXICALI
TUCSON
EL PASO
CIUDAD JUÁREZ
HERMOSILLO
BAJA CALIFORNIA
CHIHUAHUA
GOLFO DE CALIFORNIA
ALTI-PLANICIE
MEXICANA
TORREON
MONTERREY
CULIACAN
MEXICO
LA PAZ
SAN LUIS POTOSI
AGUASCALIENTES
LEON
GUADALAJARA
QUERETARO
MORELIA
MEXICO CITY

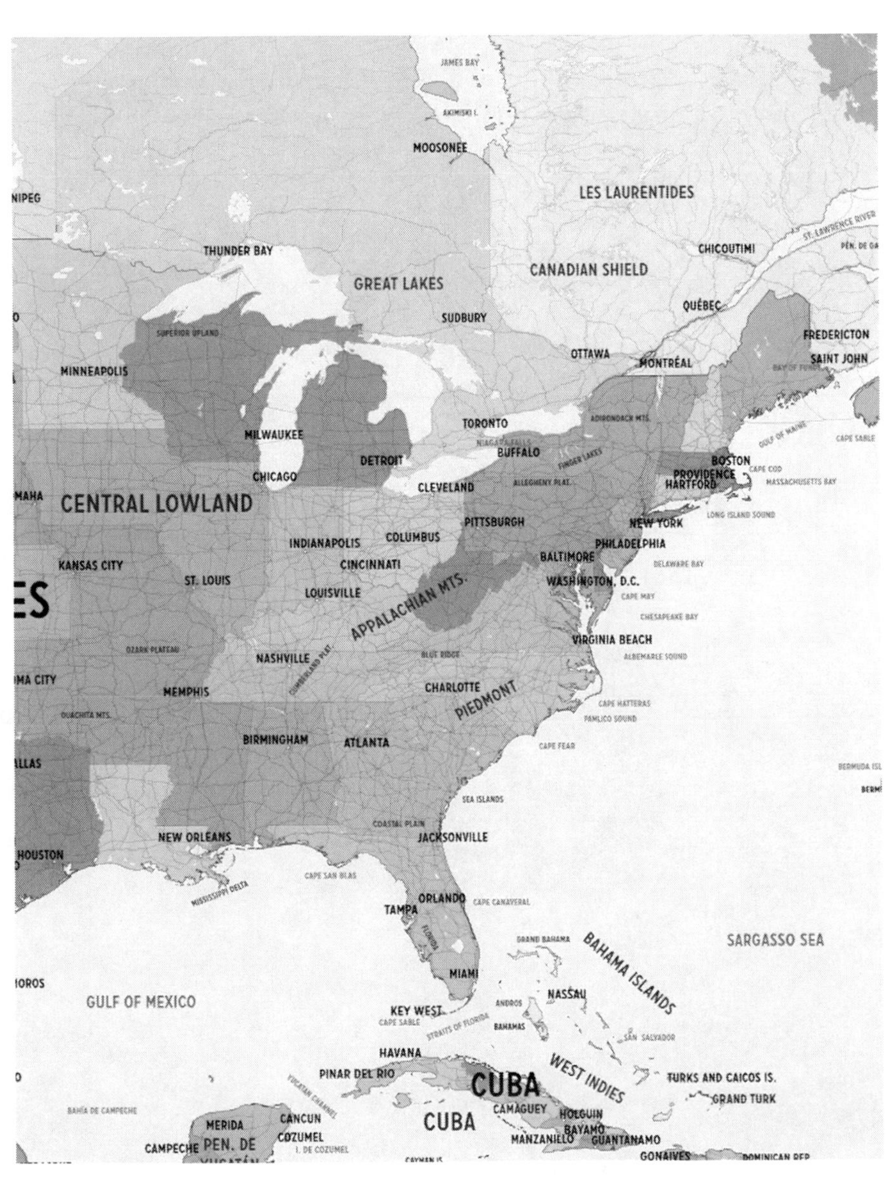
JAMES BAY
AKIMISKI I.
MOOSONEE
LES LAURENTIDES
ST. LAWRENCE RIVER
THUNDER BAY
CHICOUTIMI
GREAT LAKES
CANADIAN SHIELD
QUÉBEC
SUDBURY
SUPERIOR UPLAND
FREDERICTON
OTTAWA
SAINT JOHN
MONTRÉAL
MINNEAPOLIS
ADIRONDACK MTS.
TORONTO
MILWAUKEE
GULF OF MAINE
CAPE SABLE
BUFFALO
FINGER LAKES
DETROIT
BOSTON
CHICAGO
PROVIDENCE
CAPE COD
HARTFORD
MASSACHUSETTS BAY
CLEVELAND
ALLEGHENY PLAT.
CENTRAL LOWLAND
NEW YORK
LONG ISLAND SOUND
PITTSBURGH
PHILADELPHIA
INDIANAPOLIS
COLUMBUS
BALTIMORE
DELAWARE BAY
KANSAS CITY
CINCINNATI
WASHINGTON, D.C.
ST. LOUIS
CAPE MAY
LOUISVILLE
APPALACHIAN MTS.
CHESAPEAKE BAY
VIRGINIA BEACH
OZARK PLATEAU
BLUE RIDGE
ALBEMARLE SOUND
NASHVILLE
CUMBERLAND PLAT.
MEMPHIS
CHARLOTTE
PIEDMONT
CAPE HATTERAS
OUACHITA MTS.
PAMLICO SOUND
BIRMINGHAM
ATLANTA
CAPE FEAR
SEA ISLANDS
COASTAL PLAIN
NEW ORLEANS
JACKSONVILLE
HOUSTON
CAPE SAN BLAS
MISSISSIPPI DELTA
ORLANDO
CAPE CANAVERAL
TAMPA
FLORIDA
GRAND BAHAMA
BAHAMA ISLANDS
SARGASSO SEA
MIAMI
GULF OF MEXICO
NASSAU
ANDROS
KEY WEST
CAPE SABLE
STRAITS OF FLORIDA
BAHAMAS
SAN SALVADOR
HAVANA
WEST INDIES
PINAR DEL RIO
TURKS AND CAICOS IS.
CUBA
YUCATAN CHANNEL
GRAND TURK
BAHÍA DE CAMPECHE
MERIDA
CANCUN
CAMAGUEY
HOLGUIN
CUBA
BAYAMO
CAMPECHE
PEN. DE
COZUMEL
MANZANILLO
GUANTANAMO
I. DE COZUMEL
GONAIVES

CHAPTER 1 CROSS COUNTRY

AUGUST 19–22, 1958

There is no moment of delight in any pilgrimage like the beginning of it.
—C. D. Warner

ON THE EARLY MORNING of August 19, 1958, two brothers, Dick and Bill Lynam, and Jim Baydo left Puyallup, Washington to drive across the United States. This was the beginning of a trip they had envisioned for over a year and it was Day 1, launch day.

It took them a day to shake down their routine of one driving, one sitting next to the driver, and one sleeping in the rear seat. No one was tired enough the first day to sleep in the small backseat of Dick's 1949 canary yellow convertible with too many miles on it. Going hard across eastern Washington with the top down—it was balmy, Dick spotted the Russian satellite Sputnik, which he and Jim had never seen before. Sputnik was the first artificial satellite to be put into an elliptical low-Earth orbit.[1] It traveled at 18,000 miles per hour and took only 96.2 minutes to complete an orbit. As it tumbled across the sky, it picked up reflections of the sun and twinkled in its night arc.

They hit Spokane about midnight and got through it effortlessly on their new system of throughways. After winding through Coeur d'Alene and gassing up in Missoula, they were only 117 miles from Helena, Montana, with good road conditions and level ground until they started to climb.

On one of the summits, Dick hollered at Bill, who was sleeping in the back, that they were at the top of the Rockies. Bill rose up blearily and slumped back to oblivion. Arriving in Helena around 11:00, they drove on to East Helena for breakfast and picked a place called the

Cottage Café, which they all agreed later had the worst chow all the way across. From East Helena, Jim drove to White Sulphur Springs, made a short stop, and continued on across Montana to Harlowtown, where Dick did some banking and Bill took over the wheel.

From Harlowtown to Forsythe, it was a long stretch across the plains for 160 miles. Toward the end of it, they resorted to a songfest to get over the last miles to Forsythe and supper. Pulling in with the late afternoon sun, they managed an excellent meal at the Joseph Café and walked around town shaking it down a bit before starting off again. Their Bermuda shorts got quite a rise from the natives—cowboys don't wear shorts. They bid farewell to Forsythe just before dark and encountered thirty-three miles of miserable twisting road from there to Miles City, where Jim and Dick had a coffee stop while Bill slept.

They arrived in Bowman, North Dakota and gassed up just before midnight. It was considerably cooler than in Montana. The countryside began to look greener and the road improved markedly. Jim took over at Bowman and drove to Mowbridge, South Dakota. On the way, he was flagged down by a deputy sheriff, who was looking for some hot check passers driving an Edsel with Texas plates. After the sheriff took off, the three of them joked and said all cars must look alike in North Dakota, except for tractors and hay wagons. A little later on, some farmhands came by and waved and hollered, "Why don't you get your car washed?"

After pulling into Mowbridge about 4:00 in the morning, Bill took over and Dick moved up front and had a couple of hours to clear the cobwebs out of his head before he drove again.

Bill drove through South Dakota in the early dawn. It was foggy in the low spots, and he had to use the windshield wipers to remove the heavy condensation. The gentle rolling country had good roads. Thirty miles out of Ortonville, Minnesota, they stopped for breakfast.

As things turned out, they ate only two meals a day and maybe a snack. Staying awake most of the time, fortunate or not, they expended almost no physical energy except in driving.

Out of Ortonville, Dick had a short shift at the wheel and relinquished it to Jim. Bill was sleeping in the back, so Dick sat next to Jim and slept until they neared Minneapolis. Jim drove through there with much cursing and gnashing of teeth.

Minneapolis/St. Paul, without a doubt, is one of the most tiring and confusing cities to drive through in the United States. It was quite maddening. Bill took over on the other side of the twin cities and crossed the Mississippi River to a small town in the Wisconsin Lake District. They hit fairly good roads en route to Madison, Wisconsin, but numerous small towns kept them from making good time. They hit Madison in the late hours and bypassed it to connect with U.S. Highway 30 into Ft. Wayne, Indiana.

They gassed up there and proceeded through the city, trying to get on U.S.-33, but got lost. After some meandering, they got on the right track again and had a late breakfast in Decatur. From there, they pushed on to just the other side of Columbus, Ohio, where they stopped and split six bottles of "Old Dutch" beer three ways.

At that point, the end was in sight, and they felt they could relax a bit. Out of Columbus, Jim drove about twenty-five miles into West Virginia, crossed the Ohio River at Parkersburg, and ate at the end of Jim's run. The Appalachian Mountains were a sight, and Bill took over from Jim and got them as far as Salem before Dick took over. All the way from West Virginia's state line, the road had been mountainous, steep, winding, and twisting. Getting bottled up behind a slow driver meant getting stuck. As tired as they were, this tended to put an inordinate strain on their self-control. Dick took over in Salem and continued this torturous driving over some steep grades. The motor had almost no poop left. When it lost its RPMs, Dick shifted down and it roared like hell with no muffler.

They got as high as 2,800 feet, but within a few miles, they were back in a valley again, set to do it all over. After 130 miles in this fashion, Dick stopped at a tavern about fifteen miles out of Romney, where he bought six beers and retired to the back. Jim drove another sixty miles or so, cutting through a tip of western Maryland and back into West Virginia, where he handed the wheel over to Bill, got six beers for himself, and joined the party in the backseat.

They arrived in Winchester, Virginia, on the twenty-second at 11:30 p.m., checked into a hotel, unloaded the car, and took showers, which loosened them up a bit. They got to bed about 2:00 a.m. and slept for half a day.

CHAPTER 2 THE EAST COAST

August 23 to September 9, 1958

Go confidently in the direction of your dreams. Live the life you've imagined.—Henry David Thoreau

WASHINGTON, DC AND BALTIMORE, MARYLAND

THEY LEFT WINCHESTER at 3:00 p.m. the next day, heading for Harper's Ferry, thirty miles away. Stopping there for a little over an hour, they proceeded to Washington, DC, another fifty-eight miles away.

Hurricane Daisy arrived about the same time. Winds were up to 40 mph and pelted everyone with fat drops of rain. The hurricane had tracked up the east coast, offshore, and was on its last legs before turning into an extra tropical cyclone off the coast of New England. They found shelter in the YMCA just two blocks from the White House. The "Y" was on G Street, but they had to park the car on S Street to keep it legal during the day. They toured the town Saturday night on foot, but a slight squall came up and gave everything a thorough drenching, so they retired to their rooms with some imported Dutch beer and sloe gin, which did an excellent job of killing the evening.

Since they were Fenian mackerel snappers, Bill and Dick observed the Catholic rite of Sunday Mass and fish on Friday. On the twenty-fourth, they went to church at St. Matthews, where ceiling fans were turned on to circulate the sticky humid air. From there, they went back to the "Y" and fetched Jim. Picking up the Oldsmobile on the way to Mass, they all drove to Arlington Cemetery and walked to the Marine Memorial, a massive bronze statue commemorating the hoisting of the flag at the island of Iwo Jima in the Pacific theater during World War II. The oxidization of the bronze gave the figures a green patina. Overall, it was haunting. From there, they went on to the Tomb of the Unknown Soldier—with its connecting amphitheater—which is constructed of white Alabama marble. On the hour, they saw the impressive changing of the guard, which, at set intervals, pace the length of a mat and then repeat in the opposite direction, walking very stiff-legged. The sentinel marches twenty-one steps, turns, and waits for twenty-one seconds, then repeats the same number of steps in the opposite direction. Twenty-one was chosen because it symbolizes the highest military honor that can be bestowed—the 21-gun salute. The entire Changing the Guard ceremony lasts about ten minutes, and the numerous tourists have their role when it comes to saluting the flag.

After driving through rows of identical white tombstones, they went back to town across the memorial bridge and explored the Lincoln Memorial, which is Greek Revival architecture, supported by columns—thirty-six of them—one for each of the states at the time of the president's death in 1865. Inside is a mammoth statue of Lincoln seated in a chair, 19 feet tall. It's made out of Georgia marble and was sculpted by Daniel Chester French. The inscription behind the statue of Lincoln reads: "In this temple, as in the hearts of the people for whom he saved the Union, the memory of Abraham Lincoln is enshrined forever."

They walked over to the Washington Monument, and Jim thought it gave a good view of DC, but wasn't impressed with it as a structure. From the pictures and drawings adorning the walls inside, they learned there had been several false starts at erecting it. Construction began in 1848 but was halted from 1854 until 1877, partly for lack of money, politics, and the Civil War. At that point, it was only 152 feet tall. They didn't finish it until 1884, and it was officially opened in 1888, having risen to over 555 feet and was crowned with a 100 oz. aluminum apex that was considered to be as costly as silver at the time.[1] Later, in New York, they found out they went through the same process with the Statue of Liberty. They spent the remainder of the afternoon viewing the National Museum of Natural History, the Smithsonian Institute, and the National Art Gallery in quite a hurried fashion. To do justice to even one of them would require weeks, so the superficial coverage they gave them only entitled them to say they were there, not that they digested them.

From Washington, Bill drove to Baltimore with a side trip to the Baltimore Airport, in order to watch the planes. They sipped a sack of beer as they watched the landings and take-offs.

Getting into Baltimore around 9:00 p.m., they stopped and toured the "Block" of 400 East Baltimore Street from the sidewalk. A strip containing strip clubs, sex shops, and other adult entertainment vendors, it was noted as a starting and stopover place for many of the well-known burlesque dancers, including Blaze Starr. This consumed almost an hour and was interesting because the hawkers in front of the musical bars kept trying to entice them inside. They drove on to Aberdeen, Maryland, and tried to get inside the Army base where Dick had recently been stationed. When the military policeman mentioned it was closed, they drove back through Aberdeen to a wood a few miles west of town, where they slept in the car. This was fine and saved money, at the expense of a crick in the neck.

Gaining admission to Aberdeen Proving Grounds (APG) the following morning, Dick returned some technical manuals and visited some of the personnel he had known when he was on active duty. With that out of the way, they all went over to the Officers Club swimming pool and took their first dip of the whole journey. Earlier, they had gone over to the Ordinance Corps Museum and inspected the armored tanks and weapons from various different countries on display, most of them dating from World War II. Bill was impressed with a German Panzer tank that had been hit by a heat round and had a six-inch hole burned into the front of it before being deflected up and out. The path of the shell told the story.

GETTYSBURG AND PHILADELPHIA, PENNSYLVANIA

FEELING REFRESHED after their swim, Bill drove from APG to Gettysburg, Pennsylvania, getting lost only once. At Gettysburg, they checked into the Adam's House Hotel, which they later discovered was built on foundations laid prior to the Civil War. Looking forward to tramping over this historic battlefield the next day, they contented themselves with observing the natives, eating an excellent meal, and taking in a flick.

The following day began with a tour of the area, which meant looking over Little Round Top and Big Round Top, Devil's Den, and the site of Pickett's Charge. They climbed over the rock fences and trod the grass where the battle took place. Some parts of the terrain were hilly and difficult to climb, others level and grassy. The site of Pickett's Charge looked idyllic, ringed by trees with fall foliage and stone boundary fences. The temperature was in the eighties, just a little cooler than on July 3, 1863, the third day of the Battle of Gettysburg, when Confederate Maj. Gen. George Pickett, under the command of Lt. Gen. James Longstreet, led a charge of soldiers against Union forces.[2] This decisive battle resulted in over fifty percent casualties for the South of the approximately 13,000 troops Gen. Lee had marched north to Pennsylvania and then dropped down into the hamlet of Gettysburg, defended by Union General George Meade's forces. Many years later, when Gen. Pickett was asked why his charge at Gettysburg had failed, he replied: "I always thought the Yankees had something to do with it."[3]

Dick was under the impression that Philadelphia was only sixty miles away, so the next day, they were in no hurry to get going and left Gettysburg after brunch.

It turned out to be 110 miles to Philadelphia through the Pennsylvania Dutch countryside, with its unique stone tobacco barns decorated with folk art hex signs. They checked into the "Y" and unloaded the car. This was the end of the road for the Oldsmobile. It had served long and faithfully, but now someone else needed it. They headed out to South Philly, looking for used car lots to sell it. The Olds had done its duty and public transportation to New York and a ship was readily available. Several of the dealers took a look at the car and kicked the tires. It still ran and that was good enough for the third guy they engaged. He offered $35, which Dick eagerly snatched. They bid a fond adieu to the Oldsmobile, and parting with the car at that stage of the game for Dick was like giving a gold watch to an old employee he was sad to see leave, but happy that he was going. They took the subway downtown and spent the evening roaming around, acquainting themselves with the place.

The following morning, Jim and Bill went off to see Independence Hall and the Benjamin Franklin Institute of Science. Dick took in the Rodin Museum of Art and the Philadelphia Museum of Art. They knew the cracked Liberty Bell was around there somewhere, but they didn't do a very good search and missed it. They reunited again toward dark in the courtyard of City Hall and pub-crawled until bedtime.

NEW YORK CITY, NEW YORK

THEY CAUGHT THE 10:00 a.m. train for Manhattan Island, arriving five hours later. The "Y" was full and they referred them to the Le

Marquis Hotel on Thirty-first Street, just off Fifth Avenue. As it turned out, it was a better deal, and they were unpacked and settled within an hour. Jim lost the toss and was allocated the cot. That night, they took a walk up to Times Square and around the Radio City district. They were within easy striking distance of Radio City Music Hall, St. Patrick's Cathedral, Rockefeller Center, the United Nations, and Central Park. Earlier that day, they had all taken a ride on the Staten Island Ferry. It was possibly the biggest bargain anyone could ever find in New York: a nickel each way.

After Sunday Mass at the architecturally distinctive St. Patrick's Cathedral, they joined Jim, who had been exploring on his own all morning, to explore Rockefeller Center and walk up Fifth Avenue to Central Park. Strolling around leisurely, they made their way to the Bowery in the late afternoon. At one time, this part of Manhattan was a well-mannered part of town, but it had slid down the social scale. The Bowery was noted for flophouses, whiskey joints, and notable bums, but now was populated with celebrity lounges and high-priced lofts. Their visit was during a sunny day, and all the vagrants seemed content to stroll the streets without hitting-up the intruders from the West who prowled their lanes.[4]

On Labor Day, they stayed out, wandering and gawking at Gotham and took it easy. The next morning, Tuesday, they confirmed their sailing at the Arosa Line Office, which was located a few blocks from Wall Street. With that settled, Jim and Bill took the ferry to the Statue of Liberty. They both looked for names of relatives who got off the boat and were processed through Ellis Island. Photos of the lines of immigrants and the conditions of the 1800s illustrated what an important monument Ellis Island is to American social history. Bill didn't know if Jim found any of his relatives, but he knew he wouldn't find any of his. The Lynam oral history had it that an Irish relative was invited off the boat to join the Union Army to fight in the Civil War when it anchored in New York harbor. He declined and continued on to Halifax, Nova Scotia, in Canada, where the family settled before coming back to the United States for the Alaskan Gold Rush.

That night, they had sort of a farewell party. Jim was heading west, back to the Pacific Coast, and Bill and Dick were en route to Europe, to the east. They found their way to Max's Tavern down the street from the Le Marquis and faithfully promised to send John, the bartender, a postcard from every country they visited. He received one from Dublin, Ireland, anyway.

The next day, while Jim was packing for his flight home, they took in the United Nations Building, situated on the East River. Dick wore his army Bermuda shorts, and the guard tut-tutted him, saying he couldn't go into one of the meetings dressed like that.

Jim's plane left at 10:30 that evening, so they took the subway to Idlewild Airport. Jim enplaned and, by pre-arrangement, was met by his friend George Whitney at the Sea-Tac Airport outside of Seattle. He was ready to go back to work at Central Refrigeration the next day.

With Jim safely off, the two of them wandered around the recently constructed part of the airport, marveling at the varicolored fountains. Taking the subway home, they got back to the hotel at midnight.

Bill Lynam and Jim Baydo kibbitzing on a bridge over Central Park Lake, NYC.

CHAPTER 3 AT SEA—THE NORTH ATLANTIC

SEPTEMBER 5–15, 1958

The real voyage of discovery consists not in seeking new landscapes but in having new eyes.—Marcel Proust

THEY EMBARKED on the *Arosa Kulm*, which was Swiss-owned, staffed with both German and Italian sailors, and registered in Panama. Boarding time was two in the afternoon, but the ship's departure was delayed by a storm until that evening. At 7:50, the ship got underway to Plymouth, the scheduled port of entry to England. Dinner was called soon after, so they didn't see the lights of Manhattan recede. There were only fifty-three passengers on board—not many, considering the ship's capacity of 830—so they had plenty of space to make the voyage quite pleasant.

By the time dinner was over, they were out of the narrows and into the Atlantic. They dropped the bar pilot off to a waiting boat at Ambrose Light eleven miles out and departed from the United States. A member of the Sandy Hook Bar Pilots Association, their pilot was required to bring ships in and out of harbor. There were also just docking pilots who, once in harbor, bring ships to moorage and take them out. The bar pilots have to know the location of fickle currents, the channel depth, the draft of the vessel, and mast clearance to make it under bridges. If that were not enough, they need to know where the sandbars, rock ledges, shoals, sunken vessels, and buoys are, all the while looking out for kayaks, sailboats, and other ships in the right-of-way. Any mistake where a mishap were to occur on their part can bring the law down on the pilots with fines and even jail time. One of the bar pilots, Jeff McAllister, said, "There are five or six federal agencies that will crawl up your ass when you fuck up, and gladly do it."[1]

It was foggy, so they had nothing better to do than go back to bed and read after breakfast. That night, there was a dance, which broke the ice. Their fellow passengers were mostly students on vacation, but some professionals were going to overseas assignments or school. The son of a Greek American couple, whose family ran a candy store in the Bronx, was on his way to medical school in Bologna, Italy. He had to spend the first semester learning Italian before he could begin his medical studies. Dick and Bill tended to hang out with the singles found at the bar, and they narrowed acquaintances to those who could close the bar and hang out until the wee hours of the morning.

Our fellow passengers enjoying the crossing to England on the MS Arosa Kulm.

When it was clear and sunny, the deck chairs were broken out, things perked up. The food was good and there was lots of it, so everyone probably gained weight eating and sitting around. That night, there was another dance in the *Bierstube,* which was supposed to be a replica of a Bavarian beer hall. The band was made up of crew members who played an instrument or could sing, such as Senior Donatini, the ship's electrician.

The day dawned foggy and rough. Dick took a Dramamine and spent the afternoon lightly dozing and the evening reading. Bill was perhaps the better sailor and enjoyed the rough seas just fine. Tuesday the weather became worse, with winds up to Force 6 or strong breeze of 21 to 26 knots on the Beaufort sea state scale of 12. The ship rocked and plunged quite a bit, and Dick was not alone with his disturbed equilibrium.

The weather improved greatly and everybody on the boat seemed full of pep. People started walking the deck, lounging outside, and generally getting their sea legs. They had a little session of blackjack, which lasted two hours, and then a group joined them around the bar until 3:00 in the morning. They went off to their cabins a little later, after sniffing around the galley for snacks and were up late the next morning for lunch. Dick went back to bed until tea time, usually served around 4:00 p.m. There was an open-air dance scheduled that night at 8:30, and that was a novel experience, given they were 1,900 miles out into the Atlantic. The next day marked being on board for a week, and it had passed quickly. The meals came one after another, and soon it was evening, time for a little dancing in the *Bierstube.* Even with an ordered routine, the days sped by.

The ship was rescheduled to dock at Le Havre, France, and the Plymouth passengers were to take a ferry back to Southampton, but that changed. They were now going to Southampton direct instead. It was partly cloudy that day, but they made it to breakfast for the second time since New York, then spent most of the day reading. They enjoyed a few beers in the Bierstube and were in bed by 10:30. Bill, however, stayed up another six hours and joined in late for lunch.

Bright and clear with a brisk breeze from the southeast, they saw a ship, the first in five days. They were due to land some time in two days, so that night was the captain's dinner. They didn't eat much while sitting at the captain's table, although the food was good. After so many days at sea, where initially they ate like horses, now the fare was beginning to get tiresome.

They were supposed to sight Bishops Rock Lighthouse, four miles off the Isles of Sicily, Cornwall. The light is said to shine for twenty-four miles, but the fog and mists that evening obscured their view. It got its name from the eponymous chess piece—it simply looks like one. It subsequently had a helipad attached to its roof, dating from 1858, and it was eventually upgraded to an automatic station.[2]

After the dinner, there were some skits put on by the passengers. One especially good one was a knock at the entertainment director who was a hell-for-leather German organization man. *Alles ist in ordnung! (Everything Is in Order!).* One of the passengers wrote a skit that mocked an overly organized person with lots of fake German words to make the point. Several passengers played the parts that led up to the ribbing given the guy. They were a little unsure how he took it, but they themselves found it uproarious. There was more singing and dancing by the passengers, then Senor Donatini again supplied vocal solos until his voice gave out. His repertoire included *Nel blu di pinto di blu (Volare), Che Cos'e l'amore, Fratello sole sorella luna,* and other Italian goodies. By three that morning, they were ready for breakfast and their clique of eight fellow travelers scurried around the ship and dug up some hot rolls from the baker and butter from the officers' mess.

Overall, they traveled 2,815 oceanic miles according to the ship's news. Bill threw some bottles left from the party overboard with notes in them giving his address and date, with a request to know who picked it up, when, and where. He hoped to get at least one reply.

Dick playing monkey-boy in the riggings of the MS Arosa Kulm.

Land's End, at the tip of Cornwall, was in sight that night at 5:45 p.m., which put them in the English Channel, just off the coast of "Merrie England." The phrase, an archaic spelling, refers to the Victorian period and the English stereotype, a utopian conception of English society and culture between the Middle Ages and the onset of the Industrial Revolution, of a nostalgic society incorporating the thatched cottage, the cup of tea, the Sunday roast—a rather mythical landscape.[3] But they knew this was not going to be the England they'd be exploring.

Many lighthouses and small towns were visible on the English shore. Dimly, through the mist, they could see the French coast. At 10:30 a.m., they dropped anchor off Southampton, England, and were quite ready.

OUTER HEBRIDES
ABERDEEN
NORT
INNER SEAS
GLASGOW
EDINBURGH
GREAT
BRITAIN
H ISLES
BELFAST
LEEDS
ISLE OF MAN
IRISH SEA
MANCHESTER
UNITED
KINGDOM
DUBLIN
LIVERPOOL
BIRMINGHAM
IRELAND
CARDIFF
LONDON
BRISTOL CHANNEL
ENGLISH CHANNEL
LANDS END
GUERNSEY
JERSEY
NORMANDIE
PA

SKAGERRAK
GÖTEBORG
'H SEA
KATTEGAT
JUTLAND
ØRESUND
KØBENHAVN (COPENHAGE
DENMARK
ZEALAND
MALMÖ
MECKLENBURGER BUCHT
STETTINER
WADDENZEE
FRISIAN IS.
HAMBURG
BREMEN
BERLIN
AMSTERDAM
NETHERLANDS
HARZ
ROTTERDAM
ESSEN
LEIPZIG
COLOGNE
BONN
GERMANY
BRUSSELS
ERZGEBIRGE
LILLE
BELGIUM
FRANKFURT
PRAG
ARDENNES
CZECH
LUXEMBOURG
BÖHMERWALD
LUXEMBOURG
ARIS
STUTTGART

CHAPTER 4 ENGLAND

SEPTEMBER 16–19, 1958

> *To my mind the greatest reward and luxury of travel is to be able to experience things as if for the first time, to be in a position in which almost nothing is so familiar it is taken for granted.—Bill Bryson*

THEY WERE OFF THE BOAT—finally—on English soil and had a chance to stretch their sea legs in the Southampton Ocean Terminal. Southampton is in an estuary where two rivers meet—the Rivers Test and Itchen. A port for cruise ships and freight with container terminal, it was the place where the Pilgrims departed aboard the *Mayflower* in 1620 and the *Titanic* in 1912. It was also the home port for the *RMS Queen Mary and Queen Elizabeth.*[1]

Leaving Southampton, they hitchhiked to London, seventy-four miles away. Two short hops and one long one took them out twelve miles from the city. The last fellow who picked them up, Jack Morris, worked as an elevator operator on the *Queen Elizabeth* and had just come in from New York. He was on his way up to his home in London. He invited the two of them in for tea to his flat. His wife whipped up an omelet and a spot of tea. They talked about an hour and a half, and then Jack took them to the Boston Manor "underground" station, where they caught the subway to Tottenham Court Road. At that point, they were just off Piccadilly Circus, in the heart of the *Mecca of the Saxons,* wandering around for a while before finding the "Y" on Great Russell St., close to the British Museum. Billeted in a well-lit room in the new wing at a cost of $1.68 or "12 shillings the two," they got settled and walked over to see Jacqueline, aka "Goggie," one of Dick's old flames he'd met in Seattle. Goggie lived in a Queen Anne house, a nineteenth-century architecture style, that was on the estate of the former Duke of Bedford. She had married and had a baby, so they got out of there fast.

"So much for old girlfriends," Dick said, and the brothers went to a pub down the street, *The Lamb*, where they ate a dinner consisting of pale ale, cheese, and buttered rolls.

Walking back to a main thoroughfare, they caught a double-decker bus to Piccadilly Circus. The road junctions and public space of London's West End in the city of Westminster link to the theaters on Shaftsbury Avenue, as well as to Haymarket, Coventry Street, and Glasshouse Street. In the heart of the theater district of London, the hub could be likened to New York City's Times Square, with the glare of neon signs blinking, with traffic through, and the busy tube of the London Underground System spewing travelers onto the circus. Walking around there for a couple of hours, they took in a cinema, Charlie Chaplin in *A Night on the Town*, with Ben Turpin, made originally as a 1915 silent film with dubbed-in dialogue.

LONDON

THIRTEEN YEARS AFTER World War II, there was little evidence of visible war damage in downtown London, except for some chipped brick and stone higher up on some buildings' facades. Right away, Bill noticed that people were more polite than in the United States, saying "excuse me" or "sorry" for almost no reason. They also often volunteered helpful information without being asked. For example, a woman in a little shop overheard Bill asking for a bookstore. She waited outside until they came out, because she didn't want to hurt the shop owner's feeling, since he had a few books for sale also. She directed the brothers to a bookstore down the street.

They visited the British Museum and its fine antiquities. And, viewed the Rosetta Stone, the *Magna Carta,* documents with the signature of Elizabeth I, parts of the frieze from the Parthenon, the first copy of the *Anglo-Saxon Chronicles,* a manuscript by Venerable Bede, and a heck of a lot more. The *Rosetta Stone,* found in 1801 near Alexandria, had three different sets of inscriptions on it, all saying the same thing, but in different languages or form, and this was the key for Egyptologists to decipher the ancient Egyptian hieroglyphics, as well as the Egyptian demotic script, a precursor to a form of Arabic. The early Greek inscription, the third engraving, broke the code to the Egyptian pictographs.[2]

The *Magna Carta,* dating from 1215 and written in Latin, was also known as *The Great Charter of the Liberties of England.* It was significant, since it limited the power of the king by law and protected the people's privileges.[3]

The *Elgin Marbles* were 257 feet of sculpted bas relief marble, hijacked by Lord Elgin in 1816 from the top of the Parthenon on the Acropolis in Athens. The Greeks have been trying to get the stone work back from the British since.[4]

The *Anglo-Saxon Chronicles* cover the period from 60 BC to AD 1154. They are a collection of the annals, or yearly histories, of the Anglo-Saxons written in Old English.[5]

Venerable Bede was an English monk, who in 735, wrote *The Ecclesiastical History of the English Peoples,* a history of the English Catholic church. He was later rewarded by a later pope with sainthood.[6]

One could spend a lifetime in the British Museum and never see it all. It's packed to the rafters, and they were overwhelmed by the artifacts of history piled all around. There seemed no end of things they'd heard or read about and nestled in that building and certainly more in the basement unseen. Another curiosity was a namesake of their father, who was formerly the superintendent of the map room until 1950, Dr. Edward Lynam, a prolific promoter of the map room and scholar on the history of cartography.[7]

After the museum, they took the bus down to the oldest part of London, which had been hit heaviest by the blitz, and later made way to the Tower of London and London Bridge. The blitz was German dictator Adolph Hitler's way to bring England to its knees before invading. He wanted to demoralize the English and make them capitulate easily. Lasting from September 1940 until May 1941, with nightly bombings of London and other major English cities and ports, the event resulted in 40,000 deaths, 140,000 injuries, and 1,000,000 homes lost. The blitz continued until Hitler moved his bombers to invade Russia. Some block fronts were missing buildings in the interior. Only the jagged teeth of foundations remained, though most of the debris and litter had been removed. The gutted buildings they saw starkly contrasted with the new construction under way—eighteen years after the raids.[8]

They crossed the Thames on London Bridge, which was supported by the original 600-year-old Elmwood piles. London Bridge was falling down by 1962, but that wasn't the first time. The nursery rhyme of the same name has been traced to the Roman occupation in the first century, when the first London Bridge was made of wood and clay and burned to the water's edge. The bridge they walked on was built in 1831, but couldn't handle the traffic flow across the Thames. In 1967, the bridge was closed and subsequently sold to an American, shipped to the United States, and reconstructed in Lake Havasu City, Arizona in 1971.[9]

When they re-crossed the bridge, they came to the monument designed by Sir Christopher Wren, commemorating the Great London

Fire of 1666, where fire gutted the medieval city of London inside the Roman wall. It was estimated to have destroyed the homes of 70,000 of the city's 80,000 inhabitants.[10]

Climbing Wren's 202-foot-high monument that sported a circular staircase of 311 steps to the top, the city beneath them, they took in the view of St. Paul's Cathedral to the south, about five blocks and the Tower of London, six blocks to the north. Afterward, they sauntered over to the Tower of London and saw the "Beefeater" guards in their bearskin shakos, dressed in their distinctive uniforms, the traditional guards of the tower. The structure actually comprised an enclosure with different buildings dating back to Anglo-Norman times, from 1066 to the sixteenth century. They saw the spot where Mary Queen of Scots, Anne Boleyn, Lady Jane Grey, and other historical personages got the ax.

In the Bloody Tower, which was constructed in the thirteenth century, existed an early printing of Sir Walter Raleigh's book, *The History of the World* (1614), beside the bed where he wrote during his thirteen years of imprisonment from 1603 until 1616. James, the First, had Raleigh's head for returning from Guyana without gold. Unfortunately, in writing his history, he only reached up to 200–197 BC before the blade went snick. At his execution in 1618, Sir Walter asked to see the ax that was to behead him and exclaimed, "This is sharp medicine, but it is a physician for all diseases." The custom of the time was to embalm the head and present it to the wife. Elizabeth, Lady Raleigh, is said to have carried it in her purse at all times until her death twenty-nine years later.[11]

Starting to get a little footsore by then, they staggered through the display in the White Tower with its display of weapons and cannons, and the brothers absolutely couldn't leave without seeing the Crown Jewels kept in the Jewel Room of the Jewel Tower. Kept in an octagonal glass case, they were displayed on velvet and lit from above. The Koh-i-Noor diamond and the Star of Africa, aka the Cullinan, the largest—the size of a medium egg—set in a scepter, sparkled. The Koh-i-Noor diamond was of great interest to them, to see it and know its fascinating history. Koh-i-Noor means "Mountain of Light." It is not the largest diamond or the brightest, nor does it have the best color. In fact, it has a streak of gray in it, so it doesn't equate with the Great Mogul, the Hope Blue, the Cullinan, or the Jonker. However, as a stone with a history of murder, torture, and intrigue, it reigns supreme. Captured by the British after the second Sikh War in 1849, it is a diamond of dispute and claimed by India, Iran, and Pakistan. Belief has it the stone carries a curse, because all the men who have owned it have either lost their throne or suffered setbacks. The curse goes back to a Hindu text from 1306 and states: "He who owns this diamond will own the world, but will also know all of its misfortunes. Only God or a woman can wear it with impunity." Queen Victoria is the only reigning British monarch who has ever worn this 105.602 carat stone. The story goes on to say that if the monarch is male, the stone is passed to a spouse—just to be safe.[12]

While in the Tower, they saw all sorts of saltcellars, ceremonial maces, the spoon used to anoint the king, state crowns set with innumerable diamonds, rubies, emeralds, and an assortment of other precious stones.

Strolling along the Thames embankment after the museums, they enjoyed seeing the boat traffic and the scenes along the river. Crossing over to the east side of the Thames on the Tower Bridge completed in 1894, which was a combination bascule and suspension bridge. Bascule, or seesaw in French, was for the drawbridge part, which works on a pivot and has a heavy weight at one end to balance the greater length at the other.[13] The towers of the bridge contain the gears and mechanisms for raising the bridge center span lifts, whereas the London Bridge was built on Roman arches. After walking down the east side of the river as far as the London Bridge, they took the bus back to the "Y."

After resting a while and cleaning up, they had dinner at the *Brassier* restaurant, which featured an orchestra playing Viennese Waltzes. They both had braised beef in wine sauce, tossed salad, milk, and coffee, for $2.75. By then, 8:00 p.m. had rolled around, so they decided to take a walk through the Soho district. Although there were quite a few nightclubs in the area and a few prostitutes soliciting on the sidewalk, it was pretty tame. Apparently, the brothers didn't look like playboys, as they were never approached, but continued to tramp around a lot of narrow lanes and side streets until about 10:30, sampling the local brew occasionally and finally ending up just a few blocks from the "Y."

Thursday morning, two expeditions lay ahead: one to the Hostel Organization on John Adams Street, the other to the Inland Waterways Association (IWA) on Emerald Street. The hostel told them to wait until the first of October before joining, because that would give them memberships through all of 1959. Of course, they only wanted a place to stay while in England.

They also sought the help of the IWA in the hope of getting some free rides on the canal barges that ply the myriad canals and waterways of England. Staff were kind enough to inform them that the workers on these barges make their homes aboard. Some barges have no more than a seven-foot beam or less, which would hardly accommodate two "long johns" like themselves, let alone the barge master and his family. As far as working aboard, papers were required, which would take too much time to acquire. The unions had their finger in the pie too. After these two fruitless excursions, they decided to hitchhike to Edinburgh,

375 miles north. Their mode of travel, hitchhiking or tramping—"trampin," as the English referred to it—was merely to save funds. They started by taking the bus from London to get to the outskirts of the city, making it to the North Road, some 12 miles out, at Barnett.

M1—THE NORTH ROAD

THEIR LUCK WAS GOOD for the first eight hours. They were able to get rides from five to fifty miles at a time. The people who picked them up ran to no one class; rather, they were from a cross section. A Colonel Blimp-type left the impression of being friendly enough, but who never quite got over his reserve. Blimp was a cartoon character from the 1930s, who was satirized as pompous, irascible, jingoistic, and stereotypically British.[14] Their Blimp implied that, as Yanks, they didn't quite make the cut. A potato merchant from Biggleswade, returning from London after delivering produce from his farm, chatted away and told them that for about 100 miles on the highway north of London, a group of ladies had a concession in prostituting to the lorry drivers who swarmed the road at night.

After the potato merchant dropped them off, they got a ride in a Jaguar, hitting a straight stretch of road at up to 110 mph with only the parking lights on, a leftover practice from nightlight restrictions during World War II, so that German aircraft would not target traffic on the motorways. They passed through the eastern edge of Sherwood Forest, Robin Hood's hangout, twenty miles from Nottingham, where they got out at the village of Stamford.

The history of Nottingham went back to AD 1100. Most of the houses were half-timbered and looked ancient. They had a half pint of bitters at a pub called *The Greenman*, which had been in operation as a tavern since AD 1400, and found out that the term "bitters" has a gradation of terms indicating alcohol content by volume (abv). It goes from: best bitter, 4.2–4.7 percent; special bitter; extra special bitter; and premium or strong bitter, 4.8 percent abv or greater, not to mention Boy's bitter, under 3 percent abv. The terms are associated with cask beers and also related to the amount of hops in the beer. Drinkers are said to have a hard time distinguishing between the types of bitters. By 1830, the terms pale ale and bitters were synonymous, and some brewers only refer to their product as pale ale.[15]

In speaking with those at the bar, they said America was far ahead of England, and they were the tail of the dog that wagged and not the dog. Agreeing reluctantly that Americans were ahead of them in many respects, it was only tactful on their part of the brothers to remind them that they did a thing or two in the field of aviation and many other sectors to cheer them up.

They then caught a ride with an American Air Force man, who took them as far as Brawty. Walking out of town about a quarter mile to a trucker's café, they soon caught a ride with a lorry driver to Doncaster, where they had to walk over a couple of bridges to get out on the highway.

The Honorable Joe Blackburn, the ex-mayor of Pontefract, picked them up next. While driving, he gave a monologue on the traditions and beauties of York and recommended seeing its walled city, one of the few in England.

"You Yanks need to see Pontefract. It's mentioned in Shakespeare's *Richard III*. Our history goes back six hundred years," he said. The gentleman must have belonged to the local version of Kiwanis or Rotary, since he was all for boosting the image of his city. The brothers told him that on the way back, they'd be sure to stop in and thanked him for the ride. Quickly, they hitched another ride in Ferrybridge and were let out in the middle of nowhere late that night. Thumbing for three quarters of an hour before walking a half mile on, a lorry driver offered a ride. He was an interesting sort, born and raised in India, heading for Newcastle-on-Tyne. They could have rode on with him but decided to get off at Scotch Corner, which was the most direct route to Scotland. They stood there amusing themselves for about an hour and a half without too much strain, but after that, they started to get cold, since it was raining lightly. That's about the time they asked themselves what the hell they were doing in northern England at 5:30 in the morning, standing in the roadway and absorbing dewfall.

A restaurant light turned on down the road, so they went there for breakfast and finally met a driver who was going their way. They passed through some rolling terrain and verdant country on the way past Penrith on up to Carlisle, just below the Scottish border. That's where they had tea, outside of Carlisle, and then stood in the rain again until a lorry picked them up going to Glasgow.

Originally headed for Edinburgh, they didn't feel like standing in the rain anymore, so they changed plans on the spot and decided for Glasgow. They crossed the Scottish border at Gretna Green, famous for quickie marriages—records show some ten thousand in one year. Scottish law was more lenient regarding marriage age—sixteen versus twenty-one years of age on the English side of the border and no need of parental consent. Marriage arrangements are still the prime industry in this village—going strong since 1754. This was the Scottish answer to Las Vegas and Niagara Falls. About five thousand marriages a year are performed here. An oil lorry driver picked them up from there and drove on into Glasgow.[16]

CHAPTER 5 SCOTLAND

SEPTEMBER 19–20, 1958

Travel is fatal to prejudice, bigotry and narrow-mindedness.—Mark Twain

EXHAUSTED, THEY ARRIVED in Glasgow, Scotland, at 2:40 p.m., approximately twenty-four hours later and 400 miles from London. The lorry driver left them in the center of the city, a slummy part of town. The area was very grimy, the inhabitants burned a lot of coal, so buildings over twenty years old were black or streaked with soot. The temperature was brisk, but there were quite a few kids running around in short pants playing kickball on the cobblestone streets with streetcar tracks. They took a double-decker streetcar, vintage about 1915, to the "Y" and got rooms. It felt good to take baths and do the laundry, which had been piling up. After getting squared away, they took a walk down to the city center about three blocks away and found a pub.

After downing a few and becoming famished, it took a while to find a decent restaurant. After dinner, they felt well enough to go exploring but saw nothing more exciting than a few "Teddy Boys," a British subculture style of clothing affected by young men after World War II, influenced by the Edwardian era mode of dress for dandies. Typically, it featured pegged trousers, long coats, and embellished waistcoats. It was somewhat similar to the "zoot suits" that became popular in the United States about the same time.[1]

There were a lot of redheads in town, and most of the women were fair-skinned. From deduction, they assumed that the nippy air made the calves of their legs and their cheeks exceptionally rosy—characterized by a "peaches and cream complexion." For night life, however, Glasgow probably hit the bottom of the pickle barrel.

Everything closed at 9:30, and people deserted the streets by 10:00. This was the effect of the Liquor Licensing Act of 1853, which restricted pub hours that were not loosened until its overturn in 1976.[2]

They checked their bags at Glasgow Central Station and purchased tickets under a huge glassed-in shed. A key feature of the station, a glass-walled bridge called "Heilanman's Umbrella," made them chuckle, because it seemed a very appropriate name, given how much it rained. They took a tram to the Glasgow Museum, next to the University of Glasgow. Two hours was enough for the museum, so they headed back to town and caught a bus for Paisley, 9 miles out and across the River Clyde.

They looked in the phone book for the sister of Dick's friend, Mary, from Galveston, Texas. Her name was in the phone book, but the phone was out of order. After a couple of false starts, they got headed in the right direction and found the address without any trouble. When Mrs. Leckie, Mary's sister, saw them coming up the walk, she thought, "There go two Americans." She told them later that when they turned into her door, all sorts of things raced through her mind. They said hello at Mrs. Leckie's door and explained Dick's friendship with Mary. She invited them in and made them welcome.

Meeting, the family, including Tommy, the dog, who had been lost for a fortnight, they were so absorbed in talking that they forgot the time and were very pressed to make the 9:00 p.m. ferry to Belfast, Ireland. They accomplished this by walking over to Glasgow Road and catching the bus to the city, hopping over the River Clyde, and grabbing a cab to the train depot to get their bags. Then, it was off to the pier, making it to the gangplank at 8:55, just minutes away from the ferry's departure. Just like that, they were on their way to Ireland . . .

CHAPTER 6 IRELAND

SEPTEMBER 21–26, 1958

The use of traveling is to regulate imagination by reality, and instead of thinking how things may be, to see them as they are.—Samuel Johnson

THEY TRAVELED SECOND CLASS, which included a berth at an extra $1.12. The boat had a bar downstairs, where they met a fellow, Pat, from San Diego, who was also traveling around. He was an Irishman who worked in Glasgow and was going over to see his mother in Belfast. Later, they ran into a couple of Irish nurses on their way home. They sat talking in the bar until midnight and then called it a night. At 6:00, bright and early, they were up as the boat was about to dock.

A cup of tea put them right, and they disembarked onto the Emerald Isle, four blocks from downtown Belfast. Nothing was open so early, and Pat accompanied them for breakfast and they finally found an open restaurant at the Great Northern Railroad Station. After breakfast, Pat went northwest to Londonderry, and the brothers went to Mass, preparatory to leaving for Dublin, to the south. In looking for churches to attend in the phone directory, they found there were twenty-four Catholic churches in Belfast. The Holy Cross Church they attended had a very intricate, multicolored mosaic floor around the altar, which was a work of art.

Afterward, they took a bus to the edge of town. The journey to Dublin was approximately 100 miles. They caught their first hitchhike in all of Ireland and pumped him for all the local lore they could get, and the stories lasted as far as Banbridge. The next hop was a lorry tanker full of milk. The truck driver had friends in Miles City, Montana, which was quite a coincidence, since they had just passed through there on the drive across the country. He dropped them at Newry, where a doctor took over. They crossed the border with him into the Irish Free State, a.k.a. Eire, The Republic of Ireland, or just called "The South," in contrast to the predominantly Protestant Northern Ireland. The good Dr. Connelly bought them a couple of Guinness after crossing over and said he had a daughter in Boston. His Irish brogue was not so difficult to understand as was the Scottish, and he was great company. He left them at Dundalk, halfway to Dublin. The doctor, like many others, expressed a far keener sense of social distance or closeness to the United States than to Great Britain in his conversation.

After walking a couple of blocks to the other side of town, another fellow offered a short hop to Castle Bellingham. It started to rain a bit as they thumbed for rides, but found protection by huddling under an overhanging tree. They noticed many thatched roofs in the south and were to see many more as they traveled. Nothing seemed to be dying for lack of water. The lawns and fields were green and the turf springy. Ireland lived up to its name as the Emerald Isle.

After two hours under that tree, they started walking toward Dublin. Two or three miles on foot and an ale later, the gods deemed them worthy of another ride as far as Dunleer, a prosperous village of about six hundred people that depended on an electrical appliance factory nearby for its bread and butter. Spending a half hour thumbing to no avail, there was no traffic. Everyone was at the Gaelic football match between the town's team and that of Drogheda, in the stadium across from the roundabout where they were loitering. While they waited for a ride on the road and were being blessed with Irish drizzle, they also listened to the crowd roar when one team or another made a goal. Then, the gates were opened and the folks drove for home. Most were locals, since no one offered them a ride.

A half hour later, the Drogheda team's bus came along and almost passed them by, but then slammed on its brakes. A head came out of the door and yelled, "Hey, you blokes jump on!" And boy, were they willing, after standing in the bone-chilling rain as long as they had! Immediately, the team found out they were Yanks and, therefore, had to know all those American songs like *The Yellow Rose of Texas, Deep in the Heart of Texas*, et al. For the next umpteen miles, their fare was singing their hearts out about Texas, Swanee, and as many other songs as the team wanted to sing. The funny thing was the team knew more of the lyrics than they did. The Drogheda's had won the match and were highly pumped up. They got the brothers as far as Drogheda itself and dropped them off on the main road. Again, they walked. The bus driver caught up to them on his way home and gave a second lift for about four miles. From there, it was "shank's mare" almost to Balbiggan. They walked along in the light of a half moon, past thatched, white-washed cottages as everyone whizzed past.

View down O'Connell Street before it crosses the River Liffe.

Finally, they flagged a bus down at 9:30 p.m. and were in Dublin by eleven. They landed at O'Connell Street, which was well lit. There were crowds of people about, restaurants open, and theaters still going. They located a restaurant, where Dick ate mutton and Bill a hamburger. Neither meal was very good. Then they found a hotel for $1.40 (10s/).

The river Liffey runs through the center of Dublin and is bisected by O'Connell Street, the main drag. Almost all of the signs in Eire are bilingual: Gaelic and English. The former is similar to Basque, in that it requires several words to express what English expresses in one word. Many or perhaps most of the pubs in Dublin buy Guinness in hogsheads of fifty-four-gallon drums from the brewery, then bottle and cork it themselves. Their Number one selling slogan is "Guinness is good for you." They also found out it can be rather bad for you.

As they caught rides or hobnobbed at bars, Dick and Bill were asked a lot of questions about the United States, and they answered as best they could, from politics to climate, to quality of life, perhaps with a bit of a spin after several Guinness, but always to their favor.

On September 23, a Tuesday, they visited the Guinness Brewery. It was reputed to be one of the largest in the world, but others have outdistanced it since. Guinness furnished free postcards, so while they waited for enough people to come for a tour, they scribbled furiously. The tour took an hour and a half, and at the end, free samples of the product were given to drink. They ran an experiment to see how long it took for a pencil inserted in a glass of Porter to fall from a vertical position in the center of the beer head to the edge of the glass—fourteen minutes! Unfortunately, they did not have the time to repeat the experiment and thereby say something definitive on the frostiness of Porter beer heads, but it was certainly entertaining.

Guinness was a paternal company to work for, as all employees were given free medical care, and according to the guide, there was a certain amount of "esprit de corps" amongst the company workers.

Bill and Dick bought rain capes that day to ward off the ever-present rain. Clad in their new gear, they left Dublin on the twenty-fourth and headed west, ending up in Sligo, north of Galway, 132 miles from Dublin. They had good luck 'trampin' and made it to Sligo on the west coast by 5:00 p.m., hitching only three rides the entire way. They crossed the river Shannon, but sad to relate, it looked like any old river. The upper stretches of the Shannon resembled Sammamish Slough in Seattle, with almost no banks and grassy fields up to the edge.

Their one big hop let them off at Boyle Abbey, a site in ruins, which had been built between 1160 and 1220. It had belonged to the Catholic Cistercian Order and was turned into a military barracks when the Protestant revolt started at the end of the sixteenth century. They passed a number or ruins of former Cistercian monasteries and churches that were burned and sacked during the Reformation, when Oliver Cromwell's troops marched through the countryside, desecrating most of the Catholic religious edifices. The church lands were turned over to English lords. Cromwell was a Puritan who tried to reform the Church of England along Calvinistic lines but failed. He was the Lord Protector of the Commonwealth from 1653 to 1658.[1]

Boyle Abbey was used as a military barracks until the end of the eighteenth century and then abandoned. Much of it had fallen down. One of the walls of the nave was buttressed to keep it from tumbling, but the rest of the stonework was in reasonable shape. Off the south transept were the kitchens, solarium, and refectory. The monks' cells were built from there out to about 200 feet in a continuous wall which enclosed a grassy courtyard the length of the church. The only part of the abbey that had a roof left was the chancel or part containing seats for the clergy and choir, but it

Ground view of Sligo Abbey, a ruined abbey in Sligo, Ireland built in 1253 as a Dominican Friary. It was destroyed by fie in 1414, ravaged during the Tyrone War of 1595 and once again in 1641 during the Ulster Uprising.

was in shaky condition. The former floor was covered with lush, verdant grass a foot high. They climbed a tower over the entrance and discovered an ancient circular stone staircase that wound around tightly. The tower went up about forty feet. From the top, they peered down the length of the nave into a courtyard on the right. They poked their noses into one of the cells that had a "no nonsense air" about it. There were places in the wall for a fireplace or a shelf and room for a bed and table. It must have been rather clammy in the winter, when the chill permeated the stone walls.

There was a "tinker," or Irish traveler, on the road with a flatbed cart pulled by a donkey in the dusk. They refer to themselves in Gaelic as "an Lucht siuil," or the walking people. His wife and two children were huddled on the cart in the rain, among a pile of possessions. The man walked up front, leading the animal. They didn't acknowledge the brothers, just plodded on by. From what the brothers gathered talking to the locals in pubs, the travelers never worked and just wandered all over Ireland bumming or stealing off the farmers, occasionally mending a pot or pan or maybe doing an odd job here and there. They lived outside year-round, sleeping in crude tents or horse-drawn wagons with their families. The travelers were supposed to be very healthy, but a British Department of Health and

Aerial view of the nave of Sligo Abbey.

Children study said otherwise, that over half the travelers do not live past thirty-nine years. Also, it was noted they were significantly poorer than the general population. Gathered from talking to the locals, Dick and Bill found there was widespread prejudice against the travelers and ostracism of the group.[2] There are said to be about 30,000 travelers living in the Republic of Ireland and another 1,500 in Northern

Ireland. Their language is called Cant, Gammon, or Shelta, and their lifestyle is similar to Romany Gypsies, but they are of a different ethnicity.[3]

They checked into a bed-and-breakfast in Sligo for $2.75 per night. On their way in to the city, they encountered Knocknarea Hill, and on top was a cairn made of fist-sized stones. According to local legend, it was the tomb of Queen Maeve, one of the Iron Age queens of Ireland. Archeologists believe it may actually date back to 3000 BC, and the old boys may have slipped Queen Maeve into the existing monument. Legend claims it's bad luck to remove a stone, but good luck to take one up to the top and deposit it.[4]

Sligo is located on an inlet a few miles from the Atlantic and is protected by a ring of small islands. Garavogue River runs through the town and empties into the head end of the inlet, providing ideal small-boat anchorage. The town had about 10,000 people, whose main occupation was agriculture. They walked out along the docks lining the inlet, then back through the village to downtown, and had high tea, which was the same as dinner, and then took in a tired movie for lack of something to do. They allowed smoking in the theaters, so everybody puffed up a storm, but there was no ventilation provided. When they came out, their eyes watered like crazy, and they realized why the picture got hazier and hazier.

The folks they met in the west of Ireland were very accommodating and easy to get along with. They seemed to have time to talk, as though two Yanks were the most interesting people in the world. There was an exception, though, when they went to a dance in a small, southern Irish town, Bally something, and after a few dances, they were invited outside. The local boys were protecting their lassies from foreign invaders and suggested they duke it out or get lost. Given their numbers, the better part of valor was to slink away, and so they did. They were perceived as the equivalent of the Vikings come to raid their little hamlet and take away their damsels.

Speaking of town names in Ireland, the words "Bally," "Ballyna," or "Ballina" are derived from the Gaelic and mean "place of." For example, Dublin in Gaelic is *Baile Atha Cliath*. The word "Dublin" is from Old Irish and means "black pool."[5]

That night, after the movies, they went into a place to get tea, and there was a young fellow who said he remembered seeing them in Dublin. He noticed because they were so tall, which seemed to intrigue the natives around there. Dick was 6'6" and Bill 6'4" and many locals queried their religion. When they said "RC," they seemed quite relieved, as though, had they been anything else, shunning would have been in order. They rejoiced with, "I'm so glad" or something to that effect.

Overnighting in Sligo, they were en route to Armagh, the ancient home of the Irish kings. Plans were changed, because the road to Armagh was so little traveled and opportunities for a ride were scarce. They did manage a lift from town with a priest to about four miles out, and then, since traffic was light, they walked a while. The road ran along a coastal plain at the foot of a range of high hills, the most prominent of which was Benbullin. They kept on ambling along until coming to a circular, roofless tower. Across the road from the tower was a small church surrounded by the Drumcliff graveyard, where W. B. Yeats is buried. Noted as a poet, he was responsible for the Irish literary revival and was a co-founder of the Abbey Theatre.[6] They walked into the cemetery and snooped around for his marker, finding it near the left side of the church. Back on the road, they boosted one another to look in the tower window. It was a disappointment, as there were only loose rocks on the floor and the top was open to the sky.

They made it to Donegal, where they ate lunch and pushed on. Ham sandwiches, tea, and pastries cost thirty cents, the cheapest ever in Eire. As they traveled north, the country began to get rockier and hillier. At Bundorass, they were along the Bay of Donegal and could see the surf breaking on the strand about three quarters of a mile in the distance. At one point, they were in view of Lord Mountbatten's estate on a low hill that swept toward the sea. The estate had a bird's eye view of the bay.

Representatives of the Irish Republican Army (IRA) planted a radio-controlled bomb in 1979 on Mountbatten's boat, killing him, two more, and injuring others. A cousin of Queen Elizabeth and the godfather of Prince Charles, he was the last Viceroy of India and presided over the end of the British Raj or rule of India.[7] The bombing was just one more event in the ongoing terrorism of the IRA against the British.

Walking outside of Donegal, a driver picked them up heading for Londonderry. They meandered around a bit on side roads and crossed the Northern Ireland frontier at Strabane. The customs officer asked if they had bought anything in the Free State, and they answered in the negative.

Crossing the River Foyle, they arrived in Derry at 7:00 p.m. One of the most ancient in Ireland, the main part of town is surrounded by a wall 400 years old. A city of just 80,000, with a Scottish background, meant that everything closed early. At dusk, the shops were all locked shut.

Prices were higher than in the south, the Irish Free State. They tried a hotel, but they wanted $2.78 or a quid each. They tried a Salvation Army hostel for thirty seven cents each, only it was way too ratty. Thinking of heading out toward Belfast, they finally found a place called Ross's Bar, a bed-and-breakfast on Waterloo Street for

$2.75, the head. The bartender/owner played the banjo and was a jazz fan. His son, fourteen years old, was quite interesting. He was studying Latin, French, and Gaelic in school. Bill put him to the test and had him read some Gaelic, so they could know what it sounded like—everyone that they encountered spoke English.

They had bacon and eggs for breakfast, which was becoming a diet staple. Everywhere they sucked it down, it was greasy. Anyone with a tender stomach had better beware. In fact, they never saw a green vegetable on a plate, but everyone seemed healthy enough. Interestingly, they were initially mistaken for Scotsmen or Australians, until people spoke them.

After looking at County Donegal, they understood why their ancestors left the place. The farmers cultivate steep hills, where the cows and sheep wore terrace-like paths in the hillsides looking for forage. It was unfortunate for them to Miss Armagh, the seat of the ancient kings, but they wanted to catch the boat back to Glasgow. They spent the night in Derry in a cheap hotel with miserable beds that sagged and felt like hammocks.

Quitting Derry at 11:00 a.m., they made it to Belfast by 5:00 p.m. They took a northerly route and passed through Colerane, Ballymoney, Ballymena, and Antrim in Ulster Province.

The symbol of Ulster is the red hand. According to legend, all the chieftains of various Pict clans were lined up in boats, and the first one ashore who laid his hand on the ground would be chief over all. The head of the O'Neill's saw he wouldn't be there first, so he cut off his hand and threw it ashore, thereby claiming the kingship.

On their way to Belfast, a young chemist took them for a ride and proceeded to give his formula for an aphrodisiac. The difference between Scotch and Irish whiskey is that the Scotch has the fusel oil removed, he said, but Irish whiskey, like Jameson's, did not. He went on to playfully explain, "Now, if this formula is to work, one needs at least five shots of Irish whiskey followed by fish and chips liberally doused with malt vinegar (acetic acid). The two, fusel oil and acetic acid, form amyl acetate, a powerful synthetic aphrodisiac. Of course, if you drink too much, you fall on your ass, or if you can't stand the vinegar, too bad, lad." From what they gathered, it was still a theoretical formula.

They had dinner in Belfast, drinking hard cider and Guinness in a pub near the terminal. Boarding the boat back to Scotland, they ran into a crowd of folks that had the same idea of getting aboard early and getting a berth for the night. They were all taken and the brothers didn't get one, so they spent the night sitting up reading, trying to doze, and taking occasional walks on deck. It was very nippy, so the walks were very short. A full moon lit the sky and the northern horizon, so it looked faintly light all night through. During the passage, they were never out of sight of land. Coming into Glasgow, they spent quite a lot of time crawling up the River Clyde at "Slow Ahead" and only covered 110 miles in nine and a half hours.

The Irish have a greater sense of social closeness to the United States than to Great Britain. To them, the United States is just a matter of a few miles to the west, while Scotland and England are far, far away. They were always asked if they knew someone's cousin or brother in Boston or New York, as though it was just around the block, and they had to tell them they lived 3,000 miles to the west of the east coast, beyond the Rocky Mountains and the Cascades in some misty dell of a place, very much like the west coast of Ireland. They embellished a little, of course, especially after a few Guinness, mentioning they caught fish from the sea—salmon, halibut, flounder—with great ease, as if they swarmed there. If they were hungry, they went moose, elk, or caribou hunting and kept the freezers full. The streams were full of trout and could be caught as easily as telling them to jump into the net. They didn't need garbage collection services, as the grizzly bears would come into backyards and eat whatever was left out for them. They kept a 30.06 rifle at the door for varmints and life was good. The Irish listened kindly and most likely had no idea whether they thought the two of them were full of bull or blarney, but they certainly believed in America, the shining land.

CHAPTER 7 BACK TO SCOTLAND

SEPTEMBER 27–30, 1958

The journey not the arrival matters.—T. S. Eliot

AT 5:15 IN THE MORNING, the tea room on board the ship opened and people came out of their stupor, gathering up their belongings. When the boat docked an hour later, Glasgow didn't look too promising. They were surprised to find a restaurant with hot water, soap, and towels in the john, which were seldom found in any but the best restaurants. They had a decent, greaseless breakfast. Another scarce item in restaurants, were napkins. Sometimes they had them, but more often, they just had to ask, because there were none.

They walked over to the Queen Street Station in time to catch a train to Edinburgh. They had a compartment extending the width of the coach to themselves. Hoping no one would join them, they glared possessively at everyone who peered in. It worked. The windows set in the opposing doors, could be raised or lowered by means of a leather strap. They left them closed as tight as possible, but smoke and steam from the coal-fired engines still entered whenever the train passed through long tunnels. They emerged into the open countryside still in the early light of morning.

Bill stretched out to shake his drowsiness, and Dick remained awake a little longer to see several piles of waste at the pit heads of coal mines scattered by the tracks. They were soon enough in the Haymarket Station of Edinburgh. Getting off downtown at the Waverly Station, they walked up the stairs and came upon Princess Street, the main street of the city. Finding a "Y" hostel was easy. It wasn't fancy, but it was the cheapest place ever: seventy cents each. Bill went to bed to try and shake off a cold, and Dick went walking around town. While walking down the street, he came across a Rolls Royce taxicab, probably fifteen years old, that looked like new. It seemed very unusual to see such an expensive car used as a taxi, even for its age.

Dick was looking for a pub, but they didn't open up till noon, so he went east on Princess, turned right at Blenheim Palace, and found a steep path that ran to the top of Calton Hill, which towers over the eastern end of the city. At the top was a tower commemorating Nelson's victory at Trafalgar and an unfinished replica of the Acropolis in Athens. Initially, it was going to be a full-sized replica, but was stopped for lack of funds. Called the National Monument, it is a memorial to those who died in the Napoleonic Wars.

To the southeast of Edinburgh, the Salisbury Crags sharply define the city's southern boundary. North and west, houses stretched out and on into the mist. Dick made an orderly retreat from the monument as the noon chimes rang and retired to a pub. His reward was a half pint of bitters.

In Scotland, again, they went back to bitters, whereas in Eire, they stuck to Guinness. After quenching his thirst, Dick headed west on Princess again and climbed the Sir Walter Scott Monument. It was a large, gingerbread-looking affair in the heart of the city, and its style could be called "flamboyant Gothic." Costing less than a nickel to go up the 287 circular stairs, it had four levels altogether, and as Dick climbed higher, the platforms at each level became smaller. At the top, two people could barely squeeze past one another. It was obvious they didn't seem worried about suicides, because they had no screens up. The top of the tower was even with the top of Calton Hill. After climbing that hill, he still had enough energy to go exploring down the west end of Princess Street and south along Lothian Road. One side of Princess was lined with shops, big stores, and restaurants, just as in any large city, but the other side had Princess Street Park, running the entire length of it.

The park was situated in a depression, with green lawns running down the side to a line of trees that marked the railroad tracks at the bottom. An open-air bandstand let passers-by on the street see and hear everything going on.

Crossing the tracks over a pair of arched bridges, Dick came to the steep side of a depression, and on top was Edinburgh Castle, perched on a rocky promontory, dominating the west end of the city. Hoary Mons Meg, circa 1449, was a medieval bombard which sat in the highest gun position of the castle and pointed its cavernous snout westward. The gun had a barrel fifteen feet long and an inside diameter of about twenty inches, and shot 400-pound cannonballs. Over the centuries, it had been fired on ceremonial occasions.[1]

Dick met Bill at the North British Hotel for breakfast and they paid with Irish Free State pound notes and took the difference in English sterling. The hostel wasn't too comfortable, so they went and searched out another place on Windsor Street, just off the road to London and five minutes from downtown.

They both covered Calton Hill and took a bus down Princess Street and got off opposite Edinburgh Castle. Walking down the hill through the park, across the footbridge, and up the opposite side, they found the hillside and a cliff merged, where they could climb rather easily until they reached the bottom stonework of the castle. Dick worked his way up by hanging on to some plant roots. He got to a level spot, and then from there, he had to use some power cables clamped to the stonework to get onto the roof of a workshop adjoining the castle. Getting that far had been hard work, and it was about that time that Bill stuck his head over the edge of the parapet above him and hollered, "What the hell you doing down there?"

Dick had gone through all his acrobatics to avoid a long walk around to the gates. Bill went just a little ways from where they began the ascent and found safety scaffolding bleachers up the side of the cliff and made his way in with a minimum amount of effort. Dick stormed the castle all right, but couldn't figure how to get down to the ground from his perch over the workshop. He climbed another wall and the other side of it had a fifteen-foot drop down to the public area, with no footholds. He eventually solved his problem by backing up to the previous wall and jumping down onto a wobbly old table, which put him in a courtyard. He then had an inkling of what Edmund Hillary and Tenzing Norgay put up with when they were the first to officially summit Mt. Everest in 1953.[2]

They walked through the castle, but didn't see anything of particular note except the Mon's Meg cannon. They declined to go into any of the museums, chapels, or the Crown Room, as they all had a tariff of fourteen cents. and they felt it would be the same old stuff as the Tower of London. The Crown Room supposedly contained Scottish regalia dating from the time when it was independent. They headed out the gate over the dry moat and strolled down the "Royal Mile," a street that used to have fashionable shops patronized by royalty. It was still a stately street with quite a few official buildings, including the city hall, or "chambers," as they called it.

They built up a thirst after a quarter of Royal Mile walking, but Sunday in Scotland is dry. Then they heard of an army club from a fellow on the street who offered directions. They finally came to the Cameronian Club on Saint Vincent Street for ex-service members, which functioned similarly to an Elks Club in the United States. According to Scottish law, the ex-military clubs are the only ones allowed to sell beer and liquor on Sunday. That was where the "boys" gathered to drink, play dominoes and darts. Bill knocked on the door, announced that they were a couple of thirsty Americans, and were welcomed in. Spending two hours there, they tried to learn how the Scots scored their dart games, while talking and sopping up the good ale. On the street again, they hopped a bus and went out to the west end, had a snack, and tried to find a movie, but once again, the Scottish Sabbath intervened. Not by law, but by custom, they closed up almost all the movie houses—the ones that stayed open donated part of their take to charity. On the bus again, they went back to the pension and ate dinner and spent the evening reading or writing. Most of the pensions they stayed at were private homes offering a bed and meals similar to bed-and-breakfast accommodations.

Monday dawned with a spot of rain that soon let up. They had an excellent breakfast at the lodging and then set out for the Leith Docks to inquire about getting a ride across the channel to Holland. At the dock offices, they were directed to several shipping companies. The best price they could offer was twenty-four dollars (£8) each. They figured that was a bit high, so they kept walking on around the docks, hoping to make a deal with some ship captain. After tramping all over the place and talking to quite a few captains and mates, it was no dice. Either they lacked the facilities to haul passengers or were referred back to the main offices. They did a lot of walking and saw a lot of ships, some of them in dry dock. At the water's edge, a few white swans were swimming among the piers.

Finding a pub, they again tried their hands at darts. Dick lost twice in a row, so he bought the lion's share of ale. Back uptown, they did some shopping and replenished their library with a volume on enology and another on French architecture. It had been two weeks since they landed in Southampton.

They gathered their belongings and cleared out of Edinburgh just before noon. The city bus took them as far as Musselburgh, and from there, they were on their own again. At the bus stop, Dick bought some biscuits and Bill got some cardboard from the woman running the store and made a sign saying: "NEWCASTLE." The shopkeeper said she didn't like Edinburgh, because it was too class-conscious. As she put it, the city had a "kippers and candelabra complex."

The sign worked. Their first hop was with a fellow who had recently been through France, Spain, and Majorca in the Balearic Islands. He detested France, especially Paris, but had nothing but good things to say about Spain. They crossed the border and were back in England, just outside Berwick-on-Tweed, and they fiddled around for an hour before a lorry driver gave a lift the remaining sixty-seven miles into Newcastle. The fellow had been in the German Army during the war, was taken prisoner, was repatriated, and then came to England in 1946 to live. He lost his wife and child in Berlin during the air raids. He said he started out in 1946 with nothing and now had a good job, owned a fleet of lorries, a car, a home of his own, and a new wife and more children, and that it would take an Englishman twenty-six years to do the same. He was obviously very proud of his accomplishments.

CHAPTER 8 A PASS THROUGH ENGLAND AGAIN

SEPTEMBER 30–OCTOBER 2, 1958

There are no foreign lands. It is the traveler only who is foreign.
—R. L. Stevenson

ARRIVING IN NEWCASTLE at 4:30 p.m., they had time to make a call at a travel agent's office. Thinking they had a deal set for a boat going from Hull to Rotterdam for $11.12 (£4), it turned out the second class accommodations were taken, and the next class was $18.09 (6/10s) each, so they decided to stay in the city and catch the next available ship across the English Channel.

Newcastle is a big bustling place that is vaguely reminiscent of London. There is coal mining, ship building, and steel factories, so it's certainly not a depressed area. One unique thing they saw were treated beech wood blocks used as paving stones in the Tyne-Tees district. They spent the early evening finding a place to stay and ended up at the Park Hotel on Jesmond Street. A movie filled their evening nicely, and afterward, they had a snack at a Chinese restaurant. It was difficult to find a restaurant open after 10:30 p.m. in England. When they were leaving the restaurant, "the coppers" arrived to arbitrate between a customer and the cashier. "The rotter took me a 'bob,'" they overheard the customer explaining that the cashier had taken advantage of him.

Checking out of the hotel, they found C. Hassel and Sons Ltd., the shipping agent, and booked passage on the *Bolton Abbey*, bound for Rotterdam, leaving at six that evening from Hull, down the coast. Checking train times, they retired to a pub for darts and bitters and then moved on to the railway station. On the way, they passed two "bobbies," i.e. British policemen, either going to work or patrolling in a Triumph sports car, a TR2—an unusual sight.

The train took them out of Newcastle and passed through Durham, Darlington, and Thirsk, among other towns, on the way to Hull, via York, where they changed trains. At York, they had time for lunch and a quick look around before the next train came. They checked their baggage with an accommodating porter and walked uptown through one of the ancient gates of the walled city. After lunch, they strolled up one of the streets past St. Martin's Church, which dates back to the twelfth century. Outside, it looked very weathered and badly beat up. There were patches in the masonry and crumbling mortar and stone on the ground, built of ancient pre-Christian Roman masonry from the Temple of Mithras. Inside, restoration was gradually taking place. As they went in the door, they saw a little box conveniently placed for visitors to do their bit and make donations toward the project. The flooring was laid with tombstones, the oldest dated to 1664. Farther down the street was Trinity Church, formerly a Benedictine priory in pre-Norman times. The roof had collapsed centuries before, but it had been replaced by a hand-hewn wooden collar roof. The tie beams and king posts looked crude, with ax marks roughing their surfaces.[1]

The first mystery plays were performed there, but they were more properly called the York Corpus Christi Plays. A Middle English cycle of forty-eight plays or pageants, covering the sacred history from the Creation to the Last Judgment, they were presented on the feast day of Corpus Christi. The records on view showed that one King Richard III paid four pence in AD 1397 for admission.[2]

With time running out, they walked back to the station on top of the city wall. The wall was quite weathered and had a parapet along the inside where, at places, the stones rose to a height of thirty to forty feet. At a low spot, they jumped to the ground ten feet below and made way to the train headed for Hull.

Departing York at 3:30, they had an hour's uneventful ride through little towns. The ship's personnel didn't want them on board early, because they had not been through Customs, so they made themselves comfortable and as unobtrusive as possible. At 5:00, they paid the thirty-six dollar fare for both, cleared Customs, and got onboard.

They were in the second sitting for dinner at 8:00, which was about the time the crew cast off and got under way. Dinner was mutton chops, boiled potatoes, and bread and butter. The passengers for the most part were a stodgy bunch, so the brothers settled down for a dull crossing. Later that evening in the lounge, they sat down to blackjack and Bass ale. Two Dutch girls, Doortje and Katrijn, joined for a while until their mothers came to claim them. They played on until no one remained in the bar. Dick did a nice job of cleaning Bill out of $8.34.

They found the night steward and, after bribing him with some Bass ale, had a big feed of toasted cheese sandwiches and tea. This steward was familiar with Vancouver, British Columbia, where they had both gone to boarding school at Vancouver College. He told them that the *Bolton Abbey* was named after an ancient abbey in Yorkshire and had been launched three months previously, in June 1958. Soon it was to have a sister ship launched named the *MelroseAbbey*, which would be a cargo/passenger ship like the *BoltonAbbey*. Ships of that type were previously named after rivers, but most of them were on their last legs or had been scrapped. The new line of ships would be named after abbeys and towns, depending on the configuration and type of ship.[3]

Bill went to bed first. Dick went out on deck. A stiff breeze was blowing, but it was not cold. The moon was full and the sky clear. He saw three or four ships coming and going in the channel. The next morning, October 2, they awoke at 9:00 with Holland in sight.

WADDENZEE
FRISIAN IS.
HAMBURG
BREMEN
AMSTERDAM
NETHERLANDS
ROTTERDAM
ESSEN
BRUSSELS
COLOGNE
BONN
GERMANY
LILLE
BELGIUM
FRANKFURT
LUXEMBOURG
LUXEMBOURG
PARIS
STRASBOURG
STUTTGART
MUNICH
LIECHTENSTEIN
ZÜRICH
BERN
FRANCE
SWITZERLAND
ALPS
GENEVA
LYON
MILAN
TURIN

STETTINER HAFF
KALININGRAD
GDANSK
HRODNA
POLAND
POZNAN
WARSAW
BREST
ZIELONA GORA
LÓDZ
WROCLAW
PRAGUE
KRAKÓW
LVOV
CZECH REP.
TATRA MTS
BRNO
SLOVAKIA
BRATISLAVA
VIENNA
AUSTRIA
BUDAPEST
HUNGARY
CLUJ-NAPOCA
ALFÖLD
CARPATHIAN MOUNTAINS
LJUBLJANA
ZAGREB
SLOVENIA
CROATIA
TRANSYLVANIAN ALPS
BELGRADE

CHAPTER 9 HOLLAND

October 2–3, 1958

Not all those who wander are lost.—J. R. R. Tolkien

AFTER BREAKFAST, they still had a couple of hours to kill, so it was back to bed. On waking, they went through a few more formalities and disembarked at 11:30 a.m., then took a tram to downtown Rotterdam. On board, they had exchanged their English money for Dutch guilders, which was not nearly as confusing as the British currency. A Dutch guilder is the basic unit. The exchange rate was 3.79 guilders to one U.S. dollar. They had pennies, nickels, dimes, and 25-cent pieces and had seen bills for 2½, 20, and 25 guilders. A 2½ guilder bill was worth approximately 75 cents.

Taking a guess at what they considered the city center, they headed for the tall buildings on foot. The center of Rotterdam was completely new. In May 1940, as the Germans were advancing on the coast, Holland was given an ultimatum to surrender. Not accepting it as quickly as the Germans wanted, Adolph Hitler ordered the bombing of Rotterdam, which was of strategic importance to Germany as a stepping stone to the invasion of England. Once the Germans occupied Rotterdam, the Allies, the USAAF and the RAF, bombed the city over a hundred times until 1943, seeking strategic targets being used by the German occupiers.[1]

Thirteen years after the war, the nucleus of the city center seemed complete in every detail, but according to a city guide, only two-thirds of the projected construction had been accomplished. The buildings ranged from the conservative to very modernistic, with great use being made of windowless walls with patterns and designs set in the stone and concrete. The sidewalks were wide and some of the downtown streets had two islands in them to enable pedestrians to make the trip across the wide boulevards in short hops. They were surprised that there was a lot of bustle downtown, but little noise—no horns honking, no buses roaring, etc. It seemed even the streetcars were muffled on their tracks. Many of the streets were paved with bricks that were blue to bluish-white.

They inquired at a hotel information center on Coolsingel Strasse, the main drag, and got a pension on Mathenesserlaan St. It was out of the city center and took ten minutes by tram. Their room was on the third floor and had western exposure, which meant a lot of light. They had a balcony overlooking apartment buildings. The room was comfortable, with thick maroon rugs on the tabletop and mantle, and the overall effect was warm and cozy. The cost was six guilders, which wasn't too bad—just a little under two dollars apiece. After they got squared away, they went back downtown and wandered around, just taking it all in.

Rotterdam was the most modern city in the world and had nearly three quarters of a million people. The food was good and cheap. That night, they had two rare roast beef sandwiches each and glasses of milk for about thirty cents, and the sandwiches were loaded with meat. Dutch beer was more like America's, but not quite so lively. They served it cold in a big glass for 40 cents Dutch, or about eleven cents U.S. Unlike England, Rotterdam's restaurants and bars stayed open until midnight. In the afternoon, they picked up a half pint of cognac for sixty-five cents, which offered warmth through the night. Earlier, they had espresso coffee in a restaurant on Coolsingel. The table and chairs were set out in the middle of the sidewalk and glassed in. They sat in there on stools and watched the people passing by while sipping a brew served in little cups akin to those in which saké is served.

The next day, they planned to get an early start and head off for Brussels, Belgium, but first, they decided to soak up more of the city. So Friday, October 3, they packed and checked bags at the Central Station and hunted up lunch to supplement their continental breakfast. They prowled around a bit and took pictures of some of the striking new buildings in the final phases of construction. Bill went to the post office to write a letter, and Dick had a cup of espresso coffee on Coolsingel. They caught the 3:30 p.m. train to Brussels via Antwerp.

Traveling south, they passed through the Dutch countryside and then headed west a bit into country that was divided up by estuaries. They saw ship-loading cranes on the docks of Antwerp. The countryside below Rotterdam was absolutely flat. The north of Holland was reclaiming the land from the sea into polders, or land that is reclaimed by diking and draining.

CHAPTER 10 BELGIUM

October 3–4, 1958

When we get out of the glass bottle of our ego and when we escape like the squirrels in the cage of our personality and get into the forest again, we shall shiver with cold and fright. But things will happen to us so that we don't know ourselves. Cool, unlying life will rush in."—D. H. Lawrence

THE TRAIN WAS ALL ELECTRIC, very modern, and covered the distance in short order. Outside of Antwerp, the signs began to change from Dutch to French. Coming into Brussels, they saw the top of the Atomium sticking up out of the landscape. The monument was the symbol of the 1958 World's Fair in Brussels. It stood 335 feet tall and consisted of nine steel spheres connected so that the whole formed the shape of a cell of an iron crystal magnified 165 billion times.[1]

View of the Atomium, the theme of the 1958 World's Fair in Brussels, Belgium.

When they got into the station, they didn't know whether they were in the center of town or not. As it turned out, they were only three blocks away. The information booth at the depot gave the address of a large housing facility set up for the World's Fair on Blvd. Louis Mettewie. They caught a tram out to the address and navigated two blocks to find the dormitory. Set out in a cleared area, it was called the "Welcome Expo '58." It was a giant dormitory, sleeping about 3,200 people, unisex fashion. It was strictly a slap-dash affair, but it offered clean sheets and breakfast to boot, for 63 Belgian francs or $1.26 American (49 Belgian francs to the dollar).

After checking in and making beds, they headed for the fair. The bus in front of the Welcome Expo delivered them to the front entrance. There was a twenty-franc tariff to get in. That night, they buzzed the place very lightly, going from the main entrance down the Avenue of Nations with a stop to see the colored fountains inside the entrance. They passed under the Atomium and tried to climb up the stairs inside one of its supports but were shooed out—exit only! While going up the Avenue of Nations, they passed the pavilions of Norway, Finland, Austria, saw France's huge exhibit, and then stopped at the Vatican's *Civitas Dei* for a sandwich and beer. The Belgian beer was good and served cold.

By the time dinner was over, the United States pavilion was the only one open, a fashion show going on, with models walking down a long inclined ramp to a platform. They wondered how in hell all of Americana was going to fit into one building. Washing machines, outboard boats, etc. were on display. They had a "typical" coffee shop, with roast beef sandwiches for one dollar. For the most part, though, it was a glorified art exhibit. However, they got through the whole thing in about an hour, took a peek through the doors of Russia's pavilion, and then headed up to the *Pavilion du Champagnes*, the long building France occupied. Inside were wine bars

Fairway and Exhibit hall, 1958 World's Fair.

representing all the different wine regions of France. Samples went from ten francs on up, and they settled for a glass of Nony Burgundy.

Moving to the Belgian section of the fair, there was a huge object shaped like a triangular-bladed concrete rapier with the handle curved down to support it. Under the blade was a suspended footbridge which passed over a monster map of Belgium to scale, with miniature factories, moving cars, greenery, and water lapping at the seashore.

Rising time was 10:00 a.m. After eating a continental breakfast of buttered bread, jam, and coffee, they took the express bus to the fair with a camera at the ready. First, they toured the Belgian education, health, and sport center at the entrance to the fair, then moved on to the Belgian electrical energy display. It had an interesting exhibit: a hemispherical aluminum cone with a gas heater in the center, which radiated the heat to another plain concave cone some eighty feet distant and opposite. The amazing thing was even though it warmed a large area which was open to the hall, neither of the metal cones were hot.

From there, they visited a large exhibit given over to city gas, its manufacture, uses, distribution, etc. Followed by petroleum and metallurgy exhibits, some large castings were displayed. Hopping from one exhibit to another in the rain brought them to the Belgian Congo building, and soon they revisited the *Civitas Dei* for more ham sandwiches and beer. The lunch was quick before heading across the mall to start the Russian exhibit. "Exhibit" was a hell of a word to use, because like the U.S. pavilion, everything under the sun was packed into it, including a big theater. Outside, there was a full-size oil well drilling rig ringed with heavy trucks and tractors. They milled about in the bosom of Mother Russia for an hour or so and moved to the Spanish pavilion but ended up in Tunisia's exhibit. They gave that a once over lightly, then stopped at the Netherlands pavilion and looked at cows and chickens. They gawked at a wave machine, with a big, plow-like hydraulic arm that pushed the water in the tank and simulated a cross-section view of a wave breaking on a beach, only it was the slanted end of the tank.

Winding behind France's building, they turned the corner and finally found Spain and viewed gallery after gallery of art on various floor levels. They passed up Great Britain because of the crowd and took a look at Germany's pavilions. They went through just one building and headed back up the concourse to pick up a corner of the Swiss exhibit on their way to the Belgium civil engineers' stressed-concrete rapier. The exhibit looked like an extraordinary dinosaur or whale with a huge fluke that was a cantilevered concrete arrow pointing at the Atomium. Although appearing to be a solid spike of concrete, it was a hollow shell, with no opening except a skylight not observable from the ground. Descending from it were cables supporting a floating concrete footbridge leading to the exhibit's entrance. The apparent counterbalance was a large hall, it too, in the air, like the head of a whale with its enormous arrow flipper jutting out from it an astounding distance. As unstable as it appeared, its three legs rested on pods, each with pilings driven over thirty feet into the ground.

They took a couple of shots of it and tried to talk the guards into letting them get on it and walk out on the point, but of course, that was not authorized. By that time, they were getting pretty beat, but

The Belgium Civil engineer's extraordinary exhibit, a pre-stressed concrete rapier that vaulted the sky.

a Belgian beer helped them grab a second wind. They stopped off at a Belgian exhibit of glasswork and jewelry on the way to the "Attractions," the carnival part of the fair.

Bill took a photo of the fountains before they rode in a cage that lifted them about 200 feet, where they were able to view the fair from above. They wandered around the carnival section and took a

Main Square in Brussels, Belgium.

ride in a revolving barrel with cars inside that ran on tracks. When they braked the car, they revolved with the barrel. They ended up at a lingerie exhibit with live screaming models—the fun house, naturally. The last obstacle they had to run through was a long treadmill, and at the end of it was a screened part of the floor with a blower underneath. There were benches along the side of the ride, and they were jammed with people watching the spectacle. One of the employees would hold up the women on the belt and give them a whirl at the end. That's when they let go of their skirts and . . . whoosh! Belgian peasants' bloomers make a quaint sight. But the underwear wearied after a while, and they headed for the tram stop and downtown Brussels. It was remarkable—they had been to the World's Fair!

CHAPTER 11 WEST GERMANY

OCTOBER 5–6, 1958

One's destination is never a place but a new way of seeing things.
—Henry Miller

A CROWDED TRAIN TRANSPORTED THEM out of Brussels at 6:30 p.m. They elbowed their way into a compartment and grabbed two seats. Stopping first in Liege, they made it into Aachen, West Germany, by 9:15. Customs was no trouble, so they were in Germany on their own. It was a ten-minute walk to the city center, where they found a restaurant. Their non-existent German handicapped them to the extent that the proprietress took them into the kitchen to have them point out what they wanted: wurst, fries, and beer. When they asked for ketchup, they couldn't get the message across, so pulled a bottle from their luggage they had acquired in Belfast. Despite all that, it was an excellent dinner, and both agreed the wurst was the best they'd ever tasted. The proprietress directed them to a hotel, which turned out to be full. Several more attempts got them set up at a pension for three dollars or 12 Deutschmarks (DM).

Aachen and the surrounding towns still had a way to go before getting back into pre-war shape. The city was on the Siegfried Line, the main German defensive barrier to halt the Allied invasion during World War II, and the city was the door to the industrialized Ruhr Basin, a huge strategic target. It took two weeks in 1944 to capture Aachen, and heavy losses were sustained by both sides. This city was Charlemagne's seat of power and the first "Reich," a psychologically important city for the Germans to defend. Although not an important city militarily, the area beyond it was flat and favorable for the Allied mechanized army. The Germans categorically refused to surrender, so American artillery lobbed over 5,000 shells into the city, and the army/air force subjected it to heavy bombardment. As they crossed the Rhine River, it was obvious reconstruction was still underway.[1]

The next afternoon, after a little hunting, they found a bicycle shop and bought two chrome-plated, bejeweled, sturdy bicycles that cost $50 (200 DM) apiece and were two of the gaudiest machines ever. They were bronze with stripping, with chromed handlebars, three-speed derailleurs, brown leather seats, and white, fat treaded tires. They had to stick around until the next day to get the brake calipers Dick wanted put on his bike. Then, they were ready to assault the highways of Europe with their own transportation.

After breakfast the next morning, they went down the street to pick up the bicycles. There was some tri-lingual horsing around, in English, French, and German, until they finally paid for them and strapped on their luggage—an AWOL bag each—on the rear fender. They made one false start, because Dick's front brakes needed adjusting. The second try took them out of Aachen.

CHAPTER 12 BELGIUM AGAIN

OCTOBER 6–8, 1958

Travel is more like the seeing of sights; it's a change that goes on, deep and permanent, in the ideas of living.—Miriam Beard

THEIR ROUTE TOOK THEM back into Belgium and they covered approximately twenty-seven miles in five hours. Most of the travel was uphill, and as proof, they found out what kind of shape they were in—not very good. They stopped at a place called La Baraque Michel and ended up staying in Belgium all the way to Luxembourg. At Eupen, they stopped to eat, rest, and get some Belgian francs. One of the languages they heard was Flemish, one of the many dialects of Dutch.

The room in the Eupen hotel was lit by a dim bulb over a sink with two candles at either side of the bed. The bed's headboard's dual compartments came with "thunder mugs." The bed itself was two single beds joined by a common footboard which made it about seven feet wide.

Situated on a high hill, Eupen allowed a vista of all the towns on the plain below—Verviers being the largest. There were many vacant lots in built-up areas, with ruined, low, brick foundations and partially exposed cellars. Many of the buildings had been refaced to cover the scars of war. That night, they had a few beers downstairs in the bar, where they met some English soldiers. They, along with American and French soldiers, manned microwave radio relay stations in their sector. Earlier that evening, they thought they were Belgians, so they didn't attempt any conversation, but after hearing them speak English and finding out who they were, the Yanks got along quite well. As usual, the Brits bought a round of drinks. One rather interesting thing, Dick and Bill were informed there was a local Belgian law that said if you ran over somebody's chicken, you had to not only pay for it, but also for as many eggs as it might possibly produce in the future. That spurred a lively discussion on the life cycle of a laying hen.

The Brits had done some research on this question and found out that it depends on the type of chicken. Using Rhode Island Reds, as an example, hens start laying after they are six months old and can lay about five eggs every six days. After a year, a hen's laying ability declines and they are considered spent and slaughtered.[1] If true, then a hen puts out about 300 eggs for an annual production of about twenty-five dozen eggs. So if they had run over some farmer's chicken, they could have been nailed for 1,225 Belgium francs or about twenty-five dollars. They kept a keen eye out for chickens on the road thereafter.

Around the La Baraque Michel area in southern Belgium, a dialect called *Walloon* was spoken. Although a Romance language, it is an enclave language or dialect—there is some dispute over which it is. Other limited use tongues in the local region happen to be Picard, Lorrain, Champenois, and Luxembourgish.[2]

They were told it was mostly downhill to Luxembourg, and they fervently hoped so. Late Wednesday morning, they were on their bikes and under way. On the way into Malmedy, Bill thought Dick's rear tire looked low on air, so they stopped to pump it up. The trouble was the air escaped faster than it went in. Dick slacked off the valve core and it blew out, and the tire collapsed. They gathered up the parts, but didn't get the valve core seated properly until they had spent ten minutes in futile pumping.

It was all downhill to Malmedy, a great relief, but what goes down must come up. The road rose on the other side of the valley, where they found a hellish lot of more valleys that day. That was how that day went: a quick ride down and a walk up the next grade. They didn't hit a level stretch until arriving in Luxembourg. They also bucked stiff headwinds and only covered thirty-seven miles for six hours of travel.

CHAPTER 13 LUXEMBOURG

OCTOBER 8–9, 1958

All journeys have secret destinations of which the traveler is unaware.
—Martin Buber

THEY ENTERED LUXEMBOURG in the early evening and kept going until they hit a little place called Heinerscheid, about three miles inside the border. On the way, they were stopped by a cop bicycling from the opposite direction. He wanted to see passports, which was puzzling, but he was satisfied, so they continued on to Heinerscheid. However, they felt somebody must have "blown the whistle" on them, because two more cops offered their attention. As it turned out, the day before, someone had held up a restaurant in a neighboring village, so when the brothers arrived in town, they were the likeliest suspects. One of the local school teachers who spoke English eventually told them the whole story and mentioned that the small country had three languages: French, German, and Luxembourgish, a German dialect. In thirty-seven miles, many languages and multiple dialects!

The northern part of the country was all agricultural, but down south, around the city of Luxembourg, they had steel mills. The country had 300,000 people spread out over approximately sixteen thousand square miles.[1]

They were staying in the Mercure Grand Hotel, where the food was delicious. Starting off with cream of egg soup, then beef steak for Bill, and pork cutlet for Dick, sliced tomatoes in oil, seasoned with finely chopped shallots and tea, it was worth pumping all day for such a meal. If it had been Britain, they would have had greasy eggs and bacon for dinner and indigestion for dessert.

Forty miles of relatively flat country lay between them and the city of Luxembourg, and they arrived the evening of October 9. They took their bags off the bikes and checked them at the railway station, then rode around town a bit and tested the local ale.

The city was cut in two by a deep ravine. At the bottom was a park, a small stream with a rock bed, and some flower gardens. The ravine was spanned by two high bridges, one of which looked like a Roman viaduct. It got dark quickly, so they brought the bikes back to the railroad depot and checked them in for a couple of days, as they planned to board the train for Paris and return in a few days. They caught the late train, which stopped in Metz, France, where they had slightly over an hour's layover, then went on to Paris, arriving at 6:45 in the morning. They met an American Air Force officer on the train who knew Paris well enough to give enough information on how to get their tour started.

CHAPTER 14 PARIS, FRANCE

OCTOBER 10–13, 1958

Even the children in Paris speak French. —Mark Twain

ARRIVING AT THE GARE DE L'EST STATION in Paris, they walked through the covered market section as they were about to open. Awnings were spread over a skeleton of shaky support piers, and low tables were being set up with fruits, vegetables, and produce of all kinds brought in from the countryside. Just marching through the aisles was a gourmet's nose tour of some of the viands of France. Fresh food everywhere included cheeses, charcuterie, roasted chickens, pates, bread, olives, pastries, artisanal confitures, honey, duck and goose confitures, foie gras, spices, vinegars, and on and on. They made good use of such markets to keep expenses down and to eat very well.

Dick enjoying bread, wine and cheese on our hotel room's fourth floor balcon.

Moving on to find lodgings, the brothers followed Boulevard Haussmann, which paralleled the Champs Elysees to the River Seine for about ten blocks until they came to the Rue d'Amsterdam, where they found a hotel in the center of things for $3.33 a day or 1,400 French francs (FF). Arriving at the hotel at 7:30 a.m., the rooms weren't made up yet, so their bags were checked, followed by some shopping for breakfast: sliced ham, a loaf of bread, butter, a wedge of cheese, and a bottle of 1955 Beaujolais. When they got back, everything was ready, and they carted the luggage and goodies upstairs and had a great breakfast. Cleaning up, they headed for Cook's Travel Office toward the Seine, behind La Madeleine, a Roman Catholic church in the eighth arrondissement modeled after a Roman temple. Cook's were out to lunch, so they had to wait to see if any mail for them had arrived.

Dick took off toward the Champs Elysees and turned up at the Arc de Triomphe and the Place de l'Etoile. After a half hour of leisurely strolling, for twenty-four cents or 100FF, he took the elevator up to the top of the Arc. There was a wonderful view of Paris, and with the aid of a map, he was able to identify many landmarks, such as the Notre Dame, the Sacre Couer Basilica on top of Montmartre Hill, the Bois de Boulogne, Paris's large park, and the Eiffel Tower. Paris was just big enough, with enough interesting things to see, that a week would go by quickly, since just walking the streets was entertaining.

With letters in hand from Cook's, which were welcome indeed, food for supper was purchased on the way to the hotel—more cheese, bread, a bottle of dry white wine, plus some pastries for thirty-eight cents or 160FF. They had bicycled all day the day before, ridden the train all night, and both of them had now walked all day. They enjoyed some solid marathon sleeping to get back in shape, and they woke thinking it was Friday and headed out to do some sightseeing and to take care of their travel needs. They had lost a day somewhere, because it was Saturday, and they needed to arrange return passage to the United States via South America immediately. When they got to the Organization Mercury Onmes agency for the Compania Colonial de Navagaceo, they made reservations post-haste, plunking fifty bucks apiece down as a deposit for the ship home. They planned to pay the rest in Portuguese escudos—perhaps saving with a good exchange rate when they got to Lisbon, Portugal, their point of departure. With that task out of the way, it was on to Notre Dame Cathedral.

Architectural detail of Notre Dame de Paris: flying buttresses and gargoyles.

Following the Rue de La Paix, they crossed the Place Vendome and went down the left bank of the Seine to the Isle de la Cite. The

Notre Dame Cathedral was familiar to them. It showed its age clearly by the worn and chipped stonework, with whole statues missing. Surrounding the church were gargoyles which extended some distance out from the roof. Built into the gutters to drain rainwater off the roof, they extended out off the side of the building so that gallons of rainwater would fall far from the building's foundation to prevent damage. Gargoyles are half-man, half-beast, fantastic creatures with eagle wings, lion talons, and serpent tails—chimeras.[1] From the rear and looking toward Notre Dame from across the Seine, buttresses encircled the cathedral from the central part of the church around to the front right side.

Walking back on the right bank of the Seine, they crossed over to the Louvre Museum in the first Arrondissement, or district, and the Jardin des Tuileries. Inside the Louvre, they walked for what seemed like miles, seeing the *Venus de Milo,* Da Vinci's *Mona Lisa, The Winged Victory of Samothrace* (Nike), and the *Angelus* by Jean Francois Millet.

Outside, they saw the date AD 1606 engraved on one of the stone piers of the Pont Royal, one of the oldest bridges spanning the Seine. Returning by bus to the Rue d'Amsterdam and their hotel, they picked up some bread, wine, pork, and cheese for a homemade dinner.

This was the night to "do Paree," so they headed over to the Folies Bergere and paid the nominal sum of ninety-one cents or 380FF for the *promenoir,* or standing-room-only area. The entire production lasted from 8:30 until midnight, with a fifteen-minute break. The costuming was on a regal scale, with even the walk-ons, or tableaus, done in a grand manner. Some of the dances were very intricate, and one scene included several of the performers dunking themselves in a stage-level tank of water.

After the show, they trooped around the corner and up the street to the Rue Bleue, where they had a beer and met two Australians who were working their way around the continent. In Paris for a four-day stint, they were going on to Glasgow to begin a job.

After swapping stories and leaving, the brothers headed toward the hotel by way of Montmartre and Rue Pigalle, the noisiest part of town. Noted as the tourist district, it had many sex shops, peep and live shows, and *salons prives*.[2] Tourists and locals were milling around and everyone seemed to have some business. The prostitutes were out to see if they could make another franc before calling it a night, and Paris nightlife was gradually winking out. The last beer of the night put them out fast, and on Sunday, they woke feeling in great shape and ready to chew up a few more miles of sightseeing.

At the Trinity Church on the Place de la Trinite, the priest said the Mass facing the people on a table altar, and another priest took the collection preceded by a tipstaff, wearing a chain and carrying a cone mace to indicate the role of the collector. The second collection was taken by a girl eight or nine years old.

They took a bus to the Arc de Triomphe from the Place de l'Etoile. After taking several pictures of the Arc, they went over to the Eiffel Tower and took the elevator to the top, the third stage on the seventy-year-old structure. They noted the structure was held together by 2.5 million rivets and was 918 feet high. It was well worth the $1.19 or 500FF ride to the top, which was practically the equivalent of an airplane ride over Paris. The view was magnificent, and they watched a boat race on the Seine. Above each window were paintings of the vistas they were looking at, with the names of the places of special interest. After taking some photos, they took the elevator down to the second stage and then walked down the stairs to the first.

The Arc de Triomphe de l'Etoile at the west end of the Champs-Elysees, Paris, France.

Walking toward the Hotel des Invalides, they stopped on the Parc du Champ de Mars and watched miniature sailboats being buffeted about by the wind on a pond. There were all kinds of boats, from crude rafts with sail made from old rags to tiny yachts that keeled over in the breeze and ran before the wind with a furious rush of sail. Although the cast-iron chairs were dotted around the pond, most were empty and the crowd was standing. They stood for a while and then sat on the chairs to watch the show, but when it came time to leave, an old man walked their way with a big leather purse slung over his shoulder that was filled with change. He had the concession of the chairs and was renting them for eight cents or 30FF apiece. Their reactions to his demands for his thirty francs gave them away as foreigners, but they eventually coughed up the coin. There were covert glances from people standing nearby holding on to their sous while they discussed the cost of seating, which ensued in awful French with much gesticulation. As they left, a wind and rainstorm came up and they made a mad dash for a convenient zinc bar. They had a red wine and each paid a nickel or 25FF for them. When they ordered another wine and paid the same amount, the waiter demanded twice the amount, claiming they had ordered Bordeaux, not the wine. Then the fun began; for what seemed ten minutes, they went around with much shaking of hands and raised voices, with the proprietress leading the show. As they wouldn't pay up, the waiter told them to *allez-vous-on*, or "Get your ass out of here," which they did. Upon departing, a fellow next to them who had not said a word during the commotion turned and said with a Scottish brogue, "Way to go, Yanks." They had the feeling they hadn't really done their bit to spread goodwill, but also that the French thought that American goodwill came from the wallet, so they didn't feel bad about it, just a bit wound up.

Back at the hotel, they closed out their stay, grabbed the luggage, and headed back to Luxembourg. Walking back to the left bank, they passed the Invalides, the Grand Palais, crossed over the Pont Alexandre III, and on to the Rue St. Lazare, where they caught a bus for the Gare de l'Est in time for the 6:20 train to Luxembourg. The trip was uneventful except for several drunken peasants who slopped up the compartment with champagne, groped each other, and sang songs while a prim little lady sat in the corner, alternating between amused and shocked grimaces. They caught a few things a tipsy peasant woman said. Dick was writing in his notepad while the train swayed and jerked along, and the woman said he wrote like her grandmother. After arriving in Luxembourg just after midnight, they checked into a hotel across from the train station for thirty-eight cents or 160 Luxembourg francs (LUF) a night.

The Eiffel Tower on the Champ de Mars can be seen from any point in the Parisian basin.

CHAPTER 15 LUXEMBOURG, SAARLAND, AND WEST GERMANY

October 14–17, 1958

What you've done becomes the judge of what you're going to do—especially in other people's minds. When you're traveling, you are what you are right there and then. People don't have your past to hold against you. No yesterdays on the road.—William Least Heat Moon

They reclaimed their bicycles and headed east out of Luxembourg City around noon. Before leaving Luxembourg proper, they passed the World War II American cemetery. There were 5,076 Americans buried there, including General Patton. Immaculate, the city was in the process of putting up some stone memorials. Down the road was the German cemetery, where they could see grey headstone crosses sticking up.

Crossing into Saarland over the Mosel River on a ferry drawn by cables, Bill noted that the Saar basin was a French Protectorate since 1947 and was in transition to rejoin Germany as one of its smallest states.[1] French money was in use, but it was moving to the Deutschmark (DM). After crossing the Mosel, they had to get up the other side of the valley, and from then on, they didn't have much difficulty. On one particularly steep stretch, they hitched onto the back of trucks and found that moderately steep hills just slowed them down, but not the trucks. A good steep hill, however, slowed the trucks down just enough for them to grab on and ride to the top in comfort. They stopped in a little town along the way and bought a bottle of wine. The shopkeeper wanted seven cents or 30LUF for the bottle alone, so they got a glass and drank the whole thing. Taking some cheese and bread for the road, they ate it not long after. Once they came down off the high hills on that side of the Mosel, the going was easy and they made good time.

About nineteen miles out of Saar-Louis, the steel mills of the Saar Basin came into sight. They made it into Volklingen by 6:15 and found an inexpensive hotel—the Malepartus. The innkeeper used to live in Detroit and spoke English with only a slight accent. He poured a drink of excellent whiskey—on the house—and the brothers enjoyed a tremendous dinner: rump steak smothered in a sauté of mushrooms, onions, baby peas, and ham, with a salad and perfect fries. It was the best meal since Heinerscheld in Luxembourg. Down the street was a steel mill that lit up the sky at night.

They had covered fifty-three miles the day before in the rain and it looked like there were a lot of hills and rain ahead. If all went well, they hoped to make it to the Rhine River by the next day and then turn south. As it turned out, they made their best time that day, covering fifty-nine miles from Volkingen, past Pirmasens, to Kaltenbock. The going was easy through Saarbrucken, even if they did get on the wrong road to Zweibrucken. It was sprinkling a little outside of town, so they stopped at a service station to put on rain capes. They reached St. Ingbert and happily stopped for a beer, chewed the fat with the bar lady, then pressed on through a shortcut she mentioned, which led to Zweibrucken. The Saar border guards gave no trouble, and they didn't even look at their passports when they found out they were Americans. Then came Pirmasens, where there was an American Army base. They pedaled on to Kaltenbock and stopped for the night and paid $3.85 (15.40 DM) for a room. The next day's travel was mostly downhill to the Rhine, forty-two miles away.

On the way, they passed a lot of bombed-out concrete gun emplacements. Those things were big enough that it wasn't worth blasting them out, yet they were too massive to bury. They hadn't seen any wooden shoes in Holland, but about thirteen miles from the Rhine, they witnessed some women wearing thick woolen socks inside wooden shoes with leather straps across the instep.

The Rhine itself was about 900 feet wide and the banks were not steep. The current was swift enough though, that river boats going upstream had a tough time. About sixteen miles from the Rhine, they passed into the wine district, and it was harvest time. There were quite a few horse-drawn carts with large wooden tubs full of grapes going to the village presses. When they rode past the slow-moving tub carts, most of the grapes looked small and were in compact clusters. From Zweibrucken down to Landau, they were following valleys that wound through the high hills. Finally, about twenty-two miles from the Rhine, they broke out onto the plain. Starting early, the going was easy. They covered about fifty miles in three hours, which put them into Karlsruhe mid-afternoon.

They changed all their French francs into deutschmarks, then rode over and got a room in a part of town that was off limits to all Americans and Allied personnel as stated in a large sign prominently displayed on the street. Taking the bikes to a service station, they washed them of all the accumulated grime. At the pace they were progressing, they'd run out of money before accomplishing everything they'd hoped to do. The brothers decided it was time to sell the bicycles and get something with a little more horsepower, perhaps motor scooters, or at least something with an engine.

They ended up hitting a few bars that night, which were full of black soldiers dancing with the German girls. One of the black GIs immediately invited them to his table and got their story. He bought a round of beer and found out they were innocents abroad. Although he was quite cordial, it was obvious they were in the wrong bar and soon departed.

The central police station was the place to find out the requirements for buying and operating motorbikes. The way the police described it, it was a three-step operation: insurance, Customs, and police. They went down to a dealer and he took care of it all, escaping a lot of red tape, because the motorbikes were only 48 cc., which classed them as bicycles with auxiliary motors and not as motorcycles. The salesman looked at the bikes and offered thirty-five dollars (140 DM) each, just shy of their asking price. That left a balance of $119 (475 DM) to pay for each of the mopeds, taking a loss of about $12.50 each on the bicycles, which was a comparatively small price to pay to get rid of them. In U.S. dollars, the mopeds were $154 each. After a few trial runs around town, they returned to the dealership to get Bill's speedometer cable replaced, and then they were off to the Rhine Valley, which was about twenty miles wide at Karlsruhe. They didn't get started until 3:30, but managed to cover forty-four miles by 9:30. Suddenly, they could travel at night, because they had headlights.

A pitcher of water and a basin in the room for washing purposes, sheets, blankets, and big feather-filled comforters or *bettdecken* were on each of the beds at the rather primitive *gasthaus* they stopped at in Lahr, which made it hotter than hell beneath the covers. Their feet stuck out at the end, which didn't make for good sleeping, but they muddled through the night. The next day, they put on double pairs of pants, shirts, coats, and rain capes to beat the cold. It was not a problem bicycling, because they were creating their own heat, but sitting without moving on the motorbikes froze them to the bone in a wintry blast. Bill said it was like outboard motoring on Puget Sound in winter without protective clothing.

They stopped at the first gas station they came across and filled up, which cost about thirty-five cents, and they each got a pair of goggles. Looking like the "Wild Ones", made forty miles to Freiburg by 1:00 p.m. and stopped for coffee. They also put on an extra pair of socks. Freiburg to Basel, Switzerland, was another forty-three miles,

FRANKFURT
PRAGUE
CZECH REP.
LUXEMBOURG
LUXEMBOURG
BRNO
STRASBOURG
STUTTGART
MUNICH
VIENNA
AUSTRIA
LIECHTENSTEIN
BERN
ZÜRICH
SWITZERLAND
ALPS
LJUBLJANA
ZAGREB
SLOVENIA
CROATIA
MILAN
TURIN
VENICE
GENOA
ITALY
BOSNIA
DALMATIA
RIVIERA
MONACO
MONACO
LIGURIAN SEA
FLORENCE
SAN MARINO
APPENNINI
ADRIATIC SEA
CORSE
VATICAN CITY
VATICAN
ROME
NAPLES
TYRRHENIAN SEA

ZHYTOMYR
KRAKÓW
LVOV
TATRA MTS.
VINNYTSYA
SLOVAKIA
ISLAVA
CHERNIVTSI
BALTI
MOLDOVA
DUBASAR
BUDAPEST
IASI
HUNGARY
CLUJ-NAPOCA
CHISINAU
ALFÖLD
CARPATHIAN MOUNTAINS
ROMANIA
TRANSYLVANIAN ALPS
BELGRADE
BUCHAREST
AND HERZ.
DANUBE
SERBIA
SARAJEVO
CONSTANTA
BALKAN PEN.
DINARIC ALPS
BALKAN MTS.
MONTENEGRO
PRISTINA
SOFIA
BULGARIA
VARNA
KOSOVO
ODGORICA
SKOPJE
TIRANA
MACEDONIA
BOSPO
ISTANBU
THESSALONIKI
ALBANIA
SEA OF MARMARA
BURSA

where Bill's gears started slipping on a steep hill coming into Basel, generally giving him a rough time. They went into town looking for an Achilles-Sachs dealer, but nobody knew where one might be. Someone in Basel said their "guarantees" were no good in Switzerland, so they found a dealership about six miles back, in Lorbach, West Germany. It was too late to do business by the time they arrived, and all the hotels were full, so they pushed into Germany until they came to Binzen. They stayed the night there in a *gasthaus* that was a few cuts above the one the night before. They wanted to get the motorbike trouble cleared up the next day and be on their way. Switzerland was more expensive than they could stand, so they decided they didn't want to spend much time there. However, they heard that the last of the passes over the Alps closed that day, so they would have to go up as far as possible and then take the train over to Italy.

CHAPTER 16 SWITZERLAND

October 18, 1958

Like all great travelers, I have seen more than I remember, and remember more than I've seen.—Benjamin Disraeli

THEY BIT OFF A GOOD CHUNK OF MILEAGE that got them almost completely across Switzerland. Earlier that morning, they went to the Sachs shop and got the moped trouble cleared up with some simple adjustments and installed a new taillight for Bill's bike. They started out from Basel by noon, heading southeast for Zurich, fifty miles away. Traveling along the Rhine for quite a while, they noticed the river narrowing considerably before veering away to the south. There was no sign of the Alps before Zurich.

As three sail planes orbited overhead, they immediately asked about the roads over the mountains, finding out they wouldn't hit high mountains on the route until Austria. Blasting through the downtown section of Zurich on their mopeds, they rode along the eponymously named lake shaped like a banana, which led out of Zurich. It was colder than hell, so Bill got a pair of Bermuda socks out of his pack and put them on over his gloves. The snow-covered foothills were in the distance, but the tops of the mountains were in the clouds. It got dark when they were about two hours outside of Zurich, so they switched on the headlights and could see the mountains lowering down over them.

They arrived in Walenstadt, a town ringed by mountains. The road ahead went up the mountainside several thousand feet in a series of switchbacks. They could see the lights of towns they had driven through below in the distance. Coming down the other side, they took the bikes out of gear and free-wheeled down the mountain, keeping the motors going in order to have lights. It was a scary ride down. The road was paved brick into town, wet and slick, and seemed as steep as a double-diamond ski slope. This was the fastest the mopeds would ever fly, and they hoped to make it to the bottom in one piece, only braking as the road leveled out going into town. It got colder as they descended into the valley, where all the cold air drained from the ringing hillsides. Farther into the mountains, they noticed that the valleys were hemmed in by near-vertical, sheer walls instead of gradual slopes. The destination was Sargans, almost to the Lichtenstein border, and they made it by 8:00 and put up at a *gasthaus* called the White Rose. They had covered 108 miles, which was good going on mopeds. Their shoulders were tight from leaning on the handlebars all day.

CHAPTER 17 PRINCIPALITY OF LIECHTENSTEIN AND AUSTRIA

OCTOBER 19–20, 1958

You've got to be careful if you don't know where you're going, because you might not get there.—Yogi Berra

THE NEXT DAY, they left Sargans, traveled ninety-three miles, and passed through Liechtenstein into Austria, crossing the Alps trippingly. Liechtenstein was founded in 1719 and was originally two large estates. On a small-scale map, it was merely a flyspeck. During the mid-nineteenth century, it was part of the Holy Roman Empire.[1]

They stopped in Vaduz, the capitol of Liechtenstein, a sixty-two-square-mile country, gassed up, and sent several postcards. When it began to rain, they parked the mopeds under an overhanging roof of a gas station and then frequented the nearest pub, the Rathskeller. The dark beer was Wolfsmilch and slightly resembled Guinness. Only one beer later, it stopped raining and they got underway to the Austrian border and the town of Feldkirch in Austria. They saw many of the locals in traditional dress. It wasn't a holiday, so they speculated the costumes were provided from funds of the local Chamber of Commerce. The women's costume had a gathered waist, with a full skirt and apron, while the men wore knee-length breeches, a flat black hat, and a loden or wool coat.

They came to the headwaters of the Rhine River, where the water ran down sluices and spilled over fish ladders. At Bludenz, they stopped for coffee and bumped into a fellow they had met while waiting for the ferry to cross the Mosel River in the Saar Basin. He was taking a three-year bicycling trip around the world, including South Africa and Tibet. Out of Bludenz, they started to climb and soon got into snow at Innerbraz and stayed in it all the way to Nauders.

Dick stopping to let his moped engine cool off as we head for the pass

Bill stopping to let his moped engine cool of.

LIECHTENSTEIN
ZÜRICH
FELDKIRCH
ST. CHRISTOPH
VADUZ
BLUDENZ
INNERBRAZ
LANDECK
SARGANS
NAUDERS
ZERLAND
ALPS
MILAN

MUNICH
AUSTI
LJUBLJAN
SLOVENI

They crossed Arlberg Pass at 5,000 feet on their mopeds, which they thought was not too dissimilar to Hannibal's crossing on elephants. The mopeds also proved cantankerous and had to be encouraged, kicked, and shoved in order to make it. The constant climbing overheated the engines, and they started to glow and then would balk and seize. Throwing snow on them seemed to cool them off. As the mahouts of their steeds, they'd climb some more, the mopeds would overheat, then seize. They'd wait and throw snow again on the engines that were hot enough to burn you if you touched them. They repeated the needy process every several thousand feet until the summit. Visibility was almost nill toward the top, where a snowstorm was raging and many cars were stuck or bogged down in the snow. The top of the Alps was at St. Christoph, where they rested briefly, then cruised down through many beautiful landscapes and picturesque Austrian villages.

In Landeck, they ate a dinner of ham and eggs with a spider thrown in, that subsequently was thrown out, then pressed on for Nauders, with Bill leading, since the taillight on his unit was out. Climbing again, they soon were going along the side of sheer rock cliffs with outcroppings of rock overhanging the road. Wherever the highway engineers couldn't blast, they tunneled, and where they couldn't tunnel, they bridged, leaving the mountainside with a highly variegated face.

Several kilometers before Nauders, they crossed Hockfinstermuenz Pass, then arrived at Nauders/Tirol, Austria at 8:15 p.m. They tried to get a room in an apartment house, but it was suggested they go to Nauders proper, where they checked in at the Post Hotel, paying twenty-six schillings apiece. The next day, they planned to cross another pass and head down the mountains, where sunny Italy awaited.

They woke that morning to find heavy snow falling, but without wind. Outside the window, the marketplace was in full swing, with the village people bundled up and shopping for goods in the tented stalls they could see from the hotel. The stalls around the platz were crowded, and it was business as usual under way, while all were tramping in the snow.

Open air market in the snow— Nauders, Austria.

LJUBLJANA
SLOVENIA
ZAGREB
CROATIA
ALFÖLD
VENICE
BELGRADE
BOSNIA AND HERZ.
SERBIA
SARAJEVO
DALMATIA
BALKAN PEN.
SAN MARINO
DINARIC ALPS
APPENNINI
ADRIATIC SEA
MONTENEGRO
PRISTINA
SOFIA
KOSOVO
PODGORICA
ROME
SKOPJE
MACEDONIA
TIRANA
NAPLES
ALBANIA
THESSALONIKI
PINDUS MTS.
CALABRIA
GREECE
IONIAN IS.
PALERMO
ATHENS
PELOPONNISOS
SICILIA
IONIAN SEA
MALTA

CHISINAU
ROMANIA
ODESSA
SEA OF
CRIMEA
BUCHAREST
DANUBE DELTA
CONSTANTA
BALKAN MTS.
BULGARIA
VARNA
BLACK SEA
CAPE INCE
BOSPORUS
ISTANBUL
SEA OF MARMARA
BURSA
ANKARA
DARDANELLES
ANATOLIA
LESBOS
AEGEAN SEA
TURKEY
KAYSERI
IZMIR
DENIZLI
KONYA
CYCLADES
ANTALYA
TAURUS MTS.
ADANA
ICEL
RHODES
SEA OF CRETE

CHAPTER 18 NORTHERN ITALY

OCTOBER 20–23, 1958

Kilometers are shorter than miles. Save gas, take your next trip in kilometers.—George Carlin

MAKING IT TO ITALY WAS NO TROUBLE. It was three miles to the border, then 185 miles more to Venice. The road was slushy in spots, but hard-packed with snow and ice in others. They exchanged some money at the Italian frontier, had passports stamped, and then began the big descent, which lasted all day. Just past the first village on the Italian side was a lake, Lago de Resia. Sticking up from it was a clock tower, which was all that was visible of an inundated village. Farther down was the dam that created the lake. They came upon a gradual descent for about 19 miles and then hit a series of steep hairpin curves and right-angle switchbacks that dropped them another 3,280 feet in the space of two miles, which placed them below the snow line. They spent some time gloriously freewheeling before coming down into a long valley hemmed by high mountains and eventually reaching into an orchard region where red apples were the chief crop, with some grapes on the hillsides. Further down, it began to warm up. The temperature felt comfortable while moving on the mopeds for the first time.

They got soaked splashing through wet snow and puddles, but it didn't take long to get dry on their downward cruise, with the wind streaming through their clothes. They'd covered 373 miles already on their bike engines, so they stopped to change the gear case oil and get a couple of shots of rum. The bikes certainly deserved it after the abuse they put them through. They had brought oil from Germany, but the changing process was messy. Taking advantage of the opportunity to wipe off the accumulated mud and grime gathered in the mountains, when they were through, the mopeds looked halfway presentable.

The road ahead always looked like the bottom of the valley, but they kept riding down, down, down. Outside of Merano, they dropped about 500 feet, and it got cold again. Going through the town, there was an open market in the square, and lots of people on the street. Another eighteen miles took them to Bolzano and coffee and cheese sandwiches. Skidding down into Trento in about an hour and a half, they stopped outside of town for vino and a shot of grappa, a syrupy white brandy that was bracing. They were told that it was about 70 percent alcohol, so the first sip would have a bite, but if it is a good grappa, it will warm all the way down and will have a taste of the grapes it was made from.

Many of the folks in that part of Italy are multilingual and speak both German and Italian, and the majority of road signs were bilingual. They stopped for the night in Pergine, outside of Trento, in a *gasthaus* with a couple of good beds. It was only 105 miles from Venice, the next day's destination.

So far, they had been burning about two-plus gallons of gas per day each, which was damn cheap transportation. Gas cost about fifty cents per day, which was mixed with oil at a 1:25 ratio. The mopeds were getting them across Europe quickly too, as they listened to European radio programs that featured light classical music rather than rock and roll, and they were content to find all the Elvis they wanted on the jukeboxes.

They got off on October 21 to an early start from Pergine and were on the road by 10:00. It was at least 44 miles of cold going before they got out of the rugged alpine foothills and hit level ground at Bassano del Grappa. Through the hills, they passed quite a few hydroelectric developments. It was slightly warmer after Bassano del Grappa, and there was even a weak bit of sunshine. They passed through Cittadella, which was ringed by an ancient crumbling wall. They ate in Padua—pizza and vino—and drove around the city before covering the last twenty-two miles to Venice. On the way, they passed by the slow-moving Brenta River, where women were washing clothes on the shore. The water looked muddy and too dirty to do any good for their laundry. A good part of the road from Bassano del Grappa to Padua consisted of long straight stretches bordered by large overhanging trees. Outside of Venice about nine miles, they came to an industrial section with a large oil refinery, docks, and high cranes. Just before the long causeway going into the city, they linked up with the Autostrada, a super-highway that stretched from Padua to Venice. The causeway was a six-lane highway, plus two railroad tracks and a sidewalk, which led to several parking lots and some garages. In the city itself, they could either walk or go by gondola, which cost $3.22 (2,000 lira) an hour, way over their budget.

VENICE

THEY PARKED THE MOPEDS in a garage for sixteen cents (100 lira) each, per day, and the parking attendant gave them a steer to a cheap hotel. The one he suggested went for 1,500 lira a night, whereas other places quoted about 1,800. The exchange rate was approximately 100 lira to 16 cents, 620 lira to $1. Venice was a tourist trap, so they expected things to be more expensive. After they moved into the hotel, they walked toward the main part of the city, going over bridges, through alleys—there were hundreds. Crossing the Rialto Bridge over the Grand Canal, which was built in 1540–70, they came to the Piazza San Marco with the Campanile Tower in the corner. There were pigeons all over the place. The Campanile di San Marco is the bell tower of St. Mark's Basilica and is 323 feet tall.[1] Their ramble landed them on the other side of the city. There were nine small lagoon islands off the central part of the city. Murano and Burano and seven others with the Adriatic Sea spread out beyond them. After all that tramping around the city, they were quite hungry and found a restaurant with an English menu. They anticipated the ability to read an Italian menu within a few days if they were to stay in Italy long enough.

Miraculously, they made it back to the hotel through the labyrinth of alleys without too much trouble and picked up a bottle of vino on the way to keep them company. The wine in Italy was either red or white, light-bodied, with just a little tang to it. It was much better than American wine and seemed to go with anything except pears. The room overlooked a canal and was down from the Tre Pont, where three bridges came together at the intersection of two canals. They were about 100 miles from Triest and Yugoslavia and wanted to rest and work the kinks out before any more traveling. They had covered almost 600 miles in six days and were rather "moped-pooped," to coin a phrase.

They got up mid-morning and struck out to take some pictures of Venice, or "Venezia," as the Italians preferred. Taking the same route as the night before, they landed only a few blocks off the Riva Dega Schrivani to the east, walked back by the Palazzo Ducale, and took more pictures. After plowing through the pigeon hoards that inhabited the square, came to the Campanile, and for 100 lira, were allowed to walk to the top via thirty-six inclined ramps. From the top, the lagoon that stretched away on either side of Venice was visible. The Lido, a skinny island 7.5 miles to the south, was the main land barrier to the Adriatic and acted as a breakwater. Venice wasn't very large, but what there was of it was so extremely intricate. On top of the Campanile are five bells, each with a special purpose: *The Renghiera* (aka *Maleficio*)

Pigeons and people on St Mark's Square.

to announce executions; the *Mezza Terza* to note the Senate was in session; the *Nona* announced midday; the *Trottiera* called the members of the Maggior Consiglio to meetings; and the *Marangona*, the largest, to note the beginning and ending of the work day.[2]

Descending, they crossed the square to Cook's Travel office, but they were out to lunch and wouldn't be back until 3:00. They killed the time drinking *bianca*, or white wine, and hobnobbing with the natives. When the office opened, they sauntered over and got some information, then started toward their hotel by passing the Stazione di Venezia Santa Lucia at the end of the causeway.

Retracing their steps, they got across the Ponte di Rialto, where Dick decided a shortcut could be found and started leading the way toward the back alleys, which inevitably were blind ends. At one point, they were stymied by a canal and hailed gondoliers, both commercial and tourist type, but no deal. Eventually, they got back on the main drag and arrived at the Chiesa, or Church of San Nicolo de Mendicoli, and asked a *carabinieri*, a local cop, for directions back to the Stazione. He directed them along the commercial docks to the Chiesa della Scalzi at the end of the causeway. From there, they found their way home with no trouble, after many a footsore mile. They had made a loop around the western end of the city.

Happy as they were to be home, only a short rest was afforded before they were off again to get dinner. As in Paris, they rounded up some bread, ham, cheese, vino, and butter and retired to the apartment to fix dinner. It was much cheaper to fix their own dinner than to eat out, and breakfast was at hand in the morning.

They left Venice by mid-morning and connected with the road to Trieste at the end of the causeway. The countryside was flat almost all the way to Trieste, ninety miles away. The mountains were faintly visible on their left, and at one spot, they saw snow-capped peaks in the distance. Looking back from about nineteen miles, the Campanile was still visible. Steady going through the flat farm country got them to Monfalcone. There, the hills came down to the sea and the road began to climb. The road was carved into the side of the cliff, with Trieste situated on an inverted bowl-shaped hillside. The open side of the hill sloped down to the sea with larger hills behind it. To the west, the flat plains curved along the shore of the Adriatic and ended at the feet of the barely visible Alpine foothills. At the shore's edge, the water was blue, shading to turquoise.

That afternoon, they stopped for lunch in Ciggia and ran into a wedding reception. It seemed like every time they took a break, they attracted an audience. People liked to try the bells on the bikes and to look the units over and comment. Everyone neglected the beautiful bride until they cleared out.

Bill holding up a support column outside St Mark's Cathedral, Venice, Italy.

Dick taking a break and looking over the gondola pens on the Grand Canal.

ANSODA LEMON

Lemon soda dealer delivering his product to market along one of the canals.

CHAPTER 19 YUGOSLAVIA

October 23–28, 1958

I can't think of anything that excites a greater sense of childlike wonder than to be in a country where you are ignorant of almost everything.—Bill Bryson

ARRIVING IN THE FREE PORT OF TRIESTE as the sun disappeared into the sea, they tried unsuccessfully to buy a map of Yugoslavia, as all the stores were shut. They took the road to Pola and came to the Yugoslav frontier five miles outside of the city. Their visas were in order, so all they had to do was make out a declaration form and they were off. At the border, some people were drinking a kind of banana liqueur. The brother's impression was that lemon extract would be champagne compared to the stuff they were quaffing. They changed some money just inside the border and got 400 dinara to the dollar.

On the way, they figured out Pola was the wrong road and turned east to intercept the main road to Rijeka. Pola is at the seaside tip of an arrowhead-like peninsula and would have required them to travel back again to get to Rijeka. They talked to some cops in a little place and checked directions, looking for an excuse to get warm and stay and talked awhile—all sign language, of course. Bill drew a map of the United States, showing the Seattle region, to let them know where they were from. From there, they rode up a large hill, which curved back to the north and soon ended up overlooking Trieste, now on the right track. The lights of the city were winking far below them in the night.

As they tooled along parallel to each other down the deserted travel way at dusk, a siren and flashing red light and siren howled. A Yugoslavian trooper on a white motorcycle stopped them and motioned for them to drive single file and not abreast. He looked very impressive in white leather coveralls, a white crash helmet with a red star in the center, but language was a barrier, and it took a lot of going around. He had no English, French, or Spanish, and two of them had no Slavic languages. After much gesticulation and instruction on his part, in what was either Slovenian or Serbo-Croat, they finally got the message and lined their bikes up behind each other, and he positively beamed. Bill and Dick thanked him and moved out in single file, but not before he waved them on with his only English word, "Cheerio."

When they left the leeward side of the hills, they ran into the full force of the Adriatic *bora*, a violent, cold northeasterly winter wind out of the Adriatic Sea, similar to the mistral of France or the *Foehn* of Austria and southern Germany that also comes from the north. The *bora* they experienced was not so cold, but at times, it grew so strong they could hardly make it down the hill in first gear, as it tried to blow them off the track. As they reached a lower altitude, it diminished somewhat and they found a small town and had supper of *zuppa de legumes*, or vegetable soup, goulash over some thick spaghetti, and some lousy Yugoslavian vino *bianco*. Yugoslavian wine was not nearly as good as the Italian, and they didn't have any vino *rosso*.

After supper, they traveled 6.2 miles over the Yugoslavian hills and dales in the moonlight to Rupa, a small town that had a hotel of sorts. The first thing the hotel wanted to know was whether the brothers had passports. It took a lot of fooling around to explain things to the innkeeper's daughter, who was conducting the interrogation, and for her to write it down. After that ordeal, they each had a glass of stuff labeled medicinal brandy and retired to their chamber. The place wasn't air-conditioned and it wasn't needed. It was cold outside and the wind was blowing hard and moaning through the wooden shutters in the room, while bright moonlight peeked through like a distorted spotlight on the creaky furniture. The wind would sound eerie any place, but especially in that house, hit with moaning buffets in the wilds of Yugoslavia.

When people saw the "D" for Deutschland decals on the bike's rear fenders, they thought the two of them were German. As soon as they opened their mouths, that quickly changed to being Englishmen or Scotsmen, because of Dick's Scotch plaid cap.

Up by 9:15, they had to settle for a cup of tea with medicinal rum in it until they reached Rijeka. The riding was up and down for a while until they began descending from the hills. Along the way, they passed many small natural circular depressions in the stony countryside. At the bottom of these depressions, soil had collected and was under cultivation. Most of the patches were no bigger than a backyard garden, but looked well cared for.

Rijeka lay at the head of a gulf on the northern coast of Yugoslavia. The city was tacked onto a rather steep hillside. When they stopped for gas outside of Rijeka, there was a fellow sitting at the gas station that had been in the United States for thirty some years and had spent time in Tacoma, close to their home. He'd returned to Yugoslavia to retire.

They met quite a few people who spoke English. But, it was a European English with a continental intonation, not American. The people there were more curious than the Italians they had encountered. When they drove up on mopeds, people simply gathered around and peered at the machines. If they talked to any of them, they told them they were Americans, saying "Amerikanski" or something like that. From their demeanor, it seemed they thought that was OK. It took a little while to get oriented and find a restaurant, and ended up eating beef steak for breakfast.

They thought they'd continue down the coast, but outside the restaurant, Dick talked to a fellow who said the road to Dubrovnik was rough and not so good. He also wanted to buy some American dollars from them at 50 percent more than the official rate, or 600 dinara per dollar. They told him to meet back at the restaurant and they went down to the shipping office and found a ship that left by 4:00 p.m. That allowed some time to kill, so they spent the time exploring the hills behind Rijeka. They met their friend on time, but he wanted cash and not a traveler's check. They thanked him anyway for the road advice, double-checked on what he said, which everyone confirmed, and went and booked a second-class passage to Dubrovnik at $7.50 (3,000 dinara) each—1,200 of which went for the mopeds' transport. They were led to believe that second class included a cabin, but it actually meant they just got a ride on the boat and had to sleep wherever they could, so they paid the difference for first class. The total cost was about ten dollars apiece to travel the 373 miles to Dubrovnik from Rijeka by sea. They had an outside, two-bunk cabin on the *Partizanka*. It was a good-sized ship, painted white and kept in decent shape. En route, the ship was to stop at Zadar, Split, and Makarska.

Leaving Rijeka on time, they steamed for two hours down the rugged coastline, weaving through a number of large offshore islands. Coastal mountains marched up to even higher mountains behind them. If they had been a little farther north, those mountains would have been covered with snow. The landscape was rocky with scrub trees and appeared to be barren land. They anticipated arriving in Dubrovnik the next evening, which would leave them approximately 311 miles from Greece.

The ship stopped in Split at 7:00 a.m. on October 25 to discharge some light cargo and passengers. Dick took a walk around the harbor to the National Bank and changed some money. At that point, they were far enough south to run into palm trees. The town of Split was situated on a hillside with a bit of level ground at the water's edge and the hills behind were bare rock. That entire morning, they had been looking at those high barren hills, with their spotty green patches of trees and shrubs near the shore. The hills rose steeply to what looked like 1,500–2,000 feet, presenting a dismal, sterile landscape. On Dick's ramble in town, he found that the Roman Emperor Diocletian retired there and died in AD 315. [1]

The ship was run by a bunch of greasy bastards. When shipboard, they had them over a barrel. When the brothers wanted a cabin the night before, they had to pay to be in first class and then pay for the cabin on top of that! That didn't include meals, which were tacked on to the rest of the bill. Then, the crew made them get out of the cabin by 7:00 a.m.

They stopped in a small place called Makarska, which had a hidden harbor that the ship had to back out of. Steep slopes ran halfway up the hills behind the town and then became sheer cliffs. The road that ran down the coast was cut into the face of this cliff. The town of Makarska must have had a tough time communicating with the rest of the country by land. It had been cloudless all day and the sun felt good.

Coastal Yugoslavia is dotted with hundreds of islands and the mainland is hilly, spare, wild, and mountainous. This was an area of partisan fighting only a few years before. When World War II broke out, Yugoslavia's Prince Paul declared the country neutral. A coup d'etat by the Serbs ousted Paul and replaced him with seventeen-year-old King Peter. Germany, Italy, and Bulgaria invaded Yugoslavia on April 6, 1941 with thirty-three divisions and 1,200 warplanes, resulting in the king and the government fleeing and the army surrendering.[2]

The country of Yugoslavia was an artificial construct resulting from realignment of boundaries after World War I. There were many political, religious, ethnic, and racial reasons and factions who had old wrongs to be righted. For two years after this upheaval, royalist General Draza Mihajlovic led the Serbian Chetniks in partisan warfare against the Croatian (Fascist, Nazi, or Ustashe) puppet government. The Germans created Muslim divisions and set them against Christian civilians and partisans. Joseph Broz (Marshall Tito), a Croatian Communist, campaigned against both the invaders and the Croatian fascists. He was successful in recruiting from both Serb and Croatian ethnics, because the Chetniks and Ustashe were persecuting age-old enemies. Tito eventually raised twenty-four divisions for his army. The minority Jews, Gypsies, and Muslims had fewer choices and suffered from both sides.[3]

During World War II, the Allies initially supported Mihajlovic, until they swung their support to Marshall Tito in 1943, when he had over 100,000 soldiers under his command and controlled 40,000 square miles of his homeland. Essentially, it was a civil war within a war. Between the factions, over two million citizens were killed, ranking Yugoslavia as the fourth largest loser of civilian population during World War II after Russia, Poland, and Germany.[4]

The Germans did not treat the partisans as an army subject to the Geneva Conventions. Partisans were treated as criminals and would be shot on the spot. The Germans would retaliate against civilian villagers, whom they suspected of aiding partisan guerillas. On occasion, they would machine-gun entire villages of civilians, including women and children. The partisans retaliated in kind when they captured Germans. After the war, Tito took control of Yugoslavia as a Communist country from 1944 until 1980. He was kicked out of the Comintern, Russia's coterie of nations under Communist rule resulting from World War II, when he went against Joseph Stalin's wishes.[5]

The rugged islands they were steaming past had not just a recent bloody history, but also an old one reaching back in time. The Celts drove the Illyrians south, the Romans conquered Macedonia in 168

BC, and then they subjugated the Celts by AD 16. The Goths sacked Roman fortresses along the Danube in AD 448, the Huns ravaged areas northwest of Belgrade, the Ostrogoths conquered Dalmatia by AD 463, and the Romans, under Emperor Justinian, retook the land in the sixth century.[6] More recently, in the 1990s, Serbia undertook an ethnic cleansing of the Muslim lands. Serbian leader Slobodan Milosevic engineered the multicultural dissolution of Bosnia and Kosovo with many lives lost.[7]

They arrived in Dubrovnik at dusk and at the dock had to fight off the representatives of various hotels. They headed up the hill and found a tourist office at the top. Outside the door, a woman asked if they wanted to stay at her place. She quoted a lodging price of $1.55 (620 dinara) for both. After making it clear that was all they could pay, she accepted, and they followed her into the residential section of Dubrovnik, where they settled into a clean room and then had to accompany the woman down to the police station to register. It was a far better experience than the two nights before at Rupa, because they did the writing and the cops put a stamp on their visas. After the formalities, they had an omelet and salad for dinner, washed down with terrible Yugoslavian wine. Dick observed how they must let goats trample the grapes and ferment the juice in old tennis shoes.

All of Yugoslavia seemed to be on hillsides. There was one wide street in Dubrovnik that ran along the length of a level stretch, from which narrow alleys ran off. No cars came into this section, because it had an ancient wall around it and was constructed mainly of limestone. The section dead-ended, blocking any thoroughfare. The stones in the oldest part of that wall had some of their surface dissolved and seemed to run together as if they were melted. The joints were just barely discernible.

They joined the natives for a "red hot" Saturday night in Dubrovnik by promenading up and down the main street. Stopping at a bakery, they had some pastry, and Dick tried a shot of cherry brandy that was dark brown and sweet and made a good after-dinner drink. Later on, they both tried a shot of maraschino liqueur, which was white, viscous, sweet, with a bite, and faintly reminiscent of tanned leather. It was distilled from Dalmatian cherries from Zadar, just north of there. It appeared, from the looks of their cigarettes and liqueurs, that they imported no foreign brands, but made all the products themselves. Plum brandy, or slivovitz, is the national drink, along with its companion, cherry *kirsch*. They also had the nerve to call some of their brandy, Cognac, an appellation restricted to brandy from the eponymous region in France.

It was only 8:00 p.m. when they got out the mopeds, went down to the docks, where there were several bars, and had more cherry brandy at an outside table across the street from the harbor. It was so balmy they hardly needed coats, and all the shops had their doors open. The moonlight reflected off the white limestone, making it very light out. They had worked hard to get down into this kind of weather. They ended up back at their digs an hour later and took one last jaunt up a steep flight of stairs until a wall at the top of the hill stopped them at a dead end. The buildings were so close around, they could hear people talking across the alley on either side. They were safe though, since they didn't understand a word.

They had to go back down the hill to the docks to get gas from the "Yugo Petrol" station, and then were off at 11:00 on a beautiful Sunday morning. They went to Mass earlier in an ancient church, the Dubrovnik Cathedral, richly decorated with paintings and what looked like silver fixtures.

Dick had trouble with his chain rattling against his rear fender, but got it straightened out by bending the fender in. Since the bikes were identical, Bill did the same to his moped, should he have the same problem. About eleven miles out of Hercegnovi, they ran out of paved road and the hills became steeper. Outside a village called Gruda, a motorcyclist passed Dick going rather fast, and when he caught up with Bill, he beeped his horn and ran into Bill's rear end! The guy and his bike ended up in the ditch, and all Bill got was a few scratches on his rear left shock absorber. The guy didn't understand English, but Dick gave him hell for going so fast on such a lousy road, to no linguistic avail. They helped the guy get out of the ditch and into the next village. In Gruda, they bought him mighty shots of slivovitz, and he went merrily on his way while the two of them supplemented their meager breakfast with risotto, tomato sauce, and meat. The last stretch into Hercegnovi was over a particularly rough surface, and they were worried about their tires. From there, they thought the road would be paved all the way to Greece.

They were scofflaws again, riding abreast and not tandem or single files skimming along the shoreline, passing through villages and honking at the natives to get out of the way. The next stop was Kotor, at the other side of a deep and bulbous-shaped inlet. They were supposed to connect with a ferry to save the long trip around by road, but they missed it. They had been told the road would be good the whole way, so they forged on, but unfortunately, the road gave out into more of a goat track than a road. "Good" apparently had a different meaning in these latitudes. After a bouncy ride, they rolled into Kotor ready to tell Marshall Tito where to shove his road.

Kotor is an ancient city tucked under a high ring of cliffs at the farthest reach of the inlet. Coming in, they saw a large ship tied up, with flags waving and people trooping up and down the gangplank. Their simultaneous thought was: *Is this ship going our way?*

They went into town and asked around and found out it was a new cargo/passenger ship of 10,500 tons, heading to a port near Athens,

Greece. The greatest problem was seeing if they could get aboard. Bill buzzed over to the Putnik office, which was the name of the National Travel Bureau throughout Yugoslavia. The fellow there was helpful. He contacted the ship's agency in town and squared it with them. After the captain's approval, they got on the ship for fifty dollars (30,000 dinara), which included everything. They gave the captain money that night and made plans to arrive shipside at 7:00 the next morning "mit der mopeds." They were the first passengers the *MSZeta* ever carried, so they expected things to be rather plush. She had just finished outfitting after being launched in Gdansk, Poland. However, things were a bit confused shipboard because of the open house they had all day, and the fellow from Putnik was nice enough to find them a room to stay onshore that night.

Our ship, the MS Zeta departing Kotor harbor, Yugoslavia.

Earlier in the evening while waiting to see the captain, they walked up a road, watching the stars come out and waited for the moon to come up over the cliffs behind Kotor. Looking down the channel, the Big Dipper was perfectly framed by the cliffs on either side. They could see the glow of the moon and the shadow of the cliffs on the other side of the inlet. While standing around trying to throw rocks high enough to catch the moonlight, a bright light was moving on the water. It was a boat with a gas lantern in the bow. A man was standing up spearing fish in the clear water while another one rowed. The boat passed under the low bridge they were on, so they were able to look down and see exactly what the fishermen were doing. The lantern in the bow attracted the fish, frozen by the strong light, so all he had to do was spear them. The bowman got a big one right below us. By that time, the moon had come up through a saddle in the cliff. It was so bright that it illuminated a cloudless sky, making it look like daylight.

Dick looking out on walled city of Kotor, Yugoslavia with the Adriatic beyond.

The man from the Putnik office said they were in what used to be the Kingdom of Montenegro, or "Black Mountain." Before 1918, Yugoslavia was the Kingdom of Yugoslavia and not an alliance of states, but a centralized country, ruled by a king in Belgrade. It was comprised of six Balkan states: Croatia-Herzegovina, Croatia, Macedonia, Montenegro, Serbia, and Slovenia. After World War II, they each became autonomous under the rule of Marshall Tito's Communist regime.[8] The man's hometown, Cetinje, was 31 miles up in the mountains and had been a capital city for 400 years. The Yugo comes from a Greek word meaning "to yoke," or join. Kotor itself goes back to the seventh century, as does Dubrovnik. In Kotor, there was a walled central section, and at the main entrance, there was a Latin inscription which said the wall was completed in 1657. Construction began in the twelfth century and took 500 years to complete. The central section was for pedestrian traffic only. In the part of the city they stayed in, the women still went to a common well for their water.

On board the ship again the next morning, there was much horn blowing and waving. A twenty-ton crane hoisted their mopeds on deck like they were a couple of paper dolls. The cabin was as nice as they had hoped. There was a double-decked berth, a private john, two full-size closets, and a sitting room with a desk, couch, and chairs. Two large portholes were nicely curtained. However, when the ship was built, somebody went key-happy. Between the doors, the closet, desk drawers, and bedside table, there were eleven keys; only one used was for the outside door.

The ship tried to feed them salami for breakfast, but they held out and got eggs and a pot of tea. After breakfast, they went exploring through the shaft alley, up a long ladder into the dry food storage compartment, the steering gear compartment, and up into blackness, which turned out to be one of the after-holds. They followed it forward past casks of wine until they came to the engine room. The engine was Italian-made, under Swiss license, Sulzer, a real monster with seven cylinders and 4900 HP. Since they were the first and only passengers, they ate with the ship's officers and captain in their dining salon. At lunch, they put flagons of wine on the table. It was no chore polishing off one between them.

There were Yugoslavian Navy PT boats moored nearby that took off after lunch, but just put-putted out to a tug and stopped. The captain told them they would leave later that afternoon, and it was 2:30 before they cleared the dock with half the town looking on and waving. The captain was going out slow, giving everything a good look. In one spot, he went into a large cove and turned the ship in a full circle. At Hercegnovi, the captain dropped the Customs official and some other officials who rode up the inlet with us, then finally cleared for the Adriatic Sea at 4:45 p.m. Later that evening, the coastline was all but invisible, and the full moon was well up. Bill took a color picture of the sunset, framed by the porthole, just as it dipped into the horizon at dusk. They toasted a good-bye to Yugoslavia and its lousy liquor.

Dinner was a fine meal with many flagons of red wine. They wore out the good nature of the dining room steward, so they caught his assistant unaware and thus procured another flagon. They sat around the salon and smoked, twiddling with the shortwave radio until it was time to take a walk on deck. Climbing the after mast to the top, about 80 feet off the water, it wasn't as shaky as the *Arosa Kulm's* mast. They tried to find somebody to deliver more wine, but had no luck. At least Yugoslavia's prices allowed them to smoke all they wanted, since cigarettes were only eighteen cents or 70 dinara for a pack of twenty. They weren't bad cigarettes, even though they burned faster than hell.

They passed the island of Cephalonia and were due to arrive at Eleusis Bay the next morning, the home of the Greek mystery religion.

They spent the morning washing, sewing, and generally getting their kit shipshape again. Their nylon jackets were dirty, because they practically lived in them. Everything dried fast in the Mediterranean, unlike the Atlantic. That afternoon, they tackled the mopeds, cleaning off the evidence of that gritty ride from Dubrovnik.

They surmised it was too slow, expensive, and troublesome to get a pilot to wind through the Gulf of Corinth and the Corinthian Canal that separated the Peloponnesian Peninsula from the Greek mainland. All the helmsman had to do was set the desired course on a dial and turn the button to automatic. The charts were from the British Admiralty, which were the best in the world according to the third mate. As they looked to the stern, the wake was almost perfectly straight, which said a lot for the quality of automatic seamanship. They retired for a nap after washing a good chunk of Yugoslavian real estate off the mopeds. At supper, they decided to take it easy on the vino. Later, for lack of something to do, they fell to picking apart Samuel Butler's so-called satire *Erewhon*. Bill had read it, and Dick had just finished it on the *Zeta*, with a do-or-die effort. It could be said that book had all the qualifications of a satire, but was not relieved from being the most dismal thing they had ever read.

CHAPTER 20 GREECE

October 29–November 7, 1958

If you actually look like your passport picture, you aren't well enough to travel.—Sir Vivian Fuchs

THE SUN CAME UP on the starboard side that morning, about eight miles off the island of Hydra, because the *Zeta* made the turn around the Peloponnesus the night before. Stopping at Piraeus to pick up a pilot, they proceeded to Eleusis Bay. The ship hovered off the mouth of the inner harbor, and after a bit of prolonged tootling, the pilot woke up and came out to the ship. There wasn't much farther to go, but a pilot was necessary for the tight turns that were coming up. Passing a bunch of rusty Greek merchant ships at anchor, they had to make a 90-degree turn between two towers marking the channel. The anchorage was on an exposed point, and a strong wind made it difficult to get the ship under a loading boom in order to take on bauxite. Bauxite is made up of iron and aluminum hydroxides and other oxides and is the raw stuff for making aluminum. This was the cargo the ship was to take back to Poland for smelting.

It took two and a half hours to get the ship anchored, but it was still too far off-shore to swing the mopeds over onto land. Instead, a seaman swung them over and lowered them into a sixteen-foot rowboat and maneuvered them and their bags onto a small dock at the bottom of three flights of stairs. A local agent for the *Zeta* carried their bags, while they teamed up and got the mopeds to the top. The agent and customs officials went back to town in a car, and the brothers followed them in a 1948 Buick taxi.

Upon arrival, they became embroiled in minor Greek officialdom! The hassle between Customs and Immigration was apparently about how to deal with the mopeds. Customs wanted to keep their international insurance certificate in Eleusis to prevent them from selling the mopeds, but of course, Bill and Dick both said, "Nix, nix" to that! "Nix" was a negative response understood everywhere. The burden of interpreting fell on the friendly agent, but the officials understood their attitude of stubborn bafflement quite well. The brothers couldn't understand why Customs was making such a big fuss over the mopeds, and they were determined not to give up their papers. Finally prevailed upon them to draft another declaration form, which was duly signed, after a lot of fuss getting the motor numbers down correctly. The Greek officials acted like fatheads throughout the whole two-hour proceeding, which left the brothers rather teed off. They had to pay for their returning taxi ride to the ship also, because they had come for their "benefit." If it weren't for the English-speaking ship's agent, they still would have been going around in circles.

After that fiasco, it was very dark out, so they stayed in Eleusis's only hotel for the night at 20 drachmas each. The exchange rate was 30 Greek drachmas to one dollar. They found one of the few restaurants in town and ate two kinds of pasta, with lots of lamb. Walking in the door, a cast-iron vessel that looked like a huge pig-scalding pot filled with pasta and a whole leg of lamb held up by a chain that could be raised and lowered into the mix, bubbled and scented the room with the aroma of garlic, tomatoes, and spices. With some pointing, they indicated they'd have some of that and the various types of pasta. Drinks with dinner were the Greek version of red wine, i.e. *kokino oino*, which was a retsina, or wine flavored with pitch. It was heavy and sweet. Retsina has a history of several millennia, since wine was shipped around the Mediterranean Sea in the past in amphorae, or big jugs, and sealed with Aleppo pine resin to keep the air out, but which flavored the wine and left it tasting like a tarry plank had floated in there.[1]

After dinner, they went to their first movie since Rotterdam: an old airplane flick called *Zero Hour,* with Greek subtitles. They took a walk after and ended up buying a quarter-liter bottle of six year old Metaxas, a Greek brandy for $1.50 (45 drachmas), and took it back to the hotel. They got chummy with the owner, and although he didn't drink himself, he poured two big glasses for them, which ruined the bottle. There was just enough left for an eye-opener. Greek cigarettes were as good as American cigarettes and a bit cheaper: twenty-four cents, seven drachmas plain, or eight "mit der feelter," which were packed much firmer than Yugoslavian cigarettes, that tended to unwound, becoming a box of empty paper tubes and loose tobacco.

They packed, left their baggage at the hotel, and walked over to the ruins of ancient Eleusis. The Eleusinian mysteries took place there, referring to the rites of a cult in ancient Greece that had a special set of gods. They are still thought to be a mystery, but a little research might put a light on what they were up to.

In Greek myth, Demeter is the goddess of fertility, grain, and agriculture and is the daughter of the deities Cronus and Rhea and the sister of Zeus. She commonly appeared as a grain goddess, but her influence eventually grew to include almost all vegetation, making her into an earth mother figure. Many objects represented Demeter, ranging from ears of grain to flower baskets and pigs. In the central myth, Kore, known as Persephone by the Romans, the daughter of Demeter, was kidnapped by Hades and taken to his underworld kingdom. Demeter kept searching for her daughter and forgot to harvest the grain, which caused a famine. In her search, Demeter came to Eleusis and befriended the city's royalty. The queen of Eleusis refused to let Demeter grant immortality to her son, so Demeter revealed her true identity to the people. She demanded that the city of Eleusis build a temple to her. Their worship of her became the Eleusinian mysteries.[2]

The rites associated with Demeter were originally conducted at Eleusis, but later spread from there to Athens. The rituals probably included some singing or dancing during a reenactment of the myth for this goddess. Initiation to the rites for novices started with a march from Athens to Eleusis, where the secret ceremony took place in the temple. The initiation had many parts, the promenade being only one of them. The initiations included purification through sacred baths in streams and in the sea, as well as fasting and an unknown central ceremony. By joining this cult, members were promised a number of afterlife benefits, as commonly practiced by any good salvation cult.[3]

The Eleusinian mysteries were one of the most sacred rites of the ancient Greeks. It was forbidden for the novices to let anyone know exactly what went on during the rituals and sacred rites, and the proceedings have remained clouded. However, some hypotheses have been advanced which fit the available data, and some of the ideas have mytho-theological importance. For example, the mythological originator of the Eleusinian mysteries was named Erysibe—"ergot" (*Claviceps purpurea*). "Ergot is a fungus which grows on wheat and from which an assortment of medicinal, hallucinogenic, and poisonous substances may be derived. This is the source for magic mushroom, shrooms, and mushies, psilocybe mushrooms that can produce hallucinations."[4] A likely interpretation of the mystery associated with Eleusis, it sounds like early hippy haven shrouded in religion, *a la* the peyote cult.

They went into the museum at the ruins and saw some sculptures dating back to circa 600 BC. Roaming the ruins for a while, and spending time seeing wells, columns, and stones grooved by long-since-vanished swinging doors, then went back to the hotel, saddled up, and headed for Athens.

The road leading into Athens pointed directly at the Acropolis, crowned by the Parthenon. The main part of the city was on the left and the port city of Piraeus stretched away to the right on its own peninsula. They followed the signs to the city center, where they got embroiled in Athenian traffic. Survival belonged to the fleetest. After orbiting a while, they asked a man who happened to work for American Express if he could recommend a pension.

Finally arriving at one, the proprietress was very accommodating and gave them coffee while a room was made up. They thought the price was a little steep for the first night, $4 (120 drachmas). By the time they settled in, it was getting late, and they decided to make a quick trip up to the Acropolis. It was thirty-three cents (10 drachmas) to get in. The entrance led to the bottom, then turned left to ascend the steps of the Parthenon, the temple of the goddess Athena, protectress of the city. They didn't approach it with any reverence and instead climbed all over the stones to get good angles for pictures. Dick was chased down by a watchman who thought he had invaded some off-limits sanctuary.

Between 1801 and 1812, Thomas Bruce, the seventh Earl of Elgin, received a permit from the Ottoman authorities to remove almost half the sculptures from the Parthenon. He also took architectural components and sculpture from the Propylaea and the Erectheum[5], which now resides in the British Museum. Only rudimentary fragments of carvings of the 2,500-year-old frieze by Phidias and his assistants remained at the entrance. The Parthenon would have looked better if Elgin had left well enough alone. At the time of his "strike," the Greeks were so overwhelmed by the Turks and the Ottoman Empire they couldn't stop him. Archeological treasures can no longer be removed from the country, and the Greeks continue petitioning England for the return of the frieze and other stolen objects.

Dick and Bill scrambled around the inner part of the Parthenon taking pictures, then explored at a more leisurely pace. The most defined sculptural remnants were the caryatid sculptures of women serving as architectural support columns for the entablature of the Erectheum porch. The figures date from 421–407 BC and portray the *Maidens of Karya,* an ancient town of Peloponnese.[6]

Dick standing below the Caryatids of the Erechtheion, Athens, Greece.

Dick standing between the columns of the Parthenon at sunset. Athens, Greece.

The Agora was still extent and a little ways from the foot of the Acropolis. It is still a vibrant place for vendors and sellers of all kinds of things. It's a thirty-acre marketplace sitting below the Acropolis and for 2400 years was the intellectual center of the Western world. They'd return later to meditate on the antiquity of the place, since the feeling of age and the origin of Western civilization hallowed the place.

Excavation unearthed some of the political products from ancient times. A random lot generator used to select magistrates was found in the dig, also, voting machines and ballot spindles. And hemlock cups used to administer the death sentence by poison were found.

Socrates, who taught there, was chosen by lot to chair the citizen's assembly and pissed the assembly off over a trial of generals accused of cowardice. They eventually convicted him of corrupting Athenian youth and made him drink hemlock *(conium maculatus)*.[7]

Bill standing in front of the Parthenon. Athens, Greece.

Heading back to the pension just before sunset, they had an appointment to meet two acquaintances from Eleusis for dinner. Tassos and Eleni Collinas met them on the Syntagma, or Constitution Square, and from there went to dinner at a "taverna," or Greek restaurant, where they all had lamb and beer. In Eleusis, Tassos, a motorcycle repairman and representative for Achilles-Sachs, had thoroughly overhauled the bikes, adjusting, tightening, and tuning them, not only repairing the bikes, but at no charge. All he wanted was that they let the Achilles-Sachs people in Germany know what good service they received. Tassos mentioned he'd been to their plant to learn about Sach's engines. Later, they sent a glowing letter to Sachs headquarters and made Tassos out to be a Greek god of motorcycle repair. After dinner, they took a promenade down the street, had dessert at a shop, and parted company. Although they did show them around some, the whole justification for their coming to Athens from Eleusis was English conversation practice.

Next day found them in Piraeus, about nine miles away, where they had a late breakfast of soup, lamb, and beefsteak. They walked out to the end of the small peninsula and ended up playing basketball with a bunch of kids. It was four against three, with Dick and Bill on opposite sides. They lost track of the score and dropped out after half an hour.

Taking a ride along the shore of the Saronikos Gulf, they pulled up and watched as the sun set behind the Peloponnesus. Out of curiosity, they stopped at the Athens airport to find out the fare from Athens to Seattle. Via Rome, Milan, Paris, and then to San Francisco over the Polar route, they could fly first class for just under $800, or economy class for just over $500. That night, they helped the concierge at the pension move eight U.S. Navy sailors into the hotel, who were on their way to Cyprus for consulate duty. The sailors were loaded down with duffel bags and didn't mind the help.

In the morning, they rolled out for church, unable to tell whether it was a Roman rite or not. Bill went on an excursion to Mt. Parnas. After Mass, he went over to join Tassos and Eleni, and they headed out of Athens. As Bill later recounted, Tassos was also driving a Sachs moped, but with more ccs, that could ride circles around him. It was nice out when they stopped for lunch and a beer before heading up the mountain. The road wound back and forth across the full length of the mountain. It was an uneventful ascent. The only thing slowing them down was Bill's lack of horsepower. The Collinas were nice enough to throttle back to his speed so he could finally conquer Parnas, albeit at a snail's pace. At the top, the Greek Air Force had a radar dome manned by approximately fifty men. The dome was on an adjacent peak to the one they climbed. They stayed at the top for half an hour and did a lot of rubbernecking. To the west, Athens was framed in a hazy southern exposure. Eleni collected some *jee*—at least that was what it sounded like—and explained what it was by humming a Christmas carol—mistletoe.

The entire trip took five hours and they covered about forty-one miles. Mt. Parnas was 4,636 feet high and they coasted all the way down. When they got back, Bill thanked Tassos for all the work he had done on their bikes and took his leave to get some dinner. He found Dick in the restaurant Kissos, which they had been frequenting—the owners spoke English and the food was generally very good.

The following day started out as a hunt for a friend of Dick's who was in the Greek Army he'd met at Aberdeen Proving Ground, but nobody had ever heard of the address, so they ended up climbing Mount Parnitha, another mountain on the north side of Athens from

Parnas with the mopeds. Several thousand feet above the city, they could see the Aegean Sea shimmering in the distance and the Plain of Marathon. Coming down the mountain, they stopped in a town for a late lunch. From there, headed for Piraeus, but got the same story from the shipping lines there as in Athens, that there were no convenient ferries to Italy. They got back to Athens at dusk and rode the mopeds to the Pynx, a hill across from the Acropolis. It was on the Pynx that citizens of ancient Athens met in forums to listen to the famous orators of the day. There were still a few ruins at the top of the hill. Their plan for the next day was to leave Athens and head for Corinth and on up to Corfu, a Greek island off the coast of Greece and Albania that had a ferry to Italy.

They got off to a late start after a minimum of getting organized and hit the right road to Eleusis and Corinth. Passing through Eleusis, running along the bay for quite a while, noticed how the water was so clear they could see deep into its emerald translucence. They stopped and dipped their hands in and found it was warm. Along that stretch of road, a Ford passed by with Washington State plates. It took them by surprise so much they didn't have time to wave, and they couldn't go fast enough to catch him.

A stiff head wind most of the day slowed them down. They crossed the Corinth Canal, empty of any ships. Looking down from the bridge, the water was about 250 feet below and the sides of the channel were almost vertical on this four-mile-long canal. The canal took twelve years to dig and was finished in 1893.[8] Crossing the bridge put them on the Peloponnesian peninsula, which by virtue of the canal, made it an island. They stopped in Corinth for a late lunch. A small place, the city had a population of 25,000, but probably expanded during the summer for the tourist trade. The road hugged the Gulf of Corinth and passed through innumerable villages. The road narrowed, and they were almost squeezed off by trucks, where the only place to go was over a bulkhead and onto the beach.

It started to rain at dusk. The local wind, the *Etesiae*, vanished soon after and they started to make good time. They found that by bending over, they increased speed by just over one mph. They stopped in Aiyion for the night, 112 miles from Athens. Every time they were passed by oncoming trucks on the narrow road, the lights blinded them through their rain-spattered goggles, and it was just a matter of time before they missed a turn or hit a donkey cart or a bicycle on the side of the road.

At the hotel in Aiyion, they met a fellow from Baltimore, who was born in Greece and had come back to look the country over. He helped by interpreting, which expedited matters. That night, they ate dinner in one restaurant, had coffee in another place, a dessert in a third place, all in the Greek manner. About twenty-five miles from there, they planned on taking a ferry over to the mainland and leaving the Peloponnesus and expected to be close to Corfu by the next evening.

Dick's carburetor began leaking just as they were ready to leave Aiyion. Tom, their fellow American and interpreter, found a shop where they could get it repaired, then he went off sightseeing. After an hour and a half of messing with the machine, the mechanic figured out what was wrong and replaced the part to the tune of $3.34 or 100 drachmas.

The day was clear and they finally left at noon. It started to rain after an hour on the road, so they donned capes to fend off the intermittent showers. At Rion, they took the ferry, a landing craft tank (LCT), a World War II relic now put to commercial use. Landing at Attirion, five miles across the mouth of the Gulf of Corinth, where it opened to the Ionian Sea. On board, fellow passengers were members of a Greek Army band with their instruments, a shepherd with a flock of sheep running around among them bleating, most likely seasick, and a few other passengers standing on higher components of the vessel, probably to avoid stepping into sheep scat.

Greek Army musicians standing among the sheep on the WWII LCT barge that took us across the Gulf of Corinth.

Back on the mopeds, they climbed to Messalongian, twenty-two miles away. The final phase of the day's journey took them to Arta, 84 miles away. Four hours later, it was dark and they took a brandy break at Amphilokia, where the mopeds drew a crowd of about thirty or forty people. Most of them were in the street, but more were headed over, and they kept hearing the people shouting, *Germanoi,* so the local cops went into action, shooing them away. The "D" for Deutschland, i.e. Germany, on their license plates drew a lot of comments, favorable or not, they didn't know. "Nicht sprechen Grec."

Someone said that, "a special providence looks after children, fools, drunks, and the USA." Perhaps it was that day that they, blithely ignorant of what Greece had gone through during World War II, received the blessing of this providence. Although it was only a little over a decade after the end of the war, the local memory had been seared with the atrocities of the Germans during the war, and to have Germans trooping through the villages and sites of former violent offences would have been painful to the locals.

Greece was invaded in 1939 by Italy, then Germany too, by Hitler's armies, to save his Axis ally Mussolini's ass. He was losing then, and the Bulgarians on the eastern side jumped in and appropriated some of the country. As a result, the different factions, Communists, non-Communists, and non-aligned people created a resistance movement against the Germans. Over two million resistance fighters did everything they could to harass the German occupation. The Germans in turn created death squads, deported over 60,000 Jews to Auschwitz, demolished their homes, businesses, graveyards, and synagogues, executed 100 Greeks for every German soldier killed, burned down and leveled villages where resistance was found, took all the crops they could, resulting in over 100,000 Greeks starving to death, and conducted a scorched earth policy against the Greeks, pillaging and destroying homes and people. Over 400,000 Greeks, mostly civilians, died during the war. The Germans capitulated and left Greece in August 1944, when the Germans surrendered to the Russian Army in Stalingrad. As the Russians moved closer, the Germans retreated to their homeland. Greece, though, was not over its trouble, as the Communists tried to take over the country in a civil war that lasted until August 1949. It was finally rebuffed with British and American support to the Greek government.[9]

The village crowds dissipated as they told them they were *Amerikanos* and waved their pathetic little American flags to dispel any notion that they were Germans. The local cops were a boost too, since they reinforced the idea and shooed away the crowds.

As they continued to Arta, they came onto rough roads. Bill's headlamp was weak, so Dick led the way, twisting all over the highway in order to avoid the numerous chuckholes. Contrary to what one might think, weaving all over the highway was not dangerous or even very hazardous, as they had it all to themselves, not counting the sheep. The roadway was fleeced with sheep, driving, bleating, and hogging the whole road. Three times, they almost decimated flocks of them that were being led down the road by shepherds they never saw. Luckily, they heard their bells and only grazed their flanks. They arrived at Arta and promptly found a hotel, thanks to the hard work of the hotel's advance man, a boy about fifteen or so who caught them and asked if they needed a hotel. He had to work for his money and was in competition with other kids trying to get business. In order to keep the mopeds upright, they only went as fast as the kid could trot.

Out of Arta the next morning, it was a fairly short run of 100 miles to the ferry boat in Corfu. Shortly, they passed more flocks of sheep, which they honked out of the way. Coming upon a large group of women at a stream doing their washing, they watched them beating their clothes with big wooden cudgels and hanging them on bushes to dry—either electricity or washing machines had not been delivered at the time.

Farther on, was a straight stretch, where the locals had spread grain on one side of the road to dry and for storage. Their assumption was this was a bumper crop that year, and they didn't have sufficient storage facilities. Or, maybe, this was their storage system. They'd seen the same thing in North Dakota, where seldom-used side roads by a granary were piled high with wheat, oats, or barley when the bins were full. A little girl was going along with a broom, sweeping the stray kernels back to the pile.

Forty-five miles from Arta, the road became hardpan dirt, even though the map indicated it was macadam. At first, it wasn't too bad along the seashore, but as it turned inland, it got rocky, and they began taking a beating. After twenty-five miles of that, Dick ran out of gas at the bottom of a steep climb, so Bill went ahead to the next village to get gas. Meanwhile, Dick pushed his moped for two hours and covered five miles, meeting Bill at the road's summit. Bill put the gas in Dick's moped, but it leaked out of the carburetor, just as it had in Aiyion. The float valve was fouled and wouldn't feed properly. Fortunately, it was downhill all the way to a village. It took a little while after arriving to find someone who spoke English. They found a man who repaired bicycles, who found another float somewhere and got the bike going—temporarily! Three miles out of town, it went "kaput" again, so Bill towed Dick back to the village. Watching the bicycle repairman, they spotted what the float was—he'd whittled a wine cork as a float, with the needle through the center. After a little soldering, they were off again in the twilight, hoping they wouldn't spend the night out in the Greek scrubland. They had thirty-two miles to cover, and if Dick's bike quit again in the middle of nowhere, they would just have to make a fire and settle down for the night.

Dick had a copy of *Time* magazine earmarked to start the fire, but it proved unnecessary. The moped kept ticking away until they got to Parmythia, where they found they had missed a turn in the road. The saving feature to that mistake was that they only had eight miles to go before they came to a hard surface road to take them to Igomenitsa. It was a long eight miles, and the last part was down a steep mountainside, much of which was under construction. The roads were in deplorable condition until they hit asphalt for the last leg of the journey into town. They even had a long downhill glide but couldn't go fast, because their lights didn't shine forward far enough to see on the winding road.

They got into Igomenitsa at 10:00, found accommodations at the Hotel Acropolis, then had dinner. They thought they were out of the hinterlands then, because they found restaurants that were still open, something they couldn't find back in the hills. Greek Customs willing, they planned to ferry over to Corfu, the Greek island, and from there catch the boat to Brindisi, Italy.

The next morning, they were waiting for the Customs and Immigration staff to get off the boat before sailing back to Italy. The *Etesiae* was blowing so strongly that it delayed the ferry. It was a rough ride, two and a half hours, as the high winds ruffled the Ionian Sea with whitecaps. On board, they put the mopeds under the tailgate of a truck to keep the rain off, but when they cleared the harbor, the spray-soaked them. Eventually, they wrestled them between two trucks and tied them down. Arriving at Corfu in a downpour, Bill's moped was balky because of the soaking it received on the ferry.

They hunted up the agent of the Nomikou Line and gave him fifty-four dollars or 1, 620 drachmas, to get them and their gear on the *MS Miaoulis*. They were afforded a deck class passage without meals, which they thought was stingy for a twelve-hour voyage. They hoped they were through with small shipping lines and their nickel-and-dime policies until they got to Lisbon and the final ship ride home. Their arrival at Brindisi was scheduled for early morning, so they decided to stay there and get the mopeds squared away and maybe square away with a bath too. After securing passage, they went to a restaurant along with a thirteen-year-old boy who spoke fair English and wanted to practice it. He attended the English school in Corfu.

Bill's moped finally went "kaput" completely, so they waited for the ship at a pier where there was a covered place. Bill fixed his kickstand, which had been bent out of place somewhere on the rough roads, replaced his gear shift cable, dried out his sparkplug, and was in business again.

They gave the "officials" their passports and declarations, and after a suitable period of studied peering at the bikes, they decided they were OK, so the brothers loaded them onto a small motorboat that brought them out to the *Miaoulis*. On the way out, the boat's motor sputtered and quit twice. Pulling alongside the ferry, Dick jumped onto the gangplank off the pitching boat, while Bill handed over the mopeds, one by one. Given the weather and the seas, the transfer was executed without a drop of water on the bikes.

From the ferry, they got a peek at Albania, which was about three-quarters of a mile away. Rugged, irregular hills with no signs of life up the coast was the view from their vantage point. The Albania they could see from the shores of Corfu was the sole domain of the former partisan commander, Enver Hoxha, who ran that country along both Leninist and Maoist lines of communism at one time or another. He ruled from 1941 to 1985 and ran his impoverished and backward country with an iron hand. For more than forty years, including the five years after his death, the country was sealed off from the outside world. Its people were propagandized, religion was banned, and imprisonment was common. Hoxha ran a gulag, or forced labor camp, and had many prisons, where he stashed people for trivial offences. He was known for his murderous purges, decimations for real or imagined opposition. His death squads eliminated any opposition.[10] While ruling in this fashion, he nearly ruined what economy there was during the cold war by his "bunkerization" policy of building hundreds of thousands of defensive concrete bunkers. He built them on the beaches, in the mountains, in vineyards, in pastures, and any place he could put them. He built so many that there were twenty-four bunkers for every square kilometer of land in the country. And, they were never used.[11] Anybody who invaded Albania would have a hole in their head. There isn't much there, and who speaks Albanian anyway?

Although they had no desire to visit Albania, their passports specifically said: "This passport is not valid for travel to the following areas under the control of authorities with which the United States does not have diplomatic relations: Albania, Bulgaria, and those portions of China, Korea and Vietnam under Communist control." Anyway, the brothers knew what they'd see: bunkers!

People in the United States have no idea how fortunate they are to be able to travel around freely on a continent so much larger than Europe and not have to bother with customs, immigration, and the nitwit rules that such countries have.

FRANCE
GENEVA
LYON
TURIN
BORDEAUX
MASSIF CENTRAL
TOULOUSE
RIVIERA
MONACO
MONACO
PYRENEES
MARSEILLE
ANDORRA
ANDORRA
ZARAGOZA
GOLFE DU LION
CORSE
BARCELONA
BALEARIC SEA
MENORCA
VALENCIA
PALMA
MALLORCA
SARDEGNA
BALEARIC IS.
IBIZA
MEDITERRANEAN SEA
ALGIERS
CONSTANTINE
ORAN

ALPS
MILAN
ITALY
VENICE
LJUBLJANA
SLOVENIA
ZAGREB
CROATIA
ALFÖLD
BELGRADE
SERBIA
BOSNIA AND HERZ.
SARAJEVO
DINARIC ALPS
DALMATIA
FLORENCE
SAN MARINO
APPENNINI
ADRIATIC SEA
MONTENEGRO
PODGORICA
VATICAN CITY
VATICAN
ROME
TIRANA
ALBANIA
NAPLES
PINDUS MTS.
TYRRHENIAN SEA
CALABRIA
IONIAN IS.
PALERMO
SICILIA
IONIAN SEA
CAP BON
TUNIS
MALTA
VALLETTA

CHAPTER 21 WELCOME TO SOUTHERN ITALY

NOVEMBER 8–18, 1958

(Ancora una volta, Benvenuti in Italia)

Twenty years from now you will be more disappointed by the things you didn't do than by the ones you did do. So, throw off the bowlines, sail away from the safe harbor. Catch the trade winds in your sails. Explore, dream, discover.—Mark Twain

AFTER HAVING SLEPT ON BENCHES of the Miaoulis and doing so rather well under ferry conditions, they felt up to par the next morning. The ship docked and it took about twenty minutes to satisfy the Italian authorities and exchange some money—a hell of an improvement over Yugoslavian and Greek Immigration types. The first thing on the agenda was breakfast, eating what was getting to be the inevitable omelet, tea, bread, butter, and jam (known all over Europe as "marmalada," no matter what the flavor). As in Greece, they had to send out for the tea, or they would have had to wait until they were finished and go off to a coffee shop for it. Screwy! After that, they looked for a Sachs dealer, but in Brindisi, there were only Vespa and Lambretta agencies. They gassed up and left in a light sprinkle of rain and headed for Taranto, forty-five miles away. The countryside was flat with a few gentlehills.

In Taranto, they immediately tried to find a Sachs dealer to no avail. Finding instead, a trattoria, they had some spaghetti and vino. An American aircraft carrier and three destroyers were anchored in the harbor. They watched a fellow in front of the restaurant pull in every passing American sailor for eats and beer. Of course, the sailors made asses of themselves by shouting and insisting on dancing with the waitress. That behavior made the brothers feel self-conscious about being Americans. When they left, the navy was taking over the town and the natives were set to make a killing.

Outside of Taranto, it started to rain for about twelve miles. Bill's bike conked out for a while with water in his sparkplug, so Dick pushed him for a couple of kilometers to a service station. Off again, they hoped to soon be out of the rain. It looked brighter ahead, but they could never quite catch up with that bright spot. The sky closed in, starting to pelt them with big drops. It took only ten minutes to soak their legs and fill up their shoes. The water blew up under the rain capes, crept up their sleeves, and drizzled down their necks until there were few dry spots.

Passing through a village, with both engines sputtering, they dimly saw two banners over the street, one saying "Vota Communista" and the other "Vota Socialismo." Before Matera, Bill was leading the parade, when Dick's motor suddenly died. Bill was out of earshot and couldn't hear the shouts or the bell ringing. Dick just sat there in the heavy dusk, in the midst of plowed and muddy fields, watching his brother's tail light dim out as it got fainter and fainter in the distance, finally disappearing over a hill. He felt very forlorn watching that light disappear, being stranded in the middle of Italy in such stinking weather. When Bill finally turned back, Dick had the errant moped up and running again and they made it to Matera by 7:00 p.m.

That night they splurged and stayed at a Jolly Hotel, a chain all over Italy, (*In Tutta Italia*). They had a bath, huge towels, and all the refinements. Festooning the room with wet clothes, books, and all the rest of their paraphernalia, hoping it would dry before morning. The hotel room was so comfortable they didn't check out until early afternoon. Their first look at Matera, perched high on a hill, part of the Apennine mountains, was of the residents in the village out in the town square, talking and milling around after Mass.

They left for Naples over the mountains, which were about 3,000 feet high. Matera was left behind them and they managed to cover 143 miles with nothing but a patch of fog, located high in the mountains to the east of Potenza. The fog was like a plague. All day long, it was slow going, because of the steep hills and the limited forward visibility. While driving, they had three long glides down steep hillsides. Out of Potenza, Bill came close to sailing off the road when he braked for a sharp curve at the bottom of a particularly steep hill. He arrested his bike as if he were sliding into first base at a ball game before going over the abyss. If he had gone over, he would have taken a deadly roll sixty feet down a steep, grassy hillside studded with evergreen trees. The mopeds had damn good brakes, which saved their bacon more than once.

They came across a bus in a ditch. The accident happened minutes before they got there, and people were standing around and several cars were stopped. No one appeared to be hurt. They continued to climb and spent a good part of the afternoon in the clouds. Very clammy, they stopped in a place called Tricarico for a couple of shots of grappa—for medicinal purposes. At Potenza, they stopped for dinner and ate in the warm kitchen, having the traditional Italian meal of spaghetti, mixed salad, bread and butter, and a bottle of vino *rosso*.

The topography in the south central part of Italy was dictated by the Apennines, the cordillera that runs up the whole of Italy. Even though the roads were good, they traveled mostly in the dark with their vision fixed straight ahead. Pushing to get over the mountains and down onto the west coast, about twenty-five miles from Potenza, they saw the lights of a town winking below. They coasted down the hill, through hair-pin curves, and by the time they reached the bottom of the mountain, the town was above and behind them. Their feeling was that Italy probably had the best roads in Europe. The goal for that night was Eboli, because it was out of the mountains and just a short hop from Naples. However, when they arrived in Eboli, it didn't have a hotel or "albergo," so they went five miles farther to Battipaglia, a small town where they found a cheap hotel for $1.87 (1,160 lira). The exchange rate was 620 lira to a dollar. They arrived about 1:20 a.m., which was the latest they had ever run. It took them twelve hours to cover the 143 miles, but it was worth it to get that mountainous stretch behind them.

Pushing on to Naples, they stopped at Pompeii, which was practically at the foot of Mt. Vesuvius. The top of Vesuvius was wreathed in clouds, blocking their view of any smoke or steam coming from the crater. They paid extra to get into the ruins of Pompeii after their nominal closing time. On the ticket, it said: "For compensation to the commanded staff for the service necessity in extraordinary hours."

Mt. Vesuvius, only five miles from Pompeii, blew its cork in AD 79, burying the city and its neighbor, the city of Herculaneum, under fourteen to twenty-five feet of ash and pumice. The cities were lost for 1700 years until excavations in 1748 accidentally uncovered the site. Ever since, anthropologic excavations have been under way, uncovering more and more of the cities and revealing what Roman life was like in the first century. Revealed were an amphitheater, a gymnasium with a central swimming pool, and aqueducts that provided water for many street fountains, four public baths, and a large number of houses. Also uncovered were taverns, street markets, a mill, small restaurants, two theaters, a hotel, brothels, and the infrastructure of the cities with their paved stone streets. One house had *Salve, lucru* (Welcome, money) inscribed on its floor. The speculation was that it was a trading house.[1]

In the brothels and elsewhere were found frescos with erotic wall paintings of explicit sexual acts, including bestiality. Priapus, the god of sex and fertility, adorned the walls with his giant phallus. One wall inscription, loosely translated from the Latin, stated: "If anyone is looking for some tender love in this town, keep in mind that all the girls are very friendly." This was followed by a price list for various services. When these elements were excavated and discovered, many were plastered over or removed to the University of Naples to be kept out of sight.[2]

The museum had a lot of artifacts, casts of loaves of bread as they were found, pieces of cloth, and the body of a woman and a dog in the grotesque posture of death by asphyxiation. One of the excavators came up with the idea of pouring plaster into the space left by the decomposed bodies or other objects encased in the lava flows. Most of the dead were women, children, the aged, and the infirm—those which could not flee fast enough. Some bodies were found whole, locked in enclosures. The upper respiratory tracts of the majority were found to be clogged with mucus and ash.

Most of the ruins were roofless, but the ones that had frescoes were roofed over and left in a preserved state. With no guards around to stop them, the miscreant travelers climbed a wall to get into a villa and walked on a mosaic tile floor that had been laid 2,000 years before, saw the sunken bath in a courtyard, and explored various rooms. They eventually found Phoebe's Tavola, or bar. The bar was too low to lean on comfortably, but no doubt suited the people of the times quite well. Anthropologists say that the Pompeians were about the same size as contemporary Italians. Men on average were five feet four inches tall and women, on average, were slightly over five feet. Dick and Bill found the bar stools a little too close to the floor.[3]

In their proscribed perambulations, they also found out the Romans sometimes used a sawed-off hollow column for a privy. There was a bakery with the oven intact, along with the stones for grinding the grain. The outer stucco was gone from a good deal of the buildings, leaving the bricks in the walls exposed. Some of the brick work was intricate and decorative. The ancient architects had used bricks of a peculiar shape to construct fluted columns. It was characteristic of all the Roman ruins to employ bricks rather than solid stone, as in the Greek ruins, but this reflected the type of building materials available in the two countries. At intervals, across the main streets of the ruins, large raised stones were used as stepping stones to cross a road when it rained.

They left Pompeii as the sun went down behind the Bay of Naples and headed for Naples. The distance wasn't too great, but the city fathers seemed to assume that if they were that close to town, signposts were no longer necessary, so by misdirection, they finally found the city center. Cobblestones of various size paved the streets and loosened the fillings of their teeth. They hit the downtown part and found a cop to direct them to an inexpensive *albergo*. Downtown, the entrance was in a narrow side street, though their room faced the main street. They moved in and went down a couple of doors to eat. The town had a reputation for being a sailor's town, so they were wary when they went into the restaurant, asking the price of everything.

One experience made them cautious when dealing with the natives. They took a break by the docks and were simply looking around, their bikes parked and doing the tourist thing, gawking at the scenery, when a little kid less than ten came up and said, "Hi, sailors," in good English. They thought he was the official greeter and was going to ask if they'd like to sleep with his sister or lead them on to a hotel. Instead, although he appeared to only come up to their waist, he sidled closer. They were wearing T-shirts with shirt pockets where they kept cigarettes. When the kid got close enough, he came in front of Bill and flicked the bottom of his shirt pocket, ejecting an almost-full packet of Lucky Strike cigarettes that flew into the kid's waiting hand. Dumbstruck by the effrontery of the little bastard, Bill hesitated too long as the pint-sized thief hightailed it out of there, like a cat on a hot burner, so fast there was no point in chasing him. They could get more cigarettes anyway. They'd just met a member of the juvenile Mafia.

In a Neapolitan restaurant, Dick smelled a rat when they served butter, which they never did in an Italian restaurant. When queried, they wanted over 200 lira for it, and it shouldn't have been over 80 at the most. When the bill came, they told the waiter in their best pissed-off English/Italian that the bill was unacceptable. With a great show of indignity, he knocked down the price for a half liter of second-rate vino. The bill even charged for the napkin (*tovagliolo*). The waiter, a depraved type, or a caricature of one, was disappointed when he picked up Dick's book, Boswell's *London Journal*, and thumbed through it, because there were no pictures. By signs, indicated that some of the nude statuary in Bill's book on Greek art was "hot stuff."

They hiked around the area close to the *albergo*. To call it the residential section connoted an elegance it didn't possess, and to call it the native quarter made it sound too squalid, but it definitely leaned toward the latter. They had an Elizabethan attitude about garbage disposal, as somebody almost hit Dick with an old cabbage dropped from above. They found out later that some Italians have a different attitude toward private versus public space and civic-mindedness. Whether true or not, they didn't know, but it helped explain some of the garbage problems and attitudes that persist in Naples and other Italian towns. The culture prides itself on maintaining strong family bonds, particularly in Naples, where they say children never leave home and togetherness is the norm. What this suggests is families take care of their own space with pride and dignity. However, people outside the family bond are strangers and are less important and can be treated cavalierly. By extension, this attitude applies to public rights-of-way, that the government will pick up the trash in the streets, the very government they were indifferent to. The good thing was the garbage missed Dick's head, and so they moved on.[4]

Naples and other cities didn't collect garbage during national and local elections, for some reason. And the local garbage men went on strike with some regularity for not getting paid enough, leaving piles of refuse in the streets. Part of this possibly related to the Camorra, a.k.a. the Mafia, who are firmly entrenched in local politics and trash collection, they were told. One author speculated that Naples had over a hundred clans with another 10,000 immediate associates, along with a larger group of dependents, clients, and friends that make up the Camorra and who have been a secondary but sub-rosa form of government called: "the system." Evidence of this is *omerta,* or the code of silence, noted by investigative reporters who have intruded into their enclaves like the Scampia and Secondigliano.[5] Over the last three decades, the Camorristi have been responsible for the death of over 3,000 people.[6] A suburb of Naples, Secondigliano, which has the highest murder rates in Western Europe.[7]

They were accosted by one of the local hustlers, Mario, and Dick explained that they were Scotsmen, which explained their English speech and lack of money, so he wouldn't peg them as Americans. Mario had walked up to them like an old friend and in passable English started to tell them what he could do for them, from hotels, to restaurants, to women. Mario took them to "Mama Guitars," where they tried to push a bottle of thirty-three cent (200 lira) vino for almost five dollars (3,000 lira). The brothers were consoled after he explained Americans were charged and paid, 5,000 lira for the same bottle of wine. The brothers said good-bye to this hustler, and tramped around some more. At one place, they asked the price of some big barrels of wine—$140 (86,800 lira)—and when they were through talking, the guy tried to get Bill's pen from him as a souvenir. They finally ended up, by the "toils" of another hustler, Giulio, in a cantina drinking vino. It was a very slow night for him, so he joined them and practiced his English. He was a shoemaker by day and tried to make whatever he could at night. He told them he made three dollars (1,860 lira) for a ten-hour day; even the natives don't get much leeway on that kind of pay.

Leaving the city, they went through a long tunnel like the one in Trieste and climbed some hills. The islands of Capri jutted up in the distance with Ischia to the west. There wasn't a Sachs Servizio anywhere in Naples, so they decided to push on to Rome the next day. They were gradually getting disillusioned and disappointed with the motorbikes. Too many little things went wrong with them, and they only had 1,554 miles on them. Deciding to take matters into their own hands, they would fix them on their own.

Stopping outside Naples, they disassembled both carburetors and cleaned them. Watching other people take them apart often enough gave them a fair idea of what to do. It took about ninety minutes to complete the operation on both mopeds, and they were on their way by mid-afternoon. They had a good view of Vesuvius, still an active stratovolcano with a history of eruptions every twenty years. The last eruption was in 1944, so they figured it wasn't due to give them any fireworks.

They didn't get too far before their skimpy Continental breakfast failed them, so they stopped and settled for spaghetti and some vino.

The wine was very astringent, which got them into a discussion of tannins and what affects wine taste. The poorer grades of vino made the teeth feel raspy because of the tannin content in the grape skins, pips, and seeds left in the fermented wine. The better wine controlled the way the polyphenolic substances (principally the tannins and anthocyanins) i.e. read: the skin, stems, and seeds are extracted and have a huge impact on the quality and character of the final wine.[8] Obviously, they were not drinking fine wine.

The road out of Naples on the way up the coast to Rome was straight with only negligible traffic. Outside of Formia, there was a Roman aqueduct, one of many on their path. Rome had eleven of them originally, some of which are still working. Although many were visible, they were told that the Romans constructed many of them underground to keep the water they delivered clean and so that animals or birds would not foul the water. The structures themselves were made from a combination of stone and brick, with a type of cement called *pozzuolana*. It was made with volcanic ash and lime and was extremely durable. The pitch gradients on the system could vary from 1 to 50 on up to 1 to 1,000, depending on the distance. To cross low spots, the Romans used inverted siphons, where the aqueduct on the other side of the crossing maintained the same gradient.[9]

Past Gaeta, the road, the Roman-era Appian Way, ran along the cliffs above the gulf named for the town. There were many tunnels along the way, but they rode much of the way in the dark and missed a good look at much of the scenery. They stopped outside of Terracina to get a better look at the surf. There were tremendous waves coming in fast and breaking against the cliff just below the road. When the waves broke, the trapped air against the cliff made a loud whooshing sound.

Had foresight been a friend, they might have jumped into the sea rather than struggle through the next twenty-five miles. Past Terracina, they ran into an electrical storm that had seen coming for some time. A sprinkle soon developed into a downpour much like the one out of Matera. They did all right for a while by putting their feet up on the gas tanks and tucking the rain capes as far down as they would go. Before too long, though, Bill's machine picked up enough water to short out. His unit was very tender in that respect. Dick got behind him and gave him a push to get him started again. The third short out came in an especially heavy burst of rain. While trying to maneuver to give him another shove, Dick's handlebar got tangled up with his cape and they both spilled. Bill suffered the worst damage. His throttle cable broke in the melee, and that put him out for good. They got to a service station up the road and rigged a towing cable from Bill's old throttle cable that had broken in Corfu. They learned to save their old cable for just such an emergency. Dick tied one end to the back of his moped and gave the other end a few turns around a pair of pliers, which made a comfortable handle. If something came up, Bill could always drop the pliers and dive for cover.

A tailwind had helped, but the rain had slowed them considerably. They expected to make Latina without further ado, but 4.3 miles outside the town, it started to rain again, letting go with thunder and lightning all around. The downpour practically submerged their mopeds, killing Dick's motor. It was a two-mile hike into Latina in the heavy rain. Italian cypress trees that were 40 to 60 feet tall lined both sides of the road and Dick thought they stood a good chance of getting hit by lightning. Flashes were hitting the ground close by—one strike hit one of the trees nearby, and they heard it sizzle from the electric bolt, yet never caught fire. It just blew some branches off and sung with its boiled sap, offering a scary night melody. The repeated strikes were momentarily blinding.

They sloshed into Latina in the middle of the road, pushing their dead bikes, arriving about 9:00 p.m., and took the first pension they came to. A sorry, bedraggled sight as they trooped in the pension door and stood dripping gloppy puddles on the floor, they prayed for sunshine the next day so they could get their clothes dry. They damned the mopeds for being unreliable pieces of junk and the people who made them to hell and farther!

After delaying a while in Latina, waiting for the rain to stop, they managed to replace the broken cables and were off to Rome by noon. Their clothes partially dried during the night, but not their soggy shoes. They finally got smart and packed wads of newspaper inside, the top of their AWOL bags, to absorb the rain. They had some success at this and only had to throw away soggy newsprint after running in the rain.

They felt no more kindly disposed toward Sachs that day. They had counted on them having a dealer both in Latina and Rome, thus a quandary existed over the bike problems, looking for a dealer in town, the automobile club said there wasn't one. They had nursed the things all the way to Rome, and they were so mechanically fouled up they didn't know if they could even get rid of them.

CHAPTER 22 ROME TO VENTIMIGLIA

NOVEMBER 8–18, 1958

Everyone, soon or late, comes by Rome.—Robert Browning

ON THEIR APPROACH TO ROME, there were rolling hills with steep sides. Much of the land was under cultivation and the earth was a rich, dark rusty-red, from the iron oxides in the laterite soils, but some of the freshly plowed fields were badly eroded, because the furrows ran down the hill instead of with the contour of the land. The entrance to Rome from the south was a far cry from the entrance to Naples. There were no congested back streets, no cobblestones, and no lack of signposts. Rome had wide, smooth-surfaced streets, more proper boulevards, and plenty of signposts. There was a sharp line of demarcation between city and country. A group of modernistic new apartment houses marked the boundary, but snuggled in with them were slum houses that looked like something from the hinterlands of Georgia; they were the only slums they'd seen so far.

They came into the city on the Via Cristoforo Colombo, past many new buildings tucked under part of the ancient Roman wall around the city. Turning right from the Via San Gregorio, they ran into the Colosseum, Rome's ancient snaggle-toothed stadium, and stopped and explored. The Roman ruins lacked the grace and majesty of the Grecian ruins, because they used brick extensively, covered with plaster or mortar. All too often, what remained of the Roman handiwork imparted a sense of decay instead of the wonder that anything survived at all. The chipped and falling stucco echoed a deserted scene, transiting its way to rubble.

At the Piazza dei Venezia, they stopped to consult their maps and were lucky enough to find out from an American GI that there was a "Y" in town at a reasonable price. Directions led them down the Via Nazionale to the railway station on the Piazza dei Cinquecento. Cinquecento sounded exotic in English, but was just the Italian word for the number 500. After some searching, Dick spotted the "Y's" sign tucked away in the corner of the Piazza dei Independenza. As might be surmised, a fair amount of Rome was given over to piazzas or city squares. Like many ancient cities, it was cut up by streets running every which way, leaving odd segments of land, good only to put a statue on—like Washington, DC, only more so. At least a part of Rome's statuary was decorative and much easier on the eye, because of the great sculptors who made them.

The commemorative statues of long-dead heroes, which so often looked out of place in their surroundings or so awkward as to be grotesque, were the parking place of pigeons and a place for the homeless to hang out. Samuel Butler, in his work *Erewhon,* made the observation that all civic statuary ought to be reappraised every fifty years to determine its artistic worth, historical value, and relationship to contemporary times. The statuary that didn't make the cut should be melted down to make way for the new.

The "Y" in Rome was a new building, had central heating, hot water, and comfortable, spacious rooms. This put it on a footing with the best hotels in their price range in Europe. The daily rate was $3.55 each, or 2,200 lira. The heat meant things would dry, so they washed everything. The doors, drawers, chairs, and knobs, all had something hanging from it, plus they had acquired a clothesline in Latina and stretched it across the room in several directions, filling it with the soggy stuff.

It was raining, coming down with an air of permanency, so they limited their ramblings that night to a brief hunt for an English-speaking movie, then picked up a jug of vino *bianco,* went back to the "Y," and ate dinner in the *ristorante* downstairs. The "Y" was not as prudish as the ones stateside, with both a bar and snack bar combined. The clerk didn't raise an eyelid when Bill asked for the key with a bottle of vino in hand.

Thursday, during their second day in Rome, they gained a much more clear idea of how to get around the city. They wouldn't be able to direct a person to any place, but they could get there themselves and back again with a minimum of difficulty. Rome's traffic moved with little or no regulation, and they found the mopeds were sprightly enough to get through the confusion without getting clobbered.

After a leisurely breakfast, they set out for St. Peter's and the Vatican. Following the signs across town, they came to the Via de Conciliazione after crossing the Tiber River, which led into St. Peter's Square. They were afraid the church might be closed, but luck prevailed. The first impression of the interior was the enormous size and brilliant colors surrounding them. All the statuary was executed on a heroic scale, and the marble and mosaics all blended to create a harmony of intense, but beautiful color. It was certainly different from Notre Dame, where the interior was dark, lit by flickering candles, and only relieved by the stained glass windows. The interior of St. Peter's was spiritually elevating without sacrificing light and color. The size of the place and its architectural, historic, and religious associations shrank mankind to its proper significance. At the extreme end of the nave, at the back of the apse, was the so-called *Cathedra Petri,* or symbolic throne of St. Peter, a chair which was often claimed to have been used by the apostle, which appears to date from the twelfth century. Gianlorenzo Bernini, the seventeenth-century sculptor, created a large bronze throne in which it's housed, raised up on four supports, where it's held by the four Doctors of the Church—Saints Ambrose and Augustine representing the Latin Church and Athanasius and John Chrysostom the Greek Church. Over that was the papal crown, suspended as if someone were wearing it while sitting in the chair. Directly behind the crown was an oval-shaped, yellow alabaster-colored window, with the Dove of the Holy Spirit, which appeared to be resting on the crown.[1]

Entering the basilica, the whole scene was framed between the four huge bronze columns of the baldachin, also by Bernini, looking down the complete length of the nave. The baldachin, itself a massive canopy covering the main altar ninety-eight feet high, was adorned with olive leaves and bees—the emblem of Pope Urban VIII (1623-1644)—and vines growing up the spiraled fluting of the columns. The top was surmounted with a pediment of baroque brackets supporting a draped canopy.

Aerial view of St Peter's Square.

Set below the level of the floor was a sunken space with stairs leading down. There was a white marble figure of one of the popes kneeling, all of his garments meticulously draped in marble. This area furnished access to the crypt under the main altar, where St. Peter is said to be buried. In the left transept, there was a door over a massive piece of stonework, very intricately draped and highly polished. They had to step back to get the scene in proper perspective. It appeared like a huge piece of stiff, heavy fabric, but was really many blocks of marble cunningly fitted together to give the impression of one solid piece of stone. In places where the walls were not filled with statuary or mosaics, there were varicolored inlaid marble panels running to the roof. The marble ranged in color from jet to rose and was polished to a shade less than brilliant, which gave it a painted effect. Even the floors were dressed with inlaid marble of lighter shades.

The statues on the balustrade of St Peter's Basilica represent Christ the Redeemer, St John the Baptist and 11 Apostles.

Pius XII was buried beneath a pink circular slab between the main altar and the Chair of St. Peter. The pope died while the brothers were in Paris, but they didn't find out until they arrived in Athens and read the English newspaper. Afterward, they wandered around for a while, went into the Treasury, and were treated to a concentrated display of consummate workmanship and venerable objects. Chalices of gold, filigree, platinum inlaid with diamonds, emeralds, malachite, rubies, and pearls abounded and were displayed with vestments used by the various popes, made of the heaviest cloth of gold and the most intricate, resplendent embroidery. There was a monstrance set in a base of raw emeralds, a pearl-studded chain with a pear-shaped pearl the size of a small fig, and crosses of rock crystal. The monstrance is a sacred vessel, usually made from gold or precious metal, cruciform in shape, with a small see-through glass box window in the middle that holds a consecrated host for the purpose of Eucharistic adoration. When the wafers of unleavened bread and wine are consecrated at the celebration of the Mass, they transform into the body and blood of Christ himself, known as the mystery of transubstantiation. The papal tiara, called the "Crown of St. Peter," was set with many precious stones. There were different reliquaries of the most elaborate workmanship. One reliquary was said to hold two of the thorns from Christ's crown of thorns from the Crucifixion. The thorns were set into a gold base and projected upward inside a glassed-in portion at the top of the reliquary. They had an angular side, were about 1.5 inches long, came to a very straight needle point, and were brownish-black in color. Another reliquary held fragments said to be of the True Cross.[2]

From the Treasury, they took the elevator to the roof over the nave and from there ascended some killer stairs that were circular, switchback, and sideways canted to get to the top of the dome. They went inside the dome about halfway up, which put them over the main altar and looking down on the baldachin. One of the guards stood across the width of the dome, faced the wall, and said something in a normal voice, but the acoustics were such that the sound traveled

The Egyptian sotto stele in the middle of St Peter's Square from one of the side fountains.

along the wall and was amplified to almost twice the normal volume at a distance of approximately eighty feet. Known as the whispering gallery, where whispers can be heard at great distances because of the circular enclosure of the structure that carries the sound wave around, even in other parts of the gallery. Dick got on one side and whispered, "Hey, turkey, can you hear me?"

From across the dome, Bill went, "Gobble, gobble," in a sotto voce whisper that was amplified greatly by the acoustics of the architecture. From the other side, Dick heard him loud and clear. The inside of the dome was covered with mosaics in all the brightest colors, and although they were hundreds of years old, they hadn't dimmed an iota. From the floor below, the mosaics looked like carefully wrought paintings but were composed of porcelain bits, each as small as a penny.

The top of the dome provided a commanding view of Rome, with most of the city to our right, the Roman Forum to the far right, and the Tiber River running through the heart of the city. Behind St. Peter's were gardens, a fern-covered grotto, and the papal coat of arms carved in topiary shrubbery.

The Vatican Gardens from the top of the Basilica.

From the Vatican, they went looking for the offices of *The Rome Daily American* newspaper to inquire about a friend of Dick. Although she wasn't there, the sports editor on the day showed them around the whole place and they gladly met a few of the editorial staff. That little side trip brought them to dusk, and since Dick had no taillight at the time, they started home. It took no more than fifteen minutes to cross town. And before night's end, they finally got a lead on a place that, perhaps, could fix the mopeds. They planned to take the bikes there the next day, then pay the rest of their return fare home at the travel agent's office.

After delivering the mopeds to the shop, they changed their reservations out of Lisbon from February 13 to January 13. They thought a little caution wouldn't hurt and maybe they could get back to the United States with a few dollars left.

Rome had its nightlife all right, but it cost money. They didn't indulge much. There was a notable paucity of English-speaking movies in town considering the number of Americans there. Americans could buy cigarettes at the embassy, but when they inquired, they found out the cigarettes were only for military personnel. As civilians, they felt discriminated against.

Getting the bikes out of hock, they made a quick trip over to St. Peter's to see the Sistine Chapel. They arrived half an hour too late and decided to see the Colosseum once again instead and do a better job of it. They took a couple of pictures of the Colosseum and clambered around in the upper galleries. The Colosseum was not too interesting after all, so they went over to the Roman Forum on Palatine Hill. Climbing over an iron picket fence, which had a little sign on it that they couldn't translate, *l'entrata vietato ecetto al personale ufficiale*, descended into a subterranean level lit by grates in the ceiling. There were some mutilated frescoes on the wall and some very picturesque passages that resembled movie sets, except they were the real thing. They found some beautifully inlaid mosaic floors that most tourists never saw.

From the Forum they went to the Catacombs of St. Callixtus and took the tour. The catacombs were dug by both the Christian and Jewish communities of Rome, where their dead were buried underground. The more numerous Christian catacombs were dug between the second and fifth century in the soft tufa rock formed from the deposit of streams or springs. It was cheaper for the Christians to bury their dead underground than in above-ground expensive plots. Also, they followed the example of Christ's burial and not in the pagan tradition of cremation. They were motivated by Scripture that bodies not be altered, since one day, the dead would rise. All the Christian catacombs belong to the Catholic Church, and no one is allowed to explore them without the Vatican's permission.

There is speculation that the Holy Grail is buried in one of the catacombs under the Basilica de San Lorenzo Fuori le Mura, near the tomb of St. Lawrence, a deacon of the Church martyred in AD 258. However, the Vatican says this is bunk. Their argument is that "Christians didn't bury objects with their dead. As for now, we only found inscriptions and remains." The Church also doesn't give much veracity to the tale, since it is mentioned in an apocryphal gospel and not a canonical document. Vatican authorities denied permission to open the catacombs to look for the Holy Grail.[3] The Grail is a cup or bowl of extensive legend and myth that goes back to the Last Supper and the Crucifixion of Jesus, then on to the Arthurian legends of Britain. It is mentioned in Wagner's *Parsifal,* in the film *Indiana Jones and the Last Crusade,* and more recently in Dan Brown's book *The DaVinci Code,* where he places the Grail as buried under Rosslyn Chapel in Scotland.[4]

Overview of the Roman Forum, the central part of the city around which ancient Rome developed.

The catacombs' tour coordinator had them and the other visitors sit on a bench marked German, French, Spanish, or English, and when enough people were gathered on any one bench, a tour guide came along who spoke that language, and off they went.

After descending a long flight of stairs, there were long, narrow aisles cut into the sides up to a height of approximately twenty-five feet, where there were niches for the bodies. Many of the original carvings were still extent depicting the Greek word for fish, *ixthus*, which letters form an acrostic *Iesus Christos Theou Uios Soter*, which translates: Jesus Christ, Son of God, Savior. This was a common symbol of Christ and seen on many vehicles with variations. Also, the Good Shepherd with a lamb on his shoulders representing Christ and the souls he's saved is commonly found on sarcophagi and tombs. Other ancient symbols of Christianity they saw were the *orante*, or the open arms of a figure that symbolized the soul that lives in divine peace, the monogram of Christ, XP, where the Greek letters X (chi) and P (rho) originate. The first two letters of the word Christ were chipped into a tufa enclosure. They also found the dove with olive branch carved into the tombs, the alpha and the omega and the phoenix chiseled into tomb covers.[5]

There were tombs of quite a number of popes, whose remains had long since been removed to St. Peter's. All of the tombs or niches were carved out of limestone, called "tufa," which has strength enough to support its own weight when passages of some width are hewn. In Roman times, the Christians used to hollow out a niche in the tufa, place the corpse in it, and then seal it with a slab of marble or cement. The niche was marked with a Latin or Greek inscription on the slab, usually with some sign, such as a picture of a tool, to indicate the person's occupation. St. Callixtus's catacomb tombs ranged from 90,000 to 350,000. It had four levels, the lowest of which was about eighty-five feet underground. There are said to be miles of catacombs below and outside of Rome, some of which have been lost as vegetation grew over their opening and the memory of the place forgotten.[6]

The tour lasted about a half hour and was conducted by an Irishman who had been a tour guide for twenty-eight years. He didn't give the impression that he was even a little jaded by his tenure. He wanted to know about them and cautioned them to be very careful on the roads, when he learned the brothers were traveling on motorcycles. He may have been thinking about the local traffic. Considering the melee of cars, motorbikes, bicycles, and pedestrian traffic on the Roman streets, they had to adopt as a motto: "Full speed ahead and damn the Carabinieri" to survive the roadway free-for-all.

On "Arrivederci Roma Day." They went to Mass in the morning at the Gesu' Church, the main Jesuit church, and met one of Bill's instructors from Bellarmine High, who showed them around after Mass. He was in Rome studying for his master's degree in theology and pointed out the relics of St. Ignatius Loyola and an arm of St. Francis Xavier. The church was very ornate inside, with statues on the ceiling and walls in relief, elaborately carved altar rails, and other appointments. From the Gesu', they went back to the "Y," packed up, and went over to St. Peter's to see the Sistine Chapel, their third try to view it, and it was closed, so that was that. They took one more stroll through St. Peter's and took a couple of pictures inside. Taking pictures was forbidden, but that made it all the better. Bill rolled the film and set the lens in a corner, while Dick stood in front of him until he was ready. He sighted the camera from his hip, then Dick stepped aside, and click. That was all there was to it. There were several guards skulking around, which added some surreptitious spice to the undertaking. They were fully expecting the developed film to have a message, "Thou shalt not . . ."

They finally got out of Rome and headed for the coast, then due north. It was bright and sunny, but cold. After four days of lolling around a heated room, they had softened considerably. Stopping at Civitavecchia for spaghetti and vino at dinner hour, then pushing on through Tarquinia to Grosseto, they stopped for the night. They planned for another cold one the next day, which meant doubling pants, socks, shirts, and a double ration of grog. On top of all that went the rain capes as windbreakers. They were cold just making the preparations. It "was tough for them," as the saying goes.

From Grosseto, they were 705 miles from the Spanish frontier and had to travel 382 miles to get through France in three days. They wanted to make the trip more rapidly, because they didn't particularly like French prices and weren't sure if southern France would be any less expensive.

They made a record on Monday, November 17, by covering 193 miles, with no time to do anything but travel. The day had started with an argument with a thieving waiter over the breakfast bill in a Grosseto café. He was not budging from his bill of $2.03 (1,260 lira) for two breakfasts, so Dick figured the bill again and finally left $1.77 (1,100 lira), telling him to go to hell. Bill picked up a pair of pants for $4.84 (3,000 lira) at the outdoor market just outside the city walls. They were best described as having the feel of a horse blanket and being "rat gray" in color.

North of Grosseto, the island of Elba was not far offshore, where Napoleon Bonaparte was exiled for a while. They made it on to Pisa before dark and got a shot of the Leaning Tower in the twilight. As they walked the exterior walkway to the top of the tower, they noticed it didn't just tilt; it leaned way over. The unevenness distorted one's sense of balance. A spot of spaghetti in Pisa set them right, and then they were off again to La Spezia. They thawed out and headed inland over the Tuscan hills that went up several thousand feet. At times, they saw the Ligurian Sea in the distance by the light of the half-moon. They stopped for the night in Sestri Levante, 33.6 miles outside Genoa and 138.6 miles from France.

From Sestri Levante into Genoa, it was very hilly, taking 2.5 hours to cover the distance. It was a bright, sunny day, perfect for viewing Genoa, perched on high hills. The upper part of the city seemed very staggered and scattered because of the rugged terrain. In the sun, the city looked slightly rose-white and very clean. The Genoans were in the throes of building wide boulevards in some parts, and as a result, some of the streets were chewed up, but it wasn't nearly as bad as Naples, since Naples wasn't doing anything about their roads. The road ran along the Liguarian Sea, up hills, through tunnels, and got rough along the cliffs. The coastline, pocketed with a series of coves, sported small towns in each. Sometimes, the towns were as close as two miles from each other, but cut off from one another, except by sea or road. The shallow water of the sea was turquoise and clear when viewed from up high, and it looked good for swimming and diving. They arrived in Ventimiglia as planned after an all-day ride along the Italian Riviera, just nine miles from France.

CHAPTER 23 THE PRINCIPALITY OF MONACO AND RETURN TO FRANCE

NOVEMBER 19–22, 1958

The first condition of understanding a foreign country is to smell it.
—Rudyard Kipling

AFTER CROSSING THE BORDER, they were in Monaco almost before they knew it. They went to look at the most popular casino, The Casino de Monte Carlo, but the decision to play was easy. It and the four other casinos were closed for their national holiday (Fete de S.A.S. le Prince Souverain)—so they pushed on to France.[1] The countryside started to level out a bit, which made things easier, and Customs didn't give any trouble when they arrived. They sped on by St-Jean-Cap-Ferrat and down the hill into Nice, but didn't stop. At Antibes, Bill had a flat and they wheeled his bike to a shop for a fix. While waiting, they walked around a bit and exchanged some money, taking a small licking on the exchange. In Italy, they could have received the equivalent in lira of 455 francs to the dollar. In Luxembourg, they got 477 francs to the dollar. When they got back to the shop, the guy was putting on the second patch, but when he dunked the tube, three more holes showed up. Bill just bought a new tube instead and they were back on their way.

At Cannes, three letters were waiting for them from their dad and friends that perked them up nicely. They sat down at an outdoor café and read them over a couple of glasses of wine. After a nice sit, they headed to St. Raphael, twenty-eight miles away, for a coffee break, then inland for Le Luc and Brignoles. Somewhere in the hills it got cold, so by the time they reached Le Luc, they were frozen, but they forged on to Brignoles, fifteen miles more, and finally had dinner there. Afterward, they decided to keep on going to make up for all their delays, and they wrapped scarves around their ears and across their noses. All that, plus caps, goggles, and capes, made them look very weird indeed. Side by side, they stormed through little villages at full speed in the middle of the night, heading in the direction of Marseille and Aubagne. When they asked the cops where to find a hotel in Aubagne, the brothers had to buy them a drink so they'd show the way. One of them even led them to their room directly and pointed out the john down the hall. Two *vin ordinaries*—a small price for directions.

Pushing to get out of France and into Spain, the land of the deflated peseta, in less than two days, they simply hoped the mopeds would stand the pace. They had been running them wide open and knew they could stand only so much of that. If the bikes got them to Lisbon, they would probably be pretty well used up, not so much by the number of kilometers, but by how they had been driven. By then, they had learned how to make all sorts of little adjustments which used to cause no end of consternation.

They left Aubagne without breakfast, since there wasn't a restaurant open, but two kilometers down the road, however, they found a bakery and had the traditional repast of coffee and rolls. Shortly after, they entered Marseille over Belgian block and cobblestone roads, which did no good to the tires. The streets of Marseille were laid out much like the haphazard manner of Paris, so they stuck to the main route through the city. Besides, they were still in a hurry to get out of France. At the edge of the second suburb of the city, they stopped for coffee and sent off several postcards. Dick got a flat tire from a three-inch spike just outside of Martigues, so Bill went into town looking for a bicycle repair shop. The search took him across several bridges. He finally found a shop and got repair materials and headed back to Dick. Held up when he had to wait for two large boats to pass through the last bridge and by the time he got back to Dick, he'd found a closer tire repair shop. He had left the bike, and was leisurely sipping a *vin rouge*, talking to an English-speaking Frenchman several blocks away.

Marcel Meunier, the Frenchman Dick talked to, had flown for the Free French Air Force (Forces Aeriennes Francaises Libres) during World War II in several aircraft, including the P-63 King Cobra fighter plane. He was trained in Texas along with other Free French airmen. When Bill found them at the bar, Marcel and Dick were conversing over Marcel's training experience. The Frenchman went on at great length mentioning his Texas flight instructor, who made it a point to always anoint his instructions with the word "fucking." The flaps were "fucking flaps," the tail end of the aircraft was the "fucking empennage," and so on. But out of Marcel's mouth, it sounded more like *fooking*. Marcel insisted on buying a round of *vin ordinaire* and was enthusiastic about his contribution to the war effort. After sipping some more wine, they bid adieu and picked up Dick's bike and left for Arles.

They had lost an hour of daylight and made up for it by not stopping until Montpelier. From Martigues to Arles, it was flat country and mostly deserted. All they saw were what appeared to be targets for French Air Force planes flying around that area. The stretch, about nineteen miles, went through the Rhone River delta. The only people they saw were two highway employees working beside the road picking up rocks and turning the soil. The plain was covered with piles of rocks three to five feet high in conical pyramids. As far as they could determine, those piles didn't serve any purpose other than to make a work project. Perhaps they were depositional rocks from the Rhone's annual flooding. Regardless, they didn't stop to ask.

The countryside outside of Arles was given over almost entirely to vineyards. Beyond St. Gilles, they found a train parked in the middle of a crossing. When they asked a girl in halting French how long she had been waiting, she replied it had been fifteen minutes. They went down the tracks to the end of the train, crossed over, and were on their way to Montpelier. It had turned seasonably cold in the Rhone Valley, and all the grape vines had dark red or yellow leaves. The air was still and hazy from all the fires burning the vine pruning. The smell of vinegary smoke pervaded the overcast sky—cold and beautiful too; it was a haunting fall day.

Arriving in Montpelier in the evening, they checked out about ten hotels, trying to find a great price, then finally settled on the Lux Hotel. After moving in, they had dinner, then went looking for a French Army major Dick had known when stationed at Aberdeen Proving Ground. The major was in London, however, and his Tonkinese wife entertained them with a drink and some small talk before they departed.

They next morning, they rose up and went their separate ways to get breakfast. Neither could find anything more substantial than toast and coffee at that time of the morning. Packed and on the road by 10:00, it was the earliest they had been under way since acquiring the mopeds. The sky was overcast, threatening to rain all day and finally did later that afternoon.

At Meze, only twenty-two miles out of Montpelier, they did a quick repair job on Bill's broken clutch cable, then picked up a couple of spares to keep from getting stuck in the middle of nowhere. Lady luck must have been riding along, because Bill's cables had broken three times outside of civilization, yet replacements were always found at some bike shop close at hand.

The countryside all the way to Beziers and beyond was full of vineyards. The vines were pruned close to the ground, and the clippings being burned resulted in a smoke haze that hung in the valleys and clung against the hills. Looking up the valley, all the winegrowers (*vignerons*) had smoking brush piles blazing away, sooting the air. Stopping in one bistro for a taste of the local product, asked if there was any use for the vine cuttings. The proprietor brought out the menu and showed where one of the entrees was lamb grilled over smoking vines. He said they soaked dried vine cuttings in water and used them to add flavor to the meat while grilling.

At Narbonne, they stopped for lunch at the Hotel de Paris. It had a nice frontage, but the price was too high for what little food was served: hors d'oeuvres, pommes frites, and a single pork chop came to 759 francs a piece, or almost two dollars each. From Narbonne to Perpignan, it was more of the same, vineyards and still more vineyards. Some 18.6 miles from Perpignan, the landscape became hilly and then flattened out again coming into town.

Surrounded by abundant vineyards in the Pyrennees-Orientales region on the French border with Spain, they were traveling on the Autoroute A9-E159 (La Languedocienne/La Catalane) between Montpelier, Perpignan, and Barcelona, Spain. This was the Languedoc-Roussillon viticulture area of France, noted for its *vins doux naturels* (sweet and semi-sweet) wines and its "serious" reds, whites, and rosés. Without knowing which was which, they were looking at Grenache, Syrah, Mourverde, Carignon, Merlot, Cabernet Sauvignon, and Franc vines. Those vines produced the majority of the reds, while Chardonnay, Grenache Blanc, Muscat, and Viognier vines were used for the typical regional whites.[2]

A heavy rain began and Bill's bike conked out several times. Dick pushed him until it caught hold, so he'd go awhile, then conk, push, conk, push . . . This was Dick's main occupation for the last fifteen miles! Outside of Perpignan, a Citroen 2 CV, the tin lizzie car of France, tried to take Bill out. The driver pulled in front of him, causing him to swerve and dive off the road to avoid the car and head for a drainage ditch. Somehow, he flew over the top of the ditch, missed a telephone pole by inches, and came to a halt upright and in one piece! The damage was one slightly crumpled rear wheel rim from a hard landing after flying over the ditch. They took the driver's address. Although, he didn't speak English, he told them his mother was Australian. They decided to end their travels for that day, given the heavy rain, the moped breakdown, and the accident, all of which led them in search of a hotel for the night. After exchanging some money, they found the Hotel du Midi at $2.39 (1,000 FF) for two. Forced to change their plans of making it to Spain that day, they prayed for better weather the next day.

BORDEAUX
LA CORUÑA
PYRENEES
CORD. CANTÁBRICA
BILBAO
ANDORRA
ZARAGOZA
PORTO
SPAIN
PORTUGAL
MADRID
VALENCIA
PENÍNSULA IBÉRICA
LISBON
SIERRA MORENA
SEVILLE
S. NEVADA
VICENTE
MALAGA
GIBRALTAR U.K.
ALBORAN SEA
STRAIT OF GIBRALTAR
GIBRALTAR
ORAN
ATLAS TELLIEN
ER RIF
RABAT
FEZ
CASABLANCA

MASSIF CENTRAL
GENOA
ITALY
RIVIERA
MONACO
MONACO
LIGURIAN SEA
FLORENCE
SAN MARINO
MARSEILLE
APPENNINI
GOLFE DU LION
CORSE
VATICAN CITY
VATICAN
ROME
NAPLES
MENORCA
TYRRHENIAN SEA
SARDEGNA
MALLORCA
CAGLIARI
BALEARIC IS.
PALERMO
MEDITERRANEAN SEA
SICILIA
CAP BON
CONSTANTINE
TUNIS
VALLETTA
GULF OF GABÈS

CHAPTER 24 SPAIN: COSTA BRAVA

NOVEMBER 22–NOVEMBER 26, 1958

I have found out that there ain't no surer way to find out whether you like people or hate them than to travel with them.—Mark Twain

THERE WAS NO LETUP IN THE RAIN, but they were determined to get to Spain, rain or shine. The nineteen miles to the border town of Le Perthus was easy. It was a climb over the Pyrenees and the mountains were low at that point. Crossing without difficulty from Spanish Immigration authorities, as they were headed downhill into Spain, they bumped into the juggernaut of petty Spanish bureaucracy. The Customs clerks demanded a carnet, or passport, for the mopeds. No one spoke English, they weren't about to let them go on without one, and they couldn't offer how to get one. Thankfully, an Englishman taking a car into Spain, who was getting the same runaround, gave an inkling of where to get the carnets.

The Automobile Club of France issued them at Perthus, so they returned to France, only to find they wouldn't issue them, for some unknown reason. They said they would have to go all the way back to Perpignan, to their main office. They argued with the agent fruitlessly. Crossing the street to another place that advertised the carnets, they were told they weren't allowed to be sold the carnets. They must have been looked dejected, dripping puddles of water on the lady's floor from the capes, and hopping from one foot to another to try and warm up. She made out two documents. Whether it was pity or they were screwing up her clean floor, they didn't know, but they did everything except hug and kiss her. They returned back through the hills and passed through Customs with no difficulty.

It was getting late when they finally cleared Customs. Bill's throttle cable broke again, so Dick pushed him all the way to Figueras in the rain, about 15.5 miles, as they weren't about to go back. It was sloppy going all the way in, but they made it in decent shape and found a hotel and some dinner. By the time they changed out of wet clothes, they were ravenous, but they went down to dinner and the proprietor and his family and all the help were eating. They wouldn't serve Bill and Dick until the dining room was officially open. The brothers had to sit at a table next to them and read a book and suffer. They were nice enough about it, but oh, so firm. Everything was so much cheaper. They wondered why they had spent so much time elsewhere. While they waited, they discussed making it to Barcelona the next day.

Before saying adios to Figueras, they went to a late Mass in a rebuilt church. The back of the church was old and the stones discolored with age. They surmised the rest of it had been damaged in the Spanish Civil War (1936–9) because the apse was new. The ceiling was a quadripartite groin vault interspersed with ribbed arch vaults, illuminated by six stained glass windows set in the curve of the apse. They noted that people in the United States were eating turkey, celebrating Thanksgiving, while they had to settle for traveling in the rain like a couple of wet turkeys.

A short way out of Figueras before it started to rain, and the remaining seventy-six miles to Barcelona got them thoroughly soaked. The seacoast was the Costa Brava, famous for its resorts. The rain and fog obscured what must have been beautiful. They tucked their feet up on the gas tank, pulled the capes over their knees, and perched there as they drove along.

They made a stop in Gerona for a brandy, and then rum, to keep the chill off. Sitting with their knees drawn up and their feet crossed on the bikes put their tired legs to sleep after a while. The only movement they made was to shake the water out of the folds of the capes and pull them down again. The less movement they made, the less water ran down their necks.

Both bikes were threatening to give up by the time they made Barcelona. Dick had no rear wheel brakes after part of the linkage fell off. Such quality moped merchandise! Dick got teed off at his motor dying and slammed it to a stop on wet pavement. Starting to flip, he just bailed out and rolled head over heels and let the damn thing go. It actually ran a little better after that.

There was a hotel on a side street with a room and shower for $1.80, or 90 pesetas, 50 pesetas equaling $1. They unloaded another round of soaked jock bags full of wet clothes all the way to the bottom. There were handkerchiefs on the chandelier, moped parts on the doors, shirts and T-shirts on the clothesline. The line ran from the shower out to a tall, heavy cabinet with mirrored doors. Bill was in the shower trying to get some slack out of the line when, out of the corner of his eye, he caught sight of the top-heavy cabinet crashing down, breaking off one of the doors and nearly flattening the camera on the table in front of it. He let out a loud croak, and they both watched in disbelief as the old thing propelled itself to the floor. Only providence spared those heavy mirrored doors—and us—from any real damage. They pounded the hinges back into shape and re-hung the door and set the cabinet upright. They laughed at the thought of the maid coming along and giving the door a jerk. She would have one hell of a surprise.

They went around the corner to a restaurant and treated themselves to a full course meal and had enough room left to squeeze in a ham omelet and two bananas after. Trying to totally fill up, they went to another cafe and had coffee and pastry, topped off with a

Malaga. The Malaga is a sweet fortified wine from Pedro Ximenez and Muscatel grapes, named after its Spanish city of origin. This dessert wine acted as a kind of energy booster for them with its sugar content. Heading back to the hotel, they stopped for another Malaga, and it was there that Bill was faced with a crucial decision: to eat or not to eat more. There was a bowl of snails in rich red sauce on the bar, and Bill asked how much they were. The bartender gave him a sample with a toothpick as a tool to dig out the meat. After a couple of tries, he extracted a stringy black mess and regarded it with something less than relish as he popped it into his mouth. This was a moment of truth. He slid it all the way down his throat before saying it didn't taste too bad. Oh, magnificent courage!

They covered a bit of Barcelona, both on foot and on the mopeds. Not quite bounding out of the sack just before noon that day, they headed out and easily accommodated themselves to the rhythm of the country. Before their late breakfast, Dick was approached by one of the many ladies of the morning walking down the sidewalk. He was approached and genuinely propositioned. She spoke English, was tall, dressed elegantly, and admired Dick's goatee. She had obviously been in the business for a while. It was impossible to have known what her trade was other than for her approach. Bill watched with amusement as Dick told her, "I'm late for breakfast, I prefer redheads, you're too tall for me, etc . . ." She accepted the decline and strode off.

Breakfast was hearty, and they went in quest of some nuts and bolts to repair the mopeds. Later, they checked in with American Express to see if they had mail from the Portuguese Navigation Co. confirming their January reservations. There was none and they headed over to the American Consulate to inquire about regulations on selling the mopeds in Spain. They found out that to sell them legally would require no end of trouble and expense. Later "informed sources" told them they could sell them, strictly via a cash deal, in certain parts of town. Apparently, motorbikes were scarce in Spain.

They met a retired American at the consulate who told them the Canary Islands were warm year round, and that information gave them thoughts of a new destination. They were going to stop there anyway on the ship home, and why not go there and embark when the ship arrived, instead of in Lisbon?

After running by the waterfront, they brought the bikes back to the hotel and set out in search of dinner. Ending up in the oldest part of the city, they both had complete dinners. The bill was still less than a dollar apiece! Dessert was a big cream-filled pastry they happily indulged in at a bakery up the street. Coffee followed at another cafe down the street, where they convinced everyone they were Swedes. Bill expressed a very foreign-accented line of gibberish composed of Russian, Turkish, French, and English. It was too bad they didn't know a single word of Swedish. They later stopped for a Malaga at a place tucked in a corner. It was full of women who smiled and simpered. Too much eye contact—they angled over to see if they'd like to go upstairs. Instead, Bill purchased what they thought was a bottle of sherry, but which turned out to be brandy. They took the bottle of Pedro Domecq back to the hotel and sampled it. Unimpressed, they set out to find a snack and found the Spanish equivalent of a delicatessen.

Dick satisfied his long-standing craving for a tuna fish sandwich, but Bill was still holding out for pancakes, which didn't seem to exist in Europe. The Portuguese have a word for this condition, one that doesn't translate into English—*saudade*—a deep emotional state of longing for an absent something that might never be available. Bill's food desire, though, was soon to be sated when they went out to the Barcelona piers and found a shack of a café catering to the American sailors. Joe's Café had pancakes, and several stacks, slathered in butter and fake maple syrup. This helped Bill's longing go away. Bill had asked for pancakes in northern Greece and had drawn completely blank stares, even when they had a good interpreter.

That night, they went to a pool hall and started playing a soccer game on a table—foosball. The ball was the size of a ping pong ball, and sliding sticks with metal figures on them were twirled to hit the ball into the goal. This was a new innovation they'd not seen before.

The day was spent in a desultory manner, reading, going to the American Express to see if the Portuguese Navigation Co. had replied, and eventually exploring Barcelona nightlife in more depth. The trouble was the U.S. Navy was in town, and the natives were out to make a killing again. They hit several joints that wanted exorbitant prices for a Malaga, and the only entertainment they offered was a lot of ladies in the business, a few half-hearted castanet clickers, and sick violins. They decided to move on the next day, fair or foul, and take the ship to Palma de Majorca in the Balearic Islands.

They set an early wake-up call for before daylight, so naturally, they could not get a proper breakfast and staved off hunger pangs with coffee and rolls. They were in a stew when the clerk at American Express told them the boat didn't leave until 10:00 p.m. that night. They thought they'd only had an hour to get the tickets and board the ship, but now they had their bikes and bags packed and a whole day to kill. They returned to their favorite restaurant close to the hotel and ate a slow breakfast. They still hadn't taken any photos of Barcelona and set out to roam more extensively.

Visiting the end of the seawall, which enclosed a man-made harbor, they could see a carrier, the *USS Forrestal,* anchored a mile away, but the planes on her decks still looked huge. The ship was in Barcelona for six days, then scheduled to sail back to Naples for Christmas. None of the sailors they talked to were too excited about that. They didn't want to leave Barcelona, one of the best liberty ports in the Mediterranean.

Exploring in the old Roman section of town, they discovered the Romans founded the place between 10 and 5 BC. The streets were very narrow and paved with huge cobblestones. Some of the Roman wall was still standing off the Plaza de San Jaime. By nightfall, it was sprinkling rain, and they headed back to their favorite beanery and put on the feedbag again. Dick ordered rice with meat, but the meat turned out to be squid with a crawfish on top of everything. The crawfish was fine, but the squid was way too fishy for his taste. Somehow, the conversation with some patrons worked around to whether or not they wanted to sell the mopeds. If there was a chance to get out from under, this was it. They quoted $100 apiece, which came to a reasonable agreement. A fellow from the café went out in search of friends he thought might be interested. Nobody showed up, so they headed for the ship to load them on.

It was a simple operation to drive the mopeds up the gangplank and down the deck to a covered place at the stern. Bill checked what was available on board and warned they'd have to provide their own larder, so they bought bread, cheese, butter, ham, and two liters of wine. They mixed one vino *seco* and one vino *dulce,* to their taste. They were fully boarded an hour before the ship was on its way to the Balearic Islands.

CHAPTER 25 SPAIN: BALEARIC ISLANDS AND THE MAINLAND

NOVEMBER 22–DECEMBER 4, 1958

The world is a book, and those who do not travel read only a page.
—Saint Augustine

THE SHIP HAD BEEN DOCKED in the innermost part of the harbor, but headed out with a minimum of fuss, threading its way past the *SS Constitution,* a cruise ship on a winter cruise. All the navy ships had lights strung fore and aft and up the masts. As they cleared the harbor, the *USS Forrestal* was a spectacular sight, with a full view of lights the length of the flight deck and a long string of them from the bow up to the masthead and back to the stern. After sailing for an hour and a half, Barcelona was invisible, but the *Forrestal* could still be seen.

Little did they know that when they paid for a deck passage that literally meant deck. The best situation offered was a screened-in place on the boat deck with some uncomfortable wooden chairs. They sat in the bar for a while nursing a Malaga and trying to read, but the light was too dim. Bill finally gave up and went up to "their place" and stretched out on the deck, trying to sleep with his rain cape as a pillow.

Dick got hungry, broke out the provisions, and set himself up in the second class dining room. Liberating a glass from his previous travels, he poured some wine and sat there till the wee small hours of the morning, reading, sipping wine, and nibbling on cheese. Bill found him later, joining him for ham and cheese sandwiches and *vin rouge*. Afterward, Dick tried to catch a few winks back in the bar in a chair, but a steward kicked him out, so he wandered some more.

The *SS Constitution* was already docked when they arrived at Palma that morning. They were bleary-eyed and cold by the time they left the ship but found a hotel room for a surprisingly low price of $1.60 (80 Pt.). Locating a restaurant finally that could make an omelet, it took two and the usual tea, bread, butter, and marmalade to satisfy them. They always made a drawn-out production of breakfast when staying at any one place for a while, so it was hours later when they left the restaurant. Bill headed for a newsstand and Dick for the hotel. Dick was not paying attention to the wet brick street on the way and slammed on his brakes too hard to avoid hitting a truck. Spilling and sliding, he and the moped wound up under the truck, suffering only a skinned knee and a muddy pant leg.

The rest of the day they slept and nibbled on cheese to hold them until dinner. The Spanish do not dine until 8 or 8:30 p.m., so nothing was open when Dick went out to look for a restaurant. Bill decided to go see an English-speaking movie, and Dick left him in search of an open restaurant. Dick got lost somewhere in the middle of town, walking up the hill from the hotel. When he finally returned to the garage to get his moped, it was acting up and took another hour to straighten out. The hotel staff fixed him up with some "lomos," or pork and pommes frites, to keep him going after a fruitless search for an open restaurant.

Their research told them that Mallorca, sometimes spelled Majorca, the largest island, is centered in the middle of the Balearic island chain. It had a population of 350,000 people, and its dominant agricultural products were olive and almond trees. The Romans conquered the island in 123 BC, and in the sixth century, it became part of the Byzantine Empire. It was then ruled by Arabs from the eighth century until 1229. King James I of Spain united Mallorca with Spain under the crown of Aragon. The island became independent soon after but was reunited again in the fourteenth century by Peter IV of Spain. By virtue of its adherence to Aragon, Mallorca, and the Balearic island chain, it was finally ruled by the monarchy, strengthened by the marriage of Ferdinand II of Aragon and Isabella of Castile, who founded the national unity of Spain's current geographic properties.[1]

The English-speaking movie was at the Regina Theatre. Bill found it without too much difficulty, just off the Plaza Gomila, at the other end of town from where they were staying. The movie was pre-World War II vintage and a bit of a gasser. He left before it was finished. Dick wound up at dinner nearby and became engaged in conversation with a Danish painter who had resided on Mallorca for six years. Afterward, the painter invited Dick for a drink, and they went to a nearby bar the painter frequented. A Danish woman, the painter's friend and fellow artist, was there and, in the course of their conversation, informed them that the Guardia Civil was looking for her. During that afternoon at the Danish club, she had replaced Franco's portrait with that of King Frederick of Denmark and had switched the Spanish flag for the Danish flag on the façade of the building. Dick's host raised his eyebrows and Dick took his leave.

The current ruler was the Dictator Francisco Franco Bahamonde, aka the Caudillo. He declared a military rebellion and won his dictatorship over Spain in 1939, at the end of the Spanish Civil War that left over an estimated half million people dead. He aligned with Nazi Germany and Mussolini's Italian Fascists and ruled until his death in 1975. In the 1950s, there was still guerilla resistance to Franco in the hills by the *maquis*.[2]

The Guardia Civil was the Federal Military Police that enforced Franco's regime and patrolled in pairs in rural towns, functioning as Franco's chief means of social control. At the end of the 1936 civil war, Franco continued the oppression and decimation of thousands of political opponents. During World War II, Spain was neutral and isolated. It wasn't until the 1950s that Spain entered into the international community. In 1953, President Eisenhower visited, which resulted in a trade pact, and in 1955, Spain joined the United Nations.[3]

Setting off to take pictures of the city, it turned out, it was 5:00 p.m. before they got going. They dived into the old quarter of the city and found a Pirelli tire shop, where they bought some straps for their luggage and an air pump. They picked up a tip on a repair shop for the bikes and dumped them there for the afternoon. While the bikes were being repaired, they wandered around the streets, but all the shops were closed for lunch. They visited the Cathedral of Palma de Mallorca, also called La Seu, in the Catalan dialect. It's the largest church in the offshore Spanish islands, and they took pictures inside and out. Its history goes back to James I, who chased the Arabs out of Spain and arranged in his will to have it built on the site of a mosque, which was demolished by his son, James II, who got the cathedral going in 1300. It was completed in 1601, but has been undergoing revisions ever since. Anyone who kneels at the altar is also kneeling in the direction of Mecca.[4]

From there, they did a quick trip to the docks and the office of the Compania Mediterraneo for information on sailings back to the mainland. Before having dinner at the hotel, they investigated the "American quarter" of Palma, back near the Plaza Gomila. There were many restaurants featuring English and American foods, as well as American jazz. They had been craving egg salad sandwiches and pancakes since leaving the United States, so they took advantage of the cultural exchanges—because they were on the menu—and ordered accordingly. That evening, they had dinner at the hotel, did some reading, and planned a midnight moped ride around the island to see what was happening.

Going separate ways. Bill visited a place called the Jazz Workshop, but it was pretty dead. Dick went to a bar and

Dick looking for rear traffic the difficult way.

restaurant called Mam's over by the Regina Theater and drank Spanish beer, which was just so-so, and listened to the intermittent harangues of a woman who said she was a Lithuanian baroness. She railed against the British, especially Winston Churchill, the British Prime Minister during World War II. She seemed to like the Germans, loved the Poles, and hated the Russians. She kept talking about her castle, her two murdered husbands, all in good idiomatic English, with just a slight accent. It would have sounded more plausible if she hadn't kept throwing in the baroness business. After a while, her stories became boring, but nonetheless, they shut the place down at 2:00 a.m.

Dick on his moped as we explore Palma de Majorca—windmills in background.

While heading back to Mam's for breakfast the next morning, Dick took another spill on his bike. This time, he put holes in his only other pair of pants and scraped his right knee again. Gin worked well as disinfectant, and he continued to keep the knee clean with occasional brandy baths. Despite that, they had a great breakfast of pancakes and French toast for Bill, scrambled eggs and chili for Dick. They stopped at the waterfront and took pictures of the cathedral from a hill on the other side of the harbor. They walked the bikes up some stairs to take a closer look at some windmills.

They wanted to leave Palma that day, even though it was already mid-afternoon, so they decided to make the move out of town. A rain cloud passed over and they holed up in a café with a wide marquee. They picked up another nibble from the waiter at lunch about a prospective buyer for the bikes, but nothing came of it. The rain stopped and they took off on the road to Manacor, thirty miles away. During the ride, they passed many windmills, but none of them were turning. The windmills were used for both milling flour and pumping water to storage basins.[5] They had to give each other pushes as one or another of the bikes died out, but didn't think anything of it because that was a usual routine by then.

It was dark when they reached Manacor, but it was just a farming community, so they pushed on to Oporto Cristo and found a hotel for $1.40 a night. They were close enough to the beach to hear the surf. After a brief stroll, they discovered there really wasn't much there except a few bars, so they returned to the hotel to sew, shine shoes, and update their journal.

The sun shone bright and warm on Oporto Cristo the next morning. They had slept soundly in spite of the midnight snack of banana sandwiches and beer. They took a ride out of town and investigated some caves they'd heard about. It cost sixty cents to go inside, so they passed on the tour. They took another side trip to a point of land that formed one side of the harbor mouth. The entire landmass was limestone, with the softer stone extending out to sea, leaving a Swiss cheese effect. Walking out a bit on it, the surface was rough on their shoes. There was no beach, but in some places, the waves had cut caves of a sort into the rock. With photos taken, they left for Palma and headed for Mam's for a lunch of tuna sandwiches, chili, and beer.

Back in Palma de Majorca, in the main part of town, Bill broke his speedometer cable in front of a hotel, so they took a room and bath there with breakfast included. He had a spare cable, so it only took a half hour for him to install it. They took baths, did some laundry, and read for a while until dinnertime. They stopped back at the Jazz Workshop and shot dice for pesetas, but couldn't keep money on the table because the cops enforced some gambling law. After a lot of pesetas were exchanged by whoever won the throw, the net effect was more or less where they started. A tally sheet was kept, and when all was said and done, Dick owed Bill one peseta or two cents. They bought some American Chesterfield cigarettes, with the prices better than stateside. At Mam's that night, they really had a great feed: hamburger steaks, French fries, tomatoes, oodles of ketchup—which came from an American submarine—tuna sandwiches, and a bowl of chili to fill in the chinks. Afterward, they rolled, or waddled, back to the hotel, had a few post-prandial brandies, and went to bed.

They enjoyed the skimpy breakfast that came with the room and took off to the ticket office to purchase the boat ride back to the mainland. However, when they presented themselves at the ticket office, they were told the deck class was sold out. One first class passage cost twice as much for the two of them and the mopeds. They went to see the ship's purser, who, for a personal consideration, fixed them up with a second class cabin, which sure beat sleeping in a chair out on the deck. He gave a good deal on the bikes too, so they loaded them immediately before he changed his mind. They walked back to the lower part of the city for a second breakfast and picked up provisions for the boat ride. Under the impression they would be in Valencia by early evening, they only bought a few bananas and chocolate bars. Later on, they found out it was a nineteen-hour trip from Palma.

The boat cleared the harbor at midday on a beautiful sunny day. They spent the afternoon reading and wandering around deck. There was some scuttlebutt about stopping over at Ibiza, the smallest of the Balearic Islands, and sure enough, they anchored there for a few hours that evening. That gave them some time to stow away a dinner in town and look over the place. Ibiza was small compared to Palma and set in a protected harbor. The island was intensively cultivated, exporting quantities of potatoes. The ship pulled away from the main street, where it had been moored on time, and they settled down for the night.

It was a gray and dismal morning pulling into Valencia and they disembarked without a hitch and headed up a long street flanked by streetcar tracks pointing to the city about two miles away. Following the tracks through the city, through the ancient part, led them to the city center. The search for a decent hotel was futile. After checking several expensive hotels they couldn't afford, they ended up at the "Ideal Pension." The place was a dreary hole, which, coupled with the weather, didn't improve their attitude toward Valencia. Even the most colorful cities looked miserable on an overcast day. They got the hell out of there and went down to the train depot to inquire about the earliest departures, which was at 8:00 p.m. that evening.

After a wandering excursion to get back to the pension that incurred a lot of aimless running, they finally found it, scooped up their bags, tore out the registration sheet they'd filled in, and left without seeing anyone. The bags were efficiently checked at the depot, and, with the help of Alfredo, an English-speaking porter, they were guided to the railroad office downtown to make reservations and pick up tickets. In Spain, travelers hardly ever purchased tickets at the train depot, but rather they had to make reservations at the railroad office, usually at a separate location.

Their new friend Alfredo had taught himself English to better his world and perhaps to get a better job, but he found that almost impossible the way things were in post-war Spain. He had a wife and a large family living away from Valencia, but he had to live in the city in order to make more money. He outlined his plans for his son's education. He wanted nothing from the brothers, but they gave him Boswell's *London Journal*. He appreciated the gift, because books in English were expensive in Spain. He was happy for the opportunity to practice English with them, and they were delighted to make his acquaintance.

It was a good six hours until the train was scheduled to leave, so they spent the time exploring the port of Valencia and touring the *USS Ault*. Valencia had a very modern man-made harbor, and at that time of year, it was full of Scandinavian ships loading oranges. They rode out to the end of the farthermost jetty and climbed around on a narrow ledge just above the water. Growing tired of that adventure, they met a sailor from Chehalis, Washington, who invited them onboard to show them around. The USS *Ault* was a Sherman-class destroyer built in 1944 with a top speed of thirty-three knots.[6] While shooting the bull with a couple of guys next to the portside depth charge racks, the conversation somehow turned to cigarettes and they produced a carton. The brothers thanked them and headed back to town for dinner.

After a meal, they had to deliver the bikes to the station. Spanish railway regulations prohibited gas on board, so they turned the mopeds upside down in the parking lot, losing about half a tank each. Their weight limit was eighty-eight pounds (40 kg), and they tried to meet the limit to avoid overweight charges, but didn't quite make it—a small extra fee was involved. However, considering the distance they would travel, from Valencia to Algeciras, they didn't spend a lot—nine dollars apiece—for the tickets and the mopeds.

They stocked up on enough food to last until the next night, because there were no restaurants on the trains, especially in third class. Two liters of *vino negro*, a big chunk of cheese, butter, and six bread rolls filled their knapsacks. They boarded precisely at departure time for what turned out to be twenty-six hours of jolting, cramped misery. Reading was difficult, because their eyes gave out in the poor light, sleep was almost impossible due to the excessively crowded conditions, and a heater was going full blast, turning the carriage into a steam room.

Daylight found them among sharply rolling hills, treeless farming country, with occasional outcroppings of rock. Breakfast helped to snap them awake. When they changed trains at Cordoba later that morning, they also had to switch the mopeds from the baggage car. The second train wasn't as nice as the first, but it was less crowded and they stretched out and managed to catch some sleep. The train had wooden benches, which were so uncomfortable they gave them a bad time all the way to Algeciras. Reading was impossible because of the continued jolting, so their only amusement was to lean out the window. They made supper out of the last of the food, and they knew the end was near when they saw the lights of Gibraltar before rolling into the final destination.

They were so happy to get off that train they performed a jig on the station platform. After rescuing the bikes, they loaded them with their gear and a young boy directed them toward a gas station. They had supper, a damn tasty one at that, and, after asking around, found a pension to park their bags and themselves in for the night. A ride around town and a couple of coffees satisfied their sense of adventure before they collapsed back at the pension.

CHAPTER 26 GIBRALTAR AND TANGIERS, MOROCCO

DECEMBER 5–8, 1958

If you reject the food, the customs, fear the religion and avoid the people, you might better stay at home.—James Mitchener

THEIR ITINERARY INCLUDED A short trip to Gibraltar. Following the road around the bay to La Linea, a long, low, sandy neck of land began and connected the island with the Spanish mainland. The promontory rose about a mile out from the beginning of the isthmus, which was about one half mile wide. Gibraltar measured nearly three miles long, three quarters of a mile wide, and rose to 1,396 feet in height. The town had a civilian population of about 23,000 and was built on the western slope facing the bay, looking over the Spanish seaport of Algeciras. Gibraltar never figured historically until AD 711, when the Moorish conquerors of Spain came, led by Tarik-ibn-Zeyad. "The Rock" became known as Gibel Tarik, or Hill of Tarik. It remained in Moorish hands for seven centuries until its eventual recapture by the Spanish in 1462. That occupation only lasted some 240 years, until a force of Anglo-Dutch marines kicked the Spaniards out in 1704. It was Great Britain that gained sole control next by means of the Treaty of Utrecht in 1713. It took a while for the Spaniards to get it into their heads that the British were there to stay. The Spanish attempted to recover The Rock several times, but it remained in British hands.[1]

Gibraltar had its own stamps, but the money, called the pound, had the same value as the English pound. Those facts meant the economy was much the same as England's, differing only by geographic location. Pesetas were accepted everywhere except the post office or those places of business that didn't want to bother exchanging them.

They cleared the Spanish/English border but found it would cost dearly to bring the mopeds in and out again because of the paperwork, so they stored them in La Linea, Spain. Once across the border, they found a room with hot water and a shower at the Grand Hotel in Gibraltar. They took in the lay of the town that night and went to a movie.

The tour of the "Gib" wasn't until later that day, so Dick walked across the border to La Linea to check on the mopeds, while Bill went in search of another hotel for a better price. They met at Monty's restaurant for lunch, then went to the Gomez tourist office and picked up tickets for a flight to Tangiers, Morocco, the next day. The tour began on time and started with a bus ride. Seated next to them were a Mexican fellow, who was a medical student at the University of Madrid, and his companion from Puerto Rico. At Europa Point, on the southwestern tip of The Rock, they stopped and rubbernecked for a while. A sailing ship was rounding the point in a following sea with all sails unfurled. The weather was squally, but when the clouds parted across the Strait of Gibraltar, they could see the Rif Mountains on the Moroccan side.

Proceeding on to St. Michael's Cave, situated on the western slope of The Rock, some 1,000 feet above sea level, it was the first site mentioned by Pomponius Mella. Described as a shrine to Hercules, he was supposed to have set up two mountains as pillars: Mount Colpe, as Gibraltar was then called, and Mount Abyla, across the Strait in Africa.[2] During the Second World War, Nissen huts were constructed for use as an emergency hospital inside the cave, and they were still there as the tour went through, but didn't mar the beauty of the place. Stalactites hung from the ceiling, some extending to the floor, forming natural columns. The cave was lit by concealed lighting, and there were duckboard walkways to keep one's feet dry. Next on the itinerary was the apes' den, where they had a close look at some of Gibraltar's famous primates—an estimated forty apes lived on The Rock. The guide related that on occasion some found their way into town and had to be shooed back to their lofty home. Called Barbary Apes (Macaca Sylvanus), they are actually tail-less monkeys. Local lore has it that as long as the monkeys inhabit The Rock, Gibraltar will remain under British rule. During World War II, the monkey census got so low, Sir Winston Churchill ordered their numbers to be replenished. Another legend is that The Rock is connected to Africa by a fifteen-mile subterranean passage, beginning at the lower end of St. Michael's Cave and goes under the Strait of Gibraltar—how the monkeys got to The Rock.[3]

They also made note of Halley's mortar. Made from natural rock, it was used to repulse the invading Spanish during several sieges in the sixteenth century. It used a charge of twenty-five pounds of powder and was loaded with one pound stone shot.

The upper galleries, as they were called, were the next stop. They consisted of a main tunnel 672 feet above sea level, it extended 659 feet and had ten embrasures, or gun emplacements, facing La Linea and to sea in a southeasterly direction. A section of the tunnel known as "the Notch" housed St. George's Hall, had three gun emplacements, and commanded a 180-degree sweeping view of the eastern face. The guns were massive muzzle loaders on wooden carriages. There was a vaulted ceiling in the hall carved out of the rock, which continually dripped water. In 1878, the Governor of Gibraltar gave Gen. Ulysses Grant a banquet in this hall. The tour finished after they passed the Moorish castle Tarik had built when he first occupied The Rock in 711. The castle was completed in 740, but little of the original remained as the successive occupants added and strengthened it.[4]

Back in town, the guide let them off where they requested, and they said good-bye to fellow Americans. After a show and dinner, they went back to the Merchant Navy Club, where they were staying at ten bob apiece or $1.40. The next day, a side trip to fly to Tangiers for the weekend was planned, leaving the mopeds behind.

After a miserable night of chasing blankets all over their beds, they both started the day off rather cranky. They hit the deck and left in the semi-twilight to get some breakfast, which was coffee and cookies found in a bar down the street and then later found an open hotel to have a proper breakfast. After going through Immigration and checking luggage, they had to wait a while before a bus came by to deliver them to the British European Airways DC-3. It was judicious timing that saved them from getting wet during a blustery morning.

They took off with half a plane load and, while still climbing, took a picture of the SS *Cristoforo Colombo*, an Italian liner in the harbor. This ship was a sister ship to the SS *Andrea Doria* that crashed into the MS *Stockholm* in July 25, 1956 and sank off the New England coast. Later, Bill asked a passenger across the aisle to shoot a picture of Gibraltar for them, since the rough air required seat belts to be fastened for the entire trip. It was a half-hour flight to Tangiers at about 1,500 feet. They flew over the southernmost point of Europe, marked by a lighthouse that poked its nose out into the Strait.

The city of Tangiers looked neatly laid out as they flew in over the extreme northwest corner of Africa. There was a stiff wind blowing when the pilot tried to land, so much so that he did a go-around, but he made it on the second pass. They disembarked and went through Customs without a hitch. After waiting around a bit for their bags, they climbed aboard a Volkswagen bus for the seven mile ride to town, traveling through a gently rolling, treeless countryside on decent roads. The bus let them off on Blvd. Pasteur, the main street, close to the hotel they finally engaged. Once in the city, they noticed veiled women on the streets and men in long pullover garments with hoods thrown back—djellabas. The garments looked like they were made of rough wool, were brown-gray or gray and black-striped and worn as an outer garment. They alighted in a rain squall and had to beat off a horde of Moroccan touts trying to sell them on various hotels. After eluding their persistent entreaties, they took refuge in the Alhambra Café.

The proprietor was a decent sort of Frenchman who changed some money for them: one dollar for 460 Moroccan francs. He then mentioned a lot of dos and don'ts of the city: Don't deal with the boys on the street, do keep their money with them, do watch their wallets, he showed them to a good hotel in the rain, which was very decent of him. From Alsace-Lorraine, he had been a chef aboard a French liner and retired to Tangiers.

The hotel on the Blvd. Pasteur had a suitable third-floor room on the corner. After settling in, they went to the steamship office to inquire about prices to Casablanca and Dakar. As it turned out, both trips were too expensive, so they decided to skip both jaunts and stick around. Touts abounded and they must have looked like good targets.

One fellow, instead of approaching them head on, came up on our port side, swung around to the rear, and overtook them, supposedly so as not cause alarm. He pulled a ring out of his pocket and held it low for them to see and sibilantly announced, "Genuine diamond from South Africa—good price." After witnessing all those elaborate maneuvers, Bill told him to shove off in French. Browsing through a couple of book shops, ended back at the Alhambra for a late lunch. Afterward, they picked up some postcards and retreated to their digs to write and then sallied forth in search of some cheap Scotch. A long walk through town, which acquainted them properly, brought them settling for a bottle of Armagnac, one cut below Cognac. After a stop for coffee and pastry, they went back to the hotel to read and sip awhile and sipped away almost the whole bottle before going out to dinner. They later took a nocturnal stroll in the casbah. Dick tried on some canvas sneakers in a shoe shop, but they didn't make shoes for feet like his anywhere in Spain or Morocco. All the shops were closed by 11:00 p.m.

Tangiers had endured the ravages and occupancy of the Phoenicians, Visigoths, Vandals, Romans, Arabs, Spanish, French, British, and perhaps a few others.[5] The city, despite all the colonialists that had come and gone, still bore a markedly modern atmosphere about it—not clashingly Moorish, as one might have expected. It was the city, and the region, of Homer's "Cimmerian man" and the place of entry to Hades and "The Sea of Darkness."

The afternoon found them separating ways after breakfast. Dick took a walk around the southeastern section of the city, and Bill went back to the casbah to explore it further. Dick recounted to Bill later that the most unusual thing he saw and heard was a wizened old man with a wand in his hand, leading squatting children in Koranic chants. Dick went into the *Petit Socco,* or marketplace of the *ville ancienne* (old town), looking for something to photograph. He found it in the sultan's palace, which was situated on the slopes that led down to the mouth of the Mediterranean. Inside was a museum in the central courtyard, where there were seven rooms with ornately carved wooden doors. From there, he ventured to the sultan's garden and to the octagonal minaret of the nearby mosque, taking several pictures as he went. Meeting for dinner, they tried a bottle of *Chaudsoleil,* translated as "the Hot Sun," a decent Moroccan wine. Later, they found their way around several used bookstores, trading off some of their own stock for used-but-new-to-them books. The next day, they returned to the Iberian Peninsula.

A wing of the Sultan's palace exiting to the street.

Tangiers was a city that had four Sabbaths a week: on Wednesday, the Hindus had theirs, Fridays were for the Muslims, Saturday for the Jews, and Sunday for Christians, which were mostly the British. The British had rather thoroughly penetrated that part of the world.

We rolled out of the city on a bus to the airport and returned to Gibraltar on the same DC-3. We arrived at the airport in plenty of time and watched a chartered plane take off for Copenhagen before ours left for Gibraltar. The only tangible benefit received from Tangiers was their exchange rate: it was two pesetas higher than The Rock. Had we been forced to live on the official Spanish rate of forty-two pesetas to the dollar, we would have gone broke by then; we saved quite a chunk of change by getting fifty-eight pesetas for one dollar.

The return flight from Tangiers to The Rock was about as long as a short bus ride—a hedge-hop one might say. Coming in to Gibraltar, there was a good view of the landward side as the plane swung over Spain on its approach. Our bags were left at the airport as we made a final foray into the town of Gibraltar to enjoy one more meal at Monty's, which was the only good place to eat in town, in our opinion. Discovering that any coins of a country taken out cannot be exchanged, we were happy to unload the last of our Gibraltar pounds on the bus ride back to the airport.

A lot of tedious officialdom was anticipated at the Spanish border, but there was no delay other than the short form we had to complete for Customs and Immigration. Our bikes survived the two-day stay in the La Linea garage. No doubt they were subjected to latter-day versions of the Spanish Inquisition, consisting of poking, turning, and twisting all likely parts. We were not present to be "put to the question," which was always "How much?" or "How much do the bikes cost?" Dick's bike had a flat tire and was leaking gas, but it was drivable, so the garage attendant pumped up the tire—the rear one that was already multi-patched.

CHAPTER 27 SPAIN AGAIN

December 9–18, 1958

Once you have traveled, the voyage never ends, but is played out over and over again in the quiet chambers. The mind can never break off from the journey.
—Pat Conroy

THEY LOADED UP THEIR BAGS and were off from La Linea, circling Algeciras Bay. Gibraltar presented itself in several aspects. Between Algeciras and Tarifa, there was a range of high hills that gave a commanding view of the Strait. When they reached the top of the hill, a cruise liner was passing through the Strait heading westward. Later on, when they reached Tarifa, the southernmost point of Europe, they saw the same liner disappear south down the coast of Africa.

In Tarifa, they were waved down by a couple of Guardia Civil soldiers carrying what looked like Thompson M1921 submachine guns (Tommy guns.) Bill stopped and Dick kept on going, yelling back at Bill, "Screw them! Come on."

Bill, on the other hand, didn't like the idea of some provincial cop shooting him full of .45 caliber bullets and yelled at Dick, "Get your ass back here!" Bill stayed with the soldiers and tried to appease them as they began to unstrap their weapons, he yelled at Dick again to get him to come back.

Dick finally turned around and drove up, looking pissed. The soldiers then went into a routine asking for passports. Franco's soldiers were guarding a bistro and had been sitting in outdoor chairs when they came along. Dick suggested that perhaps their captors would like a glass of vino *tinto*. Sure enough, relations improved significantly when a liter of red wine was ordered and they had a couple of shots down them. The brothers paid for the jug and got the hell out of there.

Five miles farther, there was a stone tower perched on top of a high rock, accessed by a very weather-beaten flight of stairs. A guide who appeared out of nowhere took them in hand and explained that the tower was built in AD 1292 by the Moors. It was situated in such a way as to command the beach that sweeps in a great arc at the tip of Europe. In 1805, off the coast of Trafalgar, an event occurred that was commemorated throughout the British Commonwealth more than any other military event on the occasion of the Napoleonic Wars. One of Britain's heroes decisively thwarted Napoleon from invading Great Britain.

Lord Admiral Horatio Nelson led a Royal Navy fleet of twenty-seven ships against the combined French and Spanish fleet, consisting of thirty-three ships, on October 21 in a gargantuan sea battle, where the French admiral Villeneuve and the Spanish admiral Gravina were defeated. The British took out twenty-two French and Spanish ships that day with no ship losses on their side. British casualties amounted to more than 1,600 men, with 1,200 wounded and 460 dead, including Lord Nelson. France and Spain suffered over 12,000 casualties, with 3,250 dead, 2,500 wounded, and 8,000 captured. The significance of the battle was it gave Britain control of the seas and access to Spain and Portugal in order to resupply its forces against Napoleon on land. Further, it crippled Napoleon's navy, hindering his ability to supply his own troops fighting across Europe.[1] This battle probably influenced Napoleon to invade Russia, which ended in his defeat and withdrawal and spelled the end of his military adventures. Looking out to sea, they could almost envision the smoke and roar of the guns as cannonades went off crippling masts and sails, hulling ships—a massacre at sea filled with the cries of dying and wounded men bathed in black powder smoke and the din of broadsides. Except, the sea was calm, small whitecaps prevailed, and seagulls hunted for food opportunities.

They took pictures of the Moorish tower and moved on, going inland through lush farmland, where stands of cork trees lined the hills. They reached Vejer de la Frontera, situated on top of a high conical hill ten miles inland from Cape Trafalgar. Good weather had abandoned them, so they climbed the hill and found a very rustic hotel, but little else. The natives there were curious, and they were the objects of covert stares wherever they went.

The local theater that night provided some entertainment. The stage show had long comical dialogues in Spanish, with dancing and singing in between. Of course, the meaning of the dialogues escaped them, but it must have been funny, because everyone laughed like hell. They did understand a pantomime of what various nationalities did upon finding money. In a skit, a Spanish person walking along the street sees money lying on the ground. Without hesitation, he pounces on it, puts it in his pocket, and walks on; a Brit, on seeing money in the street, carefully walks over, puts his foot on top of it, simulates tying his shoe, grabs the money, and casually puts it in his pocket as though there was nothing there and he had fixed his shoe problem; and then, along comes an American, who looks at the money on the ground, takes out his wallet, and throws more money down beside it, and walks away. At the time this part was being played out, everyone in the audience turned around to see how Bill and Dick reacted. It was funny, but their lack of Castilian Spanish left them out of most of the comedy.

They met a fellow from Chicago who had been there a month, learning the language and taking it easy. Vejer was a city of white-washed houses, mostly noted for its seaside situation, its beaches, and little else, from what they could see along the Costa de la Luz. Their

Chicagoan friend left the next day for "further experiences," as he called them.

In pursuance of their new policy to slow down the pace, they got a late start from Vejer. There was no restaurant in that town, so they settled for coffee and cookies for breakfast. It wasn't too warm, but nonetheless a beautiful day to travel, with scattered fleecy clouds. About 8.6 miles farther on, they discovered Dick's tire pump was missing—swiped overnight. Driven by hunger, they took a side trip to a town called Conil on the seashore and ate at a hotel there. Conil would have been an idyllic spot to visit in the summer because of its wonderful beach, and they mulled whether to stay longer. A short discussion had them prevailing onward and they made it to Cadiz in about forty-five minutes.

From a distance, the approach to the city was reminiscent of Venice, because Cadiz sat out in the sea at the end of a long, narrow peninsula, and the countryside was flat, like that around Venice. Quite a ways out, the road began to parallel a broad flat beach, so they cut over and ran on the hard packed, wet sand. They played in the surf, zooming out toward the ocean when the waves receded. The bikes got thoroughly drenched in salt water and covered in sand. A seawall eventually cut them off, forcing them to return to the road in order to get into the city. The waterfront boulevard that they took into town led them to a vacant lot that was flooded with a forty-foot-wide mud puddle. Without a clue to how deep it was, Bill went through it at full speed, drenching himself and the bags on the back of his bike. After that, they both went through it rather slowly to splash some water up and rinse off the salt and sand—not much help, though.

After unloading at the hotel, they toured the outer circumference of the city and watched the sunset in the west. Cadiz was small, with a population of about 107,000, so it wasn't a long ride from one end to the other.

Dick picked up a piece of glass in his rear tire and, in the course of repairing it, found three more holes. That made a total of six patches on the tube, which made it a very shaky proposition indeed. The tires had taken a terrific beating and both bikes had bent rims. After getting the bikes squared away, they were directed to a restaurant by a cop, where, as it turned out, they were slightly fleeced on getting the bill. Without putting up too much of a fuss, they left and took a long walk around town and had coffee and pastry. The entire city had ancient cobblestone streets and winding alleys. Most of the larger Spanish cities had both older and newer sections. The Canary Islands were a two-and-a-half-day boat ride from there, and they really wanted to go but had to check out transportation means and prices first.

A nippy but clear and sunny day greeted them when they awoke. They checked with three shipping companies that were sailing to the Canary Islands but found that all third class space was taken and first class was too expensive. That decided the matter and they made haste to flee Cadiz, which was rather a dead hole, and plotted a road trip to Seville. Their usual routine had been to have tea with breakfast, then go out for coffee after, but that morning routine didn't happen, since it took a while to get their coffee and gas before leaving. They tried to ride on the beach again before leaving, but the tide forced them up on the soft sand. They drove by huge piles of salt that the locals obtained by evaporating sea water and were gone.

The distance between Cadiz and Seville was ninety-three miles. The road around the inlet forming the harbor of Cadiz was almost thirty-one miles, and then they turned inland to the north, going through Jerez de la Frontera. This region of Spain was the home of sherry wine, but nowhere did they see enough vineyards to account for the amount of wine and brandy that came from there. The gentle rolling hills past Jerez were fun and came out on a flat plain, which made for easier, faster travel. They made good time to Seville, one of the largest cities they had visited since Barcelona, and from their observations that night, it seemed much easier to find their way around than in most cities.

The city was located on a wide bend of the Guadalquivir River. An inexpensive but deluxe pension called the Cecil-Oriente was sufficient, because they had splurged the night before, needing hot water to get cleaned up. Places offering hot water charged a premium. Walking around a bit, getting the lay of the land, they found a hotel restaurant. The dinner was tasty and well served, and the wine was just a shade off the best.

Spanish *vino ordinario* is good, as a rule, and some was excellent. French wine varied from one brand to the next, and in Italy, the quality could go to extremes both ways. After dinner, they had coffee and promenaded, as was their usual desire upon arrival in a new locale, blissfully unaware of the impending holiday. In the United States, Christmas had turned into a gruesome ordeal because of the constant advertising and phony sentiment. A few of the local stores had some ragged caricatures of Santa Claus in the windows as decoration, but nowhere did they see frightened children perched on some bewhiskered pensioner's knee, nor did the Salvation Army tinkle their bells at them from every corner.

They were thinking that some airplanes flew out of Seville to the Canaries, but they were almost sure to be too expensive, so they expected to stay put for a couple of days. They confirmed this by heading to the airport not far out of the city on the road to Madrid, discovering the prices for airline tickets were over budget. While there, some Spanish Air Force P-40s were up and coming over the field at about fifty feet, doing complete rolls. Powered by twelve-cylinder Rolls Royce engines, they looked small compared to more modern jets. The only function those planes had, Bill speculated, would have been to keep counter-revolutionary forces under control as they were no match for a jet.

That afternoon, Dick bought a spark plug for his bike, but it only improved the performance slightly. He borrowed a typewriter to compose a nasty letter to the Achilles-Sachs Company in Sweinfurt, West Germany, taking them to task for their faulty workmanship—the bikes by then were practically junk. Bill replenished his book stock and got his shoes fixed. The repair shop did a lousy job, though, so the shoes he bought in London were screwed. The Cecil-Oriente was on one of the main plazas of Seville in the more modern section of town. After dinner, they took a stroll to the old city and were promptly approached by Antonio, boy pimp, no more than ten years old, who directed them to his benefactors—a couple of aged courtesans. They talked with them for a while, then took their leave, heading home for some letter-writing before bed.

The repetitive recording of the seedier side of life in Europe highlighted the contrast between it and the United States. In the United States, prostitution was looked at from a puritanical point of view, considered against the law, and only spoken of back-handedly. In sharp contrast, in Spain, France, and other European countries, it was open to the public, so to speak, and dealt with realistically. A U.S. city the size of Seville would have had weekly raids on the cathouses, whereas in Seville, all the girls were registered, the city participated in the income, and the profession blended in with the prevailing attitudes.

Little was accomplished except retrieving Bill's bike from the repair shop and delivering Dick's. His rear bearings were scarred and grooved, and two of them were missing. The repair shop cleaned his bike up so well it was almost unrecognizable. They drank some *vino tinto*, and Dick broke down and bought an umbrella to gratify a whim.

It rained that day, so Dick put his new umbrella to good use. Having requested a call for 10:00 a.m., and never receiving one, they missed breakfast. They both attended Mass at different times. Dick went to the earlier services and Bill, at noon. After catching a snack, they met back at the hotel. While sitting in the lobby reading that afternoon, Dick had to move to get away from rain that was leaking through a huge skylight. There were orange trees around the plaza in front, but they weren't in season—all sour and tasteless. They made good decorations though. The persistent rain kept them pinned down.

Cabin fever set in, sending them out into the street. It stopped raining and blue sky beckoned them down to the nearby river to take some pictures. Many of the citizens were out stretching their legs after three days of rain. They felt much better after their promenade and came back to read until dinner and then read again after dinner until they sallied forth to get coffee. They had been staying there for four days and planned to move on the next day. The direction they would take, how far they would go, was totally contingent upon the weather and the sputtering bikes.

Seville had a lot of plaques mentioning Miguel de Cervantes Saavedra, who lived there from 1596 until 1600. One of his occupations was as tax collector, and during his stay in Seville, he spent 1567 in prison for some money troubles he had with the government.[2] Perhaps he kept some of the Crown's pesetas for himself? As Spain's premier author, he is well remembered and celebrated in Spanish literature. While crossing Spain, Bill read *Don Quixote*, his 528-page major opus, then passed it on to Dick.

The bill at the pension was reasonable—slightly over twenty dollars (1,000 Pt.) for the four days, which included two meals a day—but they were tired of being there and wanted to head toward Portugal, ninety-six miles away. Both Dick and Bill were avid readers and had been buying books along the way. By then, they had collected fourteen English books found in various European bookshops, all in different stages of repair. Most were imported, relatively expensive, and ranged in subject from architecture to popular novels to absolute garbage that were read to pass the time while resting. But fourteen books created a lot of bulk, so to shave down the weight, they attempted to get some allowance for them or trade them for lighter ones.

They left Seville in fine fettle that afternoon but didn't get far before the gears on Dick's moped went to hell. He alternately lost first gear, then second gear. As Bill was coming back to help him, he also took a spill on a slippery spot, so they had to turn back and spend another night in Seville. The mopeds had never appeared shinier but were in abysmal shape mechanically. They took them back to the "mechanic" who had just fixed them, hoping he could do a better job the second time around. Bill had to buy a new rear tire, as his old one had the tube bulging in two places. Needless to say, they considered traveling by train if it rained.

Purchasing train tickets to Ayamonte, the southernmost town on the Spanish-Portuguese frontier, they got carnets for the bikes in order to take them into Portugal. They picked up the bikes from the repair shop, and thankfully, the bill wasn't too expensive. The mechanic gave no guarantee, and there was little confidence in their future performance.

The train pulled out of Seville that morning as scheduled and they bid no fond "adieus" to the place. They had been there too long. After a fairly painless ride along the side of some hills overlooking the Guadalquivir Valley, the train descended onto the delta at Huelva for a short stop, then chugged on to Ayamonte. They didn't feel like facing Customs on an empty stomach, so after wheeling the bikes to a service station, that had no oil, and only gas, they headed for a nearby restaurant. As it turned out, Spanish Customs didn't give any trouble, and after an hour's wait, they loaded on to a single-engine ferry with about fifty other people and crossed the Guidiana River. The river was about one-quarter mile across at that point and very muddy, probably from all the upstream rain. A brochure they were given in Portuguese described the river as "clear." Because they already had the necessary papers for the bikes, the Portuguese Customs gave no trouble either, and they found themselves in downtown San Antonio, or rather, Vila Real del Santo Antonio, a small town of about 10,000. It was well laid out in rectangular blocks. They had Shell and Mobil stations there, which were unknown in Spain. Quite a few people spoke English and seemed much friendlier.

They looked the town over, discovering that the searchlight at the edge of town caught all the chimney tops in its sweep. They sat in a cafe for a while talking with two American girls who were traveling as they were. One kept trying to order tea with lemon, but the waiter kept bringing her a slice of lemon rind in hot water.

CHAPTER 28 PORTUGAL

DECEMBER 19, 1958–JAN. 13, 1959

To travel is to discover that everyone is wrong about other countries.
—Aldous Huxley

THEY FOUND A DECENT PENSION and had a chicken dinner with brandy and cigarillos after the meal. It was the first time they'd enjoyed that fare! The fellow who ran the Shell station thought he might be able to sell the mopeds. They waited at the station while he talked to some friends to find out. He returned with bad news: no soap as far as the bikes were concerned. The town was just too small for Customs officials not to notice two such bikes—in other words, they couldn't sell them there.

The weather was unfavorable for travel the next day, with strong winds out of the west and intermittent rainfall, but they started out by taking a short side trip, four miles up the road to take a look at Monte Gordo, a village with a big sandy beach. There was a terrific onshore wind along the beach, and they had to wear goggles to keep sand out of their eyes. They pushed on, driving into the teeth of a minor gale that gusted to 40 mph. It was slow going, but thankfully there was no rain. They stayed within half a mile of the ocean all the way to Faro, thirty-two miles from Santo Antonio. That was a nice place, situated not quite halfway inland, across the width of southern Portugal, and with a few channels through the mud flats which led out to sea.

After they located a pension and settled in, Bill took his bike to a repair shop to have his clutch fixed. The mechanics tore the entire motor apart for whatever reason, but Bill wanted to see the improvement before paying.

They did make a friend—a fellow had stopped by the shop who spoke English quite well. He and his companion joined them as they went for coffee. Johnny had been all over the world, even Los Angeles. The Portuguese photographer with him had no upper front teeth, trailed along after Johnny, then sat and had coffee too. He spoke no English and didn't say a word while Johnny told stories about his travels. They said good-bye eventually, shook "Silent Sam's" hand, and returned to the pension for dinner. They had heard there was a movie in town, and when they went to investigate, they ran into "Sam" again. He attached himself to them one more time, so they bought him another coffee before the movie. Luckily, his ticket put him in a different part of the theater, but at intermission, there he was again, wagging his tail. The films were American, so the original soundtrack was English with Portuguese subtitles. Usually, except in Greece and Portugal, all American and English films were dubbed with the native tongue. They tired of Sam's constant presence, so bid him a firm goodnight. He unwillingly took the hint and disappeared into the night. They got one more cup of coffee and returned to the pension and discussed the possibility of staying in Faro another day to avoid being stuck in Lisbon too long.

The cramped beds were stuffed with straw and the pillows never ceased to rustle. The Pensao Madalena caused a restless night's sleep. Relocating to the Casa Verde for twenty more escudos a night, the place was worth every bit of the extra money, because it had a better room with a bath. At intervals during the day, they checked on how the repairs on the bike were coming, but the mechanics kept finding things wrong to fix, so they left them to their pleasure until later that evening. The cost was damn little for all the work they did on it.

Dick spent most of the afternoon writing letters and taking occasional scenic strolls for coffee. The weather in Faro was very unpredictable. It clouded up and rained hard, then changed to sunshine, like someone had flipped a switch. The northerly wind was fairly mild, coming in gusts of 10 to 20 mph throughout the day, then blasted severely that evening—an onshore breeze gone wild. It sounded like a wind tunnel as it blew down the main street, confined by buildings, giving a Venturi effect that pumped the velocity of the air around them to around 50 mph. Aeolus was doing his damnedest that night.

They took in a double feature again, and just like the night before, someone tried to snatch Dick's umbrella. He foiled the attempt by snatching it back just as it was wrenched from his hand—the usher was insistent it be put in the cloak room. The movies were in German and French with Portuguese subtitles. The German film was about ballet and science, so it didn't have much dialogue and was easy to understand from the pictures. If the weather was decent the next day, the plan was to motor to Lagos, 38.5 miles to the west.

They rousted out of their digs in Faro after a quick breakfast in the room and got under way to their next destination. During the entire trip, the headwinds kept their speed to a slow pace of nineteen mph. Dick's throttle cable broke nine miles before Lagos. He managed to get into town by wrapping a twig around the frayed end of the cable and using that in place of the throttle bar. He replaced it properly while they ensconced in the Pensao Costa d'Oiro.

While changing for dinner that night, Dick discovered he had a rash all over his body. After a shower, it had spread even more, so they knew it wasn't from being dirty. That was always a possibility, because they had been in many places without hot water for showering. Lack of cleanliness was not a matter of choice, but more a force of circumstance. He was quite uncomfortable, and they considered taking the train the next day.

Dick's rash was gone after dinner, but it had occupied their thoughts. They walked around making a tour of the town, went to bed, and enjoyed tea and cheese sandwiches the next morning. The weather had turned threatening, so they inquired at the train depot about transportation, but the train wasn't scheduled to leave until late that night. It was a cheerless prospect to run in the rain, but they loaded up anyway. They ran the bikes for a while with the umbrellas up, but that slowed them down and didn't keep them very dry. Almost nineteen miles later, they were flat out cold and damp. Bill wanted to stop for coffee, but Dick wanted to go on. Dick took off alone and didn't stop until he reached Odemira, twenty-five miles up the road. His hands were so cold he couldn't unbutton his cape, but a few cups of coffee warmed him up again. Bill arrived about twenty minutes later, cursing him, cursing the rain, cursing everything in general. His brakes had gone out on a steep hairpin curve, and he came very close to going over. He whacked his moped with his umbrella and felt better. While he was getting coffee, Dick went up the street and got a room in a pension. A couple of nuts fixed Bill's brakes and he was back in the running. After changing out of wet clothes, they set off in search of a restaurant.

They headed for Setubal, 18.6 miles from Lisbon. It didn't work for them to practice patience and wait for rainclouds to blow over before setting out for the train depot, twelve miles over rough roads. No train schedule was posted and no one knew exactly what time it left from Odemira. Their lack of Portuguese language was an issue, so they took off running in the rain again. They put their wet clothes back on, and sure enough, it started up before they'd gone two miles. It poured all the way.

Arriving in Setubal, they changed clothes in the waiting room of the station, which was quite an experience. They settled down to wait for three hours until the train came. Ironically, the sun came out just after they arrived and shone all afternoon! In due time, a modern train arrived and they boarded for the five-hour trip to Lisbon. The track route swung east through Beja before heading on a westerly direction. The train let them off across the harbor from Lisbon, and a boat ride was included in the ticket price. On the boat, they met a retired U.S. Army man who lived in Portugal. He turned out to be a good-luck friend who showed them the way to a decent pension downtown and also a restaurant for their first night in Lisbon.

LISBON

COOKS AND AMERICAN EXPRESS had their mail, but all the cards and letters they'd been sending weren't producing much response. They still hadn't heard a word from anyone except Mary Thompson and their dad. While at the shipping office checking about the passage home, Dick found out they got their wires crossed somewhere. The agents in Rome or Paris must have goofed, because the Lisbon office told them tourist class was full and they were signed up for second class, which would cost $100 more than they had. They had to wait until Monday to see whether the problem could be solved. After a morning of mild frustration, they got the bikes out and shot up to the American Embassy to see if there was a Christmas party planned. The question drew a blank, so they started to check out some addresses where they might sell the mopeds. On the second try, by God, they sold the miserable things for $135! What a relief to get rid of them! If the bikes hadn't sold, they would have chucked them into the Tagus River.

To celebrate, they bought a bottle of brandy, but discovered that cheap Portuguese brandy was practically undrinkable. Local prices for highly taxed Spanish brandy were too expensive. No matter, they were

$135 richer. What a couple of cheapskates they were, with enough cash on them to equal 3,861 escudos or $170. They rode the streetcar downtown by jumping on the tail end of the car and then jumped off when the conductor started to work his way back to collect fares. Next was to determine whether they were spending another three weeks in Lisbon or catching a boat to the Canaries and joining the ship home.

Later, they found out the moped bikes they'd purchased in West Germany were probably the last in stock of that line of 48 cc bikes. The frames were made by Achilles and the motor by Sachs at the Achillewerke Weikert & Co. KG in Wilhelmshaven-Langewerth. The company had ended production in 1957 and sold the production tools to the English company Norman Cycles Limited, who went on to produce thousands of the renamed mopeds as Norman Nippys.[1] This was probably Germany's way, in small part, of getting even with

Bill sitting atop the Castle Sao Jorge after a climb to the top of the hill and the castle.

the British for having lost the war. They hoped future Norman Nippy owners would have a better experience than they did.

They took a walk to familiarize themselves with the city and to look into a plane or ship to the Canaries. Iberia Airways and the price were out of their league, so they decided to wait until after the holidays to look into ships. Their meanderings took them into unknown territory and got them lost. Using Castelo Sao Jorge as a reference point, they started back to the Pensao Coimbra, but after half an hour's trudging, they were going in the wrong direction, heading into the older part of the city, the Bairro de Alfama. The remedy for getting home was a streetcar, which plunked them down practically at the front door. After dinner, they went separate ways and then met for midnight Mass at the Church of St. Domingos, a block from their *pensao* in the Praca da Figuiera.

Christmas in Lisbon was very enjoyable. Bill felt ambitious enough to go off on a picture-taking expedition after breakfast. He took a ferry across the harbor. Later, they ate lunch at the *pensao,* then set out to find a movie. They ended up taking an extensive walk out on the Avenida Almirante Reis, cutting over to the top of Avenida da Liberdade, then strolling the length of it to the downtown area. That long walk took the rest of the day, and they watched a beautifully clear evening produce a perfectly round, full moon, even while it was quite light out. They got hungry and decided to look for a turkey dinner someplace, ending up in the same restaurant they'd been in the night they arrived. It wasn't a very big meal, so they went back to the *pensao* to sample another. Two dinners, stuffed them completely, and they headed back to walk the Liberdade to work it off and go to the movie they'd missed earlier.

They ran into an American couple, the Ungers from Northern California, who were staying in a leased apartment and got acquainted with them over coffee. They were going to the movie also and paid for Bill and Dick's way in, so the brothers returned the favor and supplied a bottle of Madeira. Glasses procured from the bar in the foyer, they sat in their loges, sipping wine during the movie. Bill and Dick promised to drop by their apartment someday, with maps and details of the places they'd explored. The couple seemed very timid about traveling. They had got off the boat in Lisbon and were staying there for six months.

After the movie, which was a double feature of old flicks that were pure distillations of Hollywood corn, they went for coffee again. Later, they went to a snack bar, had a couple of hamburgers washed down with beer, and then showed the cooks how to make cheeseburgers with Gouda, which turned out rather well! They didn't drink much beer, because both Portuguese and Spanish beer didn't taste too good. The best beer they'd had was in Greece, but it was expensive—thirty cents a bottle.

They got up the next morning feeling ambitious enough to be on time for breakfast and then run over to American Express, collecting three letters from their dad. Later that day, they made the rounds to the different shipping companies looking for a ride to the Canaries, but had no luck, then ended up exploring the town on the other side of the main plaza, the Rossio. It had a couple of interesting bars, one of which was partially given over as an art gallery. When straying into a joint called the *Don Quixote*, they met a Portuguese musician who came to Portugal from the United States every once in a while, to get away from his wife. Bill got tangled up with a nice-looking blonde called Cecilia. They left that place in "good shape," but were in the mood for more, so they visited a little wine shop where the *vino blanco* was so good that they sat there and drank for at least an hour. They didn't make it home before 3:00 a.m.

Nor did they feel too bad when they got up in time for lunch, despite the late-night partying. The American Embassy called with the message that they had a phone call from their dad, so after lunch, they went there to call back. The call couldn't be placed on the premises, and no one knew where to send them so that they could, so they blew that off until later. Instead, they visited the California couple they'd met, talked with them a while, then headed back to the pension to eat. A second attempt to call Puyallup after supper had the same result, as they closed the circuit after 10:00 p.m.

Castle Sao Jorge, is a Moorish castle commanding a view of Lisbon and the Tagus River.

Sunday was such a nice day and they did a little exploring. They'd been looking at the Castle of St. George from a distance for almost a week. It was situated high on a hill across the square and served as some kind of military fortification ever since Roman times. The Visigoth and Moors had possession of it until 1398, when the Portuguese took it over. That timeline corresponded roughly to when

Portugal broke away from Spain and became an independent country. It might be closer to the truth to say that part of the Iberian Peninsula now known as Portugal became a national entity, while Spain, during that period in history, was divided into autonomous, warring provinces.[2]

They strolled to the other side of the castle grounds to the waterfront and rambled along the River Tagus, up to the Plaza da Commercio, where they caught a streetcar that took them to Belem, near the mouth of the harbor. They came across one of the true gems of medieval stonemasonry, the Tower of Belem! The fortress guarded the entrance to the harbor, where it connected to the sea. Built around the year AD 1500 in the era of Prince Henry, the navigator, it had been visited by great explorers such as Dias and de Gama. Prince Henry founded his school of navigation in Lisbon, so many of the trail-blazing armadas sailed from the spot where the tower stands.[3]

The design and execution of the Tower of Belem gave it an aspect of both grace and fragility, yet it remained a substantial fortress. The limestone had weathered to a creamy color and every detail stood out in the bright sun. There were no metallic stains or grime streaking its walls to mar the effect. They took several color pictures, both inside and outside the walls. After a marvelous tour, they took the tram back to town, took a shot of Plaza Pedro IV from the top of the pension, and then walked over to the telephone office for another try at calling Puyallup.

It took about forty-five minutes to get through, but their dad was home, so their efforts were rewarded. They had pen and paper ready to take down any momentous message and began timing the call. If they chewed the fat too long, it could have cost up to $60. They reversed the charges and didn't want to waste his money. His voice was a little fuzzy, but the connection was better than they'd hoped.

The Tower of Belem built in 1515 to guard Lisbon's harbor.

They could hear all right as long as he didn't speak too fast. As it turned out, he just wanted to know how they were doing and when they were coming home. His voice sounded natural and they imagined no emergency was eminent.

After that, they had a pleasant dinner and intended to go to a movie. There were long lines in front of the theater, so they decided to forget it. Instead, they took in a circus down the street being performed in an indoor coliseum. They stayed for the first half, but found it rather mediocre except for an all-girl Scottish bagpipe band. They looked very nice. The Portuguese women could take a lesson. A naturally pretty girl was a rare thing to see in Portugal. After leaving the circus, they bought a bottle of port, stopped at a couple of coffee houses, then went back to the room to sort out the next shipment of stuff home and do some reading.

Detail of the Tower of Belem was built in the Manueline style, the stonework incorporates motifs of the voyages of discovery, sculptures of historical personages, like St. Vincent and has an exotic rhinoceros sculpture.

COIMBRA

ARRIVING IN COIMBRA, they first found accommodations, the Pensao Rivoli. Once settled in, they took a walk down the main street to reconnoiter the town, stopping at the old Cathedral of Coimbra, the *Se Velha,* built in the Romanesque style and dating back to the twelfth century. It was really beat up, but still architecturally interesting.[4]

Since arriving in Portugal, they had developed a taste for the tiles, which were much in evidence throughout all the cities and villages. The tiles, called *azulejo,* decorated the inside and outside of houses, train stations, subway stations, churches, and palaces—simply everywhere. The tradition dates back five centuries and carries a noticeable Arab influence with their interlocking, curvilinear, geometric, or floral motifs. In Coimbra, even the street signs were made of tile. They were blue, with names written in great elegant flourishes. In the courtyard of what appeared to be an office building, they found large blue, glaze tile murals, which particularly enchanted Dick to the point that he wanted to bring some home.

They noticed the large, spacious dining room with varnished floors, finished in natural woods. Lunch, "suppe," was served at the *pensao* and consisted of omelets and pork chops, *costeletas de porco.*

That night, they checked out all the flicks in town, but only one was in English and they'd already seen it, so they visited different coffee shops and bars before returning to the *pensao.* Just before midnight, they went out to see how the natives would celebrate New Year's Eve.

Walking up the main drag, they could see flashes of light and then heard the sharp report of fire crackers. In the narrow streets, the acrid, sulfurous smell was eye-watering and smoke hugged the sidewalks. Scattered groups of kids galloped through the mist, dragging remnants from a junk pile tied to twine. Rusted lengths of gutter, porcelain pots, pans, bowls, tin cans, anything handy that made noise, grated over the cobblestones. On the Rue de Sofia, some teenagers dressed in gunny sacks and white towels went around beating people on the backs with reeds and raising a mild sort of hell. Cops were everywhere, overseeing the activities. As the crowd ebbed away, a bugle and drum band marched down the street, occasionally opening ranks to let a car or bus pass by. By 1:30 a.m., January 1, 1959, only a single old pan lying in the middle of the street betrayed the celebration for that New Year.

On New Year's Day, they walked around town and crossed the river on the new, modernistic Santa Clara Bridge. Coimbra looked very clean and peaceful in the early morning sunlight. Their long, circuitous walk through the old part of town allowed them a view of Coimbra waking up to a holiday morning. All the shops were closed and the only activity was that of people buying milk by the cup from vendors who carried it around in five-liter cans. They walked to the University of Coimbra, which overlooked the town and the Rio Mondego. Three new buildings dominated the square as they entered the campus: medicine, letters, and the library. The most striking characteristic of each building was the relief friezes which outlined the doors, each one symbolically portraying the different disciplines. In the courtyard of the old school, there was a statue of King Joao II of Portugal, who looked like a depiction of Henry VIII with his stubby legs and pot belly. Joao is commemorated for basing the university permanently in Coimbra.[5]

Walking back down the hill and prowling around the abandoned monastery of St. Elizabeth, they noticed it was on the same level as the riverbed, which may have accounted for the missing flooring and the submerged supporting arches in the basement. Two rickety wooden bridges spanned water-filled chasms in the floor, leading to a dead end, unless they felt athletic and wanted to climb out a windowless portal.

After lunch, they went to the "estacao" to look up schedules for the "rapido" to Porto and the bus to Figueria da Foz, twenty-seven miles away on the ocean. There wasn't a bus until 6:30 that evening, so they let it go in favor of a walk around the countryside. Once across the Rio Mondego, they again explored the monastery of St. Elizabeth. Walking up the hill by several monasteries, they found themselves in the country outside of town, where they left the road and followed a cart track through olive groves. The sun was out and it was very pleasant to be tramping around outdoors.

After making a circuit of the hills, they came to the road leading out of town, crossed it to the railroad tracks, and followed the tracks back to town. On the way, they mistreated a dead cat floating in a pond by throwing rocks at its swollen belly—it made an excellent target. At the railroad bridge over the river, the guards told them it was prohibited to cross. Pretending they didn't understand, the guards passed them on. Underneath the bridge, Portuguese washer-women were scrubbing away furiously. Dick thought they were singing mostly for their benefit, and said, "Maybe they think we're Hollywood talent scouts." A wooden footbridge allowed them to walk farther, and then they headed back to the pensao for dinner. Dick occupied that evening at the Casa Nova bar reading up on the War of 1812, while Bill indulged in an Italian film.

All indications were that nothing got their outfit going in the morning that wasn't absolutely vital. They made it out of bed in time for lunch and caught the afternoon train to Porto, seventy-two miles away. Bill sat in the coach most of the way and let a passenger practice his English on him. Dick amused himself by hanging out the open doors of the coach and throwing stones he picked up at station stops. One of those rocks hit the roadbed and bounced back up on the train two coaches down, so he stopped doing it. After innumerable stops, the train pulled into Porto in the late afternoon, crossing the Douro River on a high bridge.

PORTO

THE DOURO HAS A DEEP GORGE that cuts the city into two parts, and Porto was much more industrial than any Portuguese city they had seen so far. They took a streetcar to downtown, which was quite extensive. They found a place to stay a block from the Praca da Batalha, two blocks from Praca da Liberdade, the city center. After settling in and hanging their wash to dry, they had a hearty dinner and put away three liters of wine. After looking for a movie, they ended up seeing an incarnadined epic called *Blood Island*. During the intermission, Dick met some guy in the lobby who spoke English, and they started plotting the overthrow of the government in the electrician's control room.

Fishermen dry-docking their boats up the tiled beach.

They were still feeling pretty good from imbibing at dinner when they dropped into a comfortable place for coffee. It was there they went off on one of their long and involved hoaxes. In this case, they played the part of two Finns, but only Bill could speak English.

Things went on quite a while up in front of the café with several of the Coimbra University students. They got sidetracked from drinking coffee and were back to drinking wine again. More students came in, who after talking with them for a while, became fast friends, so they moved to the back room and took up a big table in the corner. The students wore their traditional costume of black suits with a heavy black cape about them. Bill was doing the talking for them before Bill would tell Dick what was said in Finnish. What he was saying hardly had the dubious dignity of a language—it was total gibberish—but to the students, it was Finnish. They kept this up for about two hours, during which time they got thoroughly drunk. They were easily gassed to the eyeballs, but never made one slip to spoil the illusion. It was 2:30 when the party broke up and they staggered home; maybe they didn't stagger—who would remember?

The next morning, they were hung-over heathens. The staff at the pension gave them a nourishing lunch, which reduced the shakes somewhat, and then they set out on a long walk to burn off the fumes. Crossing the gorge, they descended to the waterfront through twisting streets, following the Douro River to its mouth a couple of miles away. At the edge of town, a ferryman took them across to where the tram ran back into town. Before taking the tram, though, they went all the way out to a lighthouse that marked the river mouth and watched the breakers roll in on the rugged coastline. They walked along the rocks to a cafe on the shore where they had several cups of bracing tea. The shop sold English jam, Alaskan salmon, and other exotic condiments like Heinz mango chutney and ketchup. The sales clerk spoke English, so they took him to task over the outrageous prices for the stuff. He explained that the government put an 80 percent import tax on things like that, and the money went to support the army and pay the priests. He told them the priests were a bunch of bums that didn't do any work, so they asked him why the people didn't rise up and shoot the priests. He explained the government was too well organized for a revolution to get much of a start, that the priests kept wives and had children, all with the support of the state. While waiting for the streetcar, they advocated revolution, but the tram came before a shot was fired.

Speaking of revolution, the Portuguese dictator, Antonio de Oliveira Salazar, who ruled Portugal as the prime minister from 1932 until 1968, was a graduate of the nearby University of Coimbra. Everywhere they traveled in Portugal, they saw his hand at work. He ran a right-wing government called the Estado Novo (New State) that was religiously conservative and nationalistic. Anyone who expressed opposition to his rule or policies was a candidate for political prison. His secret police, the PIDE (Policia Internacionale de Defensa do Estado), "State Defense and Surveillance Police," was modeled after Hitler's Gestapo. Its job was to protect national security and to suppress political opponents.[6]

In their brief hitchhiking forays, the people who picked them up immediately wanted to know who they were and from where. When they found out they were Americans, they did a sort of sigh of relief and opened up on what was going on in their country. On one ride, the driver pointed out a political prison and explained how easy it was to be thrown in there by speaking seditiously. Salazar stuffed his domestic prisons with political opponents, such as at Peniche, a coastal fishing town with an old fort, and the prison at Tarrafal in the Cape

Verde archipelago off the coast of North Africa, part of Portugal's overseas territories.[7]

After lunch and a movie the next day, they checked a few hotels and found out a friend they had met in Lisbon, Jacques Singer, was in town. His concert was to be the next day. The process of killing time was driving them screwy, so they were counting the days before heading back to Lisbon and their ship.

They got cleaned up and went to a wonderful concert. At the front door, no one gave any trouble when they presented the note Jacques wrote out for them in Lisbon. The concert included Beethoven's "Egmont Overture," Brahms's "Piano Concerto # 2," Stravinsky's "Rite of Spring," and "Fantasia-Francesca da Rimini," by Tchaikovsky. It was a solid two-and-a-half-hour program. Afterward, they went backstage and said hello to Jacques and met the American consul and his wife. On the way home, they stopped for a cocoa and paid their bill at the pensao in preparation for leaving.

REGRESSA A LISBOA

THEY GOT UP WITH plenty of time to spare before catching the morning train to Lisbon. Charging into the coach, sprawling all over the wide seat, they left the peasants sorting themselves out on the platform. In no time at all, they were heading out of Coimbra, and matters were simplified by being on a through train. When approaching Vila Franca da Xira, Dick decided to get off the train to take a chance the boots he'd ordered when they traveled through the village previously might be ready.

When Dick slipped his new boots on—they fit like a glove. It took a while to convince the bootmaker that travelers' checks were as good as money. In forty-five minutes, Dick was back on the *rapido* train for the short ride into Lisbon. The train stopped up the hill from the main plaza, a five-minute walk from the pensao where he ran into Bill, who had collected a bunch of newly arrived mail. They went off to a coffee shop to read it before dinner. They were not going to make their maiden voyage out on the streets until it stopped drizzling.

It was good to be back in Lisbon after almost ten days in tiny towns. Up until then, they had been batting a thousand by not leaving anything behind during their travels, but they finally goofed and left the rain capes in a drawer at the Oporto pension. They had accumulated quite a few additions to their library: *Crime and Punishment*, Eric Ambler's *A Coffin for Dimitrios, Ideas of the Great Economists*, and *A History of Charlemagne*. Dick saved an unabridged version of *Don Quixote* for the trip on the high seas, across the mid-Atlantic.

The next day, they busied themselves with little tasks such as hunting for razor blades and procuring income tax forms from the embassy. Dick visited their California friends, the Ungers, at their apartment. Connecting later in the day with Bill, they saw double-feature movies, one of which was a perfect Hollywood gasser called *Sitting Bull*, replete with the Indians looking up to the sky for a sign from the "Great Spirit," and lots of pale faces doing contortions with an arrow in their gut—a surefire formula for "greatness" in the sticks of Europe. They stumbled out of the carnage during the scene with Sitting Bull riding to the rescue of his "white friend" and had a couple of beers to shake off the Montana dust.

Saturday, all the exchanges were closed when they tried to do some banking, so they compromised by buying a bottle of Madeira and a bottle of Cockburn's Lunch Port, retiring to their room to read and write until dinnertime. After dinner, they took in another movie, a blend of Mamie Stover and Somerset Maugham's *Rain*, called *Twilight of the Gods*, starring Rock Hudson and Cyd Charisse.

Dick sent a letter off urging Achilles-Sachs to kick through with some money for their troubles with the bikes. That went nowhere, of course. Bill stayed home nursing a cold, while Dick took a ferry ride across the harbor and walked the docks toward the mouth of the Tagus River. He doubled back and went up the bluff to the town of Almada, then strolled to the outskirts, where they were erecting a huge statue of Christ with arms outstretched overlooking the Lisbon harbor. The statue itself stood on a pedestal about 100–125 feet high. *Cristo Rei was* situated atop a base of the Sanctuary of Christ the King, and inspired by the *Christ the Redeemer* statue that overlooks the City of Rio de Janeiro in Brazil.[8]

Almada proper was originally crooked and cobblestoned, but now it was made up mostly of new apartment buildings in what looked to be a government-subsidized project. It was the first of its kind Dick had seen in Portugal, but that sort of thing was all over Italy. Washing festooned all the building balconies, which gave them that colorful Portuguese touch.

Dick wrote a letter to *Time* magazine, which was pure hokum and concerned a story in their January 12, 1959 issue about Sikkim, which is a tiny state next to Nepal and Tibet. Bored and sitting around, they cooked up some fraudulent facts about the story, suggesting a correction should be published and admonishing their fact checker for lazy work. After dinner, they went their separate ways. Bill went to look for a movie, and Dick took a stroll up the hill, where he dropped into the Don Quixote bar, walked the Avenida da Liberdade, and ended up taking in a movie too. It was crowded in the theater, so he had to sit on a railing at the top of the balcony, where the air was soupy with cigarette smoke.

The next day of furious running around got all their things done. They had to pick up the tickets for the ship, buy soap, pick up a pair

GREAT LAKES
CANADIAN SHIELD
CHICOUTIMI
SUDBURY
QUEBEC
OTTAWA
MONTREAL
FREDERICTON
SAINT JOHN
CHARLOTTETOWN
HALIFAX
ST. JOHN'S
TORONTO
BUFFALO
DETROIT
CLEVELAND
BOSTON
PROVIDENCE
HARTFORD
PITTSBURGH
NEW YORK
COLUMBUS
PHILADELPHIA
CINCINNATI
BALTIMORE
WASHINGTON, D.C.
APPALACHIAN MTS.
VIRGINIA BEACH
CHARLOTTE
PIEDMONT
ATLANTA
HAMILTON
NORTH ATLANTIC OC
JACKSONVILLE
ORLANDO
TAMPA
SARGASSO SEA
MIAMI
BAHAMA ISLANDS
NASSAU
KEY WEST
HAVANA
CUBA
WEST INDIES
TURKS AND CAICOS IS.
GRAND TURK
CUBA
CAMAGUEY
MANZANILLO
GEORGE TOWN
MONTEGO BAY
JAMAICA
SAN JUAN
SAINT JOHN'S
BASSE-TERRE
GREATER ANTILLES
CARIBBEAN SEA
LESSER
ANTILLES
FORT-DE-FRANCE
PUERTO CABEZAS
CASTRIES
KINGSTOWN
BRIDGETOWN
BLUEFIELDS
SAINT GEORGE'S
BARRANQUILLA
CARTAGENA
MARACAIBO
VALENCIA
CARACAS
BARCELONA
PORT-OF-SPAIN
PUERTO LIMON
BOCAS DEL TORO
PANAMA CITY
SAN CRISTOBAL
VENEZUELA
CIUDAD GUAYANA
BUCARAMANGA
LLANOS
GEORGETOWN
SURINAME
PARAMARIBO
MEDELLIN
GUIANA HIGHLANDS
GUYANA
CAYENNE
PEREIRA
BOGOTA
IBAGUE
CALI
COLOMBIA
BOA VISTA
GUIANA SHIELD
AMAZON DELTA

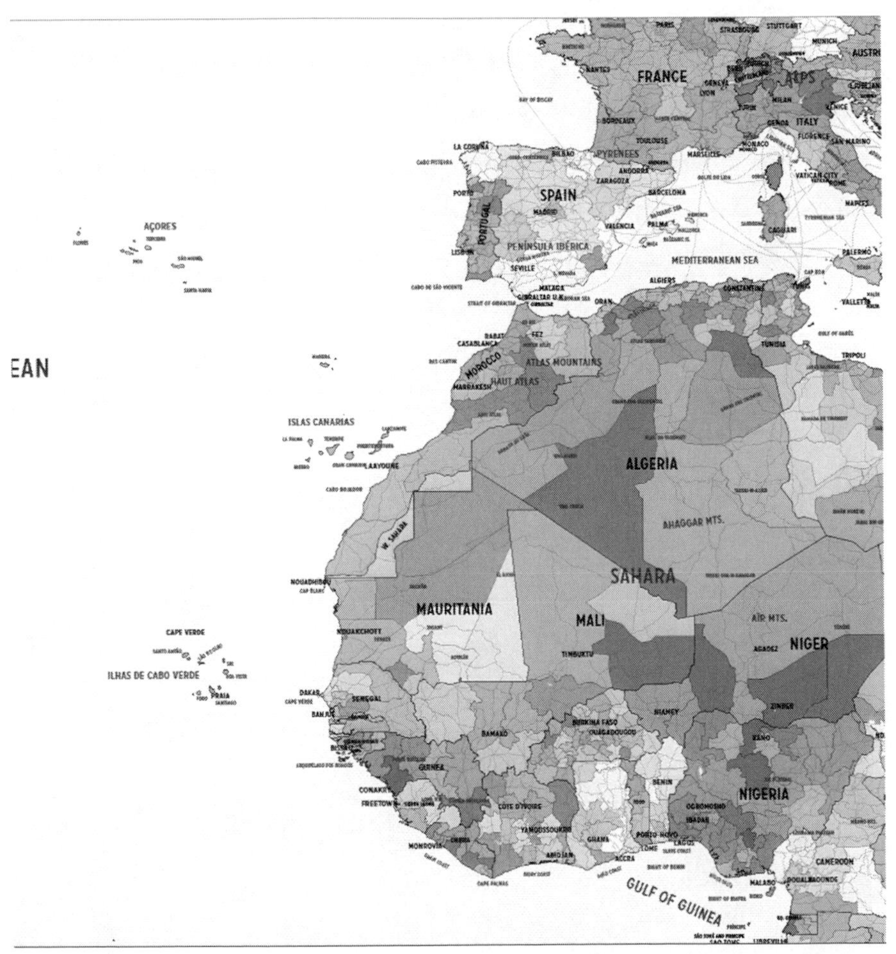
EAN
AÇORES
FRANCE
SPAIN
PORTUGAL
PENÍNSULA IBÉRICA
PYRENEES
ITALY
ALPS
MEDITERRANEAN SEA
ATLAS MOUNTAINS
HAUT ATLAS
MOROCCO
ISLAS CANARIAS
ALGERIA
AHAGGAR MTS.
W. SAHARA
SAHARA
MAURITANIA
MALI
AÏR MTS.
NIGER
CAPE VERDE
ILHAS DE CABO VERDE
PRAIA
DAKAR
SENEGAL
GUINEA
NIGERIA
CAMEROON
GULF OF GUINEA
BARCELONA
MADRID
LISBON
SEVILLE
TIMBUKTU
BAMAKO
ACCRA
LAGOS
TRIPOLI

of new pants at the tailor, buy a stock of cigarettes, leave a forwarding address at Cooks and American Express, buy a kilo of Gouda cheese for midnight snacks, get a box to put all that extra stuff in, and finally, mail home an accumulation of pictures, maps, and folders they had gathered since Rome. The pictures they sent home were pretty poor compared to the last bunch—more careful printing might have helped.

That day was the first clear day in over a week. The sun made a hell of a glare on the white buildings. The only thing Dick desired to take with him from Portugal was the tile work. They used it lavishly all over the country to decorate just about everything. They saw a lot of the blue and white azulejos in government buildings.

They were happy to be leaving the day after next. The shipping company allowed them to set up house in their cabin shipboard until the ship departed.

The Europa Point lighthouse as a ship leaves the Straits of Gibraltar for the Alantic.

CHAPTER 29 AT SEA—MID-ATLANTIC

JANUARY 14–22, 1959

No road is long with good company.—Turkish Proverb

THEIR SHIP HOME, the *Santa Maria* of the Companía Colonial de Navagaceo du Portugal, was docked just a block from the streetcar line, so it was no trouble getting uptown. There was just a light rain, but the gusty wind made umbrellas practically useless, threatening to turn their two beat-up specimens inside out. They had spent a restless night on board the night before and were glad to get off the ship for an omelet and coffee, a bolster to the meager breakfast on board. After the good eats, Bill climbed a hill to look around St George's Castle, and Dick took a walk finding some book stores and stocked up for the voyage.

VIGO, SPAIN

VIGO WAS THE SHIP'S first destination and up the coast 250 miles from Lisbon. It was a city of 150,000 that stretched along the shore for nine miles. The stop there was very short and they managed a couple of quick expeditions ashore to pick up brandy and oranges. Bill had a little trouble getting back aboard with his brandy, but somehow, Dick evaded even a raised eyebrow, even on the very same mission. The ship guards inspected Bill's packages and implied they wanted one of the bottles. He defended his hooch saying it was for tooth-brushing purposes, should they have understood and brushed past them. The Fundador brandy cost seventy-five cents a bottle and, other than medicinal uses, was for the use explained since the water in the cabin was non-potable. There was a lot of confusion at dockside because so many people boarded at Vigo. There were some difficulties with the stern line, but when it was finally cast off, they were on their way again. They noticed there were a lot of paper streamers being thrown from ship to shore and back, and a group of young nuns were gathering all they could. When they moved out of range, one of them had an armload of streamers to show for her efforts and was laughing with joy over her stash.

They stayed on deck while the ship turned away from the dock, watching the sun—favoring them with a brief appearance—before it set between the rocks, framing the harbor entrance. After the harbor was cleared, it didn't take long for the rocking of the boat in the open sea to thin the ranks of those who appeared for dinner. People kept getting up hurriedly and rushing out until the dining room was rather empty. There were also quite a few patches of sawdust in the dining room floor by the time dinner was over. After dinner, one of their table mates went outside for a minute and told them later over coffee that the lee rail was full of people. Fresh sea air often helps with seasickness. In the evening, they went to the second class lounge to see the opera film *Aida*. Large chunks of the original had been cut out, but it was good to hear what was left.

They both slept through a lifeboat drill that morning and continued snoozing until 11:00. Lunch, their first meal of the day, was tasty, and they stuffed themselves. Passenger attendance was up that day, but one lady must have had a delayed reaction, because she looked like the epitome of misery and woe as ship's staff led her out of the dining room. It was a clear, sunny day and the horizon was empty of ship sightings. They anticipated seeing more ships while traveling farther south out of the coastal Atlantic and into the shipping lanes.

Bill played ping-pong that afternoon with one of the passengers while Dick snoozed, missing tea. They rejoined for dinner and coffee and made way to the bow and took in the warm breeze and starlight. Mast lights of another ship were visible about six miles off to port, but as she drew abeam, a squall blotted it out and drove them inside to shelter. They headed toward the stern to look at the first class swimming pool. While scouting around, they climbed up one more deck, and then Bill climbed a ladder that led up to the funnel, but in the process tripped a wire that blew the horn! Naturally, he bugged out of there in a hurry.

Back at the hideout—their cabin—they prepared an empty brandy bottle with a message and then threw it off the stern. That wasn't enough, of course, so they procured another bottle from the bar and fixed it up, dating it 1954, five years before, so anyone finding it would think they had come across a near relic. Included were latitude and longitudes of where they had supposedly dropped it, wildly different from the actual position they found in the ship's newspaper. After their general prank-making, Bill procured a checkerboard from the bartender and proceeded to beat Dick at the game two times straight. The loser paid for an orange pop.

FUNCHAL, MADEIRA ISLANDS

DICK WAS UP BEFORE DAWN to watch the docking in Funchal, Madiera, the largest island of the Portuguese archipelago of volcanic islands, some 200 miles southwest of Lisbon and 250 miles north of Tenerife in the Canary Islands. He sat next to the pool as it was splashing invitingly with the ship's movement, so naturally, he went for a swim. Unfortunately, all his preparations, going below decks, putting on his bathing suit under an old pair of slacks, putting his towel under a coat, and filling a small flask with brandy to stave off the cold—even bringing a shot glass—was all for naught. The pool water that looked so good was colder than hell, so all he got wet were his legs. He settled for drinking the brandy. The pool was tile-lined with underwater lights, filled with seawater, and he hoped it would warm up after a couple of days in the sun. The seawater in the pool looked very strange, as it compensated, tilting and sloshing as the ship rolled.

A searchlight in the distance was in full view, and he watched at the bow while the *Santa Maria* overtook a ship seen earlier. The stars were extremely brilliant, and the brightest of them illumined the edges of the clouds like the moon. There was no haze or smoke at sea to diminish the light of the night sky, making the constellations appear brighter than one was used to seeing them.

Bill found him not long after, watching the sun light up the topmost peak of the island's mountains, which was momentarily obscured by clouds. The ship stopped and dropped anchor in Funchal's harbor. After a skimpy breakfast aboard, they climbed into one of the first launches going ashore. They dug up a restaurant and got some omelets, which were terrible, so they said the hell with eating until lunch.

Bill found his way along the main street to the Madeira Wine Association, Ltd. and responded to the "Visitors Welcome" sign. After comparing the free samples of vintage 1920 sweet and dry Madeira wine, he worked his way back through town, window-shopping until he came to one of the three rivers that ran through Funchal. The *Ribeira de Santa Luzia* riverbed was probably not over forty feet wide, but it was covered with enough large wire mesh, supported on a framework, to enable vines and flowers to grow out over the bed and completely obscure the river. A guide said that during the summer, it was quite a sight when the bougainvillea were in bloom with their bright blue-purple flowers extending up the river course.

Finding another place that gave free samples of wine, Bill let himself in and was served by the proprietor, Mr. John O'Leivera, who produced four bottles of Madeira wine, all different vintages, and offered samples of each. The vintages were 1930, 1920, 1915, and

1850. The last of course was the star, and was wonderfully aromatic with a body that made the others taste rough in comparison.

Mr. O'Leivera explained the blending system called the solera process. He said a succession of barrels are filled with the Madeira wine over a series of equal aging intervals, usually a year. One barrel is filled for each interval. At the end of the interval, after the last barrel is filled, the oldest barrel in the solera is tapped for part of its contents, which is bottled. Then that barrel is refilled from the next oldest barrel, and that one in succession from the second-oldest, down to the youngest barrel, which is refilled with the new product. This procedure is repeated at the end of each aging cycle. The transferred product mixes with the older product in the next barrel. None of the original barrels are ever drained until empty, so that the earliest wine always remains in its barrel. This residue wine diminishes to a small amount. Thus, through the blending process, the solera will be present after fifty or a hundred cycles.[1] Bill was able to taste original Madeira wine that was grown before the U.S. Civil War and compare the blends down through the ages.

When they returned to the ship, many Madeirans were aboard selling their wares, such as wicker baskets and chairs, carved turtles, embroidered handbags, caps, fruit, and some beautiful lace work, none of which appeared to be selling too well. Alongside in the water, there were some boys who dove for coins that generous passengers were throwing in. Dick found some leftover European coinage and flipped it over the side for their cause.

The ship drew anchor later that day, sailing for Tenerife, the largest of the seven islands in the Spanish Canary Islands. A lot of people boarded at Madeira, and their third class part of the ship resembled a human menagerie, with kids all over the place, luggage jamming the corridors, and everyone talking a mile a minute. As far as they knew, they were the only Americans in the cheapest class. Because of the crowded conditions, the service staff arranged two sittings for each meal in the dining hall, and third class, called tourist class, was almost full.

An indication of how the Spanish treated their flag was evident when a seaman took down the large ship's flag they displayed when in port and dragged it across the deck until someone picked up the tail end and helped him fold it.

The bartender was trained by then to give them their beer in a bottle and not the locally brewed beer either. They tried a bottle of Madeiran beer, and the stuff tasted horrible. They would have done better sticking to making wine. Someone had turned on the air-conditioning that afternoon, which helped keep their cabin more livable. That night, a movie was shown for their class aft on B deck, under the stars. When they went there after dinner, many people reserved their seats.

TENERIFE, CANARY ISLANDS

THE SHIP DOCKED EARLY IN THE MORNING in the inner harbor of Tenerife. Dick got up before dawn, but a lot of people were up before him, making a lot of noise. He decided not to wait for breakfast and, following the usual procedure at every port, turned in his ticket and got two landing cards. A ten-minute walk took him to the business district, where he got some coffee and a croissant to start the day. It soon became light enough to make out the steep hills just behind the city. Looking for the city center and an open restaurant, he covered a little bit of the upper part of Tenerife in the half-light. Ending up back where he started, he ate a second breakfast of tea and ham sandwiches outside at a sidewalk café. Walking around, stopping in shops here and there, he did a little comparative shopping. Dick bought a ballpoint pen for nine pesetas that had been quoted at twenty-five pesetas in another place. He picked up another bottle of brandy to supplement their larder, and managed to send off seven postcards. The local natives knew only tourists wrote postcards, so he was fair game for all the peddlers selling watches, pens, watch bands, and other assorted junk.

Dick's writing was interrupted by the sound of the ship giving a warning blast, so he wrapped things up, dropped the cards into a mailbox, and made his way back. In no hurry to board, he watched people milling about at the gangplank before boarding. Bill was found still in bed; he never set foot in Tenerife. It was mid-morning when the ship moved away from the dock, sailed around the quay, and headed due south to skirt the island.

There were so many passengers on board that all the benches on deck were full and people were cluttering the passageways. After lunch, Dick prepared another message in a bottle by sealing a note in plastic and paraffin and then putting it inside, sealing the cork again with paraffin. When they got a bit farther away from the Canaries, they planned to throw it overboard.

The next morning, all the ship's personnel were in their white tropical uniforms, due to the warm weather. The sun was bright enough to burn their skin, and they put on their Bermuda shorts for the first time since Athens. Their attire didn't shake up the natives too much when they appeared on deck.

It was such a warm, balmy day that they soon got into their swimming suits and tried out the second class pool. The water was warm but salty, turning their eyes red and making them sick when they swallowed. Underwater, the throb of the engines could be heard plainly. The ocean swell rocked the boat, making the water slosh from side to side. When diving, they had to make sure most of the water was located under the diving board.

After showering and having tea, they played cards in the lounge for a while until dinnertime and then went up to the second class lounge to see a movie. After the film, they played more cards, drank more beer, and then headed for the cabin. They set about preparing a bottle in the manner previously described but also added a lead cap over the cork sealed with paraffin. It would still be floating after the *Santa Maria* went down. And with that bottle adrift, it was time to crack a new bottle of Fundador brandy, which was easy enough normally, but the cork on the new one broke in two while being extracted, and the lower half fell back into the brandy in fragments. Dick was determined to remedy the situation with a clever idea Bill suggested: Pouring all the brandy out into glasses, he then lowered a string with a knot in it into the bottle and drew it out, forcing the cork out. After that, the problem was to pour the brandy back into the bottle without spilling it from the wide-mouthed glasses. He cast around for something to use as a funnel and found what Boswell called his "armor," i.e. a rubber. Dick snipped the end out, inserted it into the neck of the bottle, and poured away, not spilling a drop, but then the brandy tasted funny!

They started to get their sea legs and knew they had to keep themselves busy for the fifteen-day run to South America and the port of La Guaira, Venezuela, their next stop after Tenerife. But it was a zigzag journey across the Atlantic: first north to Vigo, then out to the Madeiras, then to the Canaries off the Moroccan coast, then no more landings and out into the deep until they hit the Caribbean Sea and worked past the islands of the Lesser Antilles. After that, La Guaira, the port for Caracas, Venezuela, Willemstad, which was the main city of Curacao in the Netherlands Antilles, the West Indies, past Kingston, Jamaica, a stopover in Havana, Cuba, and then finally, Fort Lauderdale, Florida, where they were to disembark. Whew! But the ship and all their company still had more nautical miles to go to make its way to Rio de Janeiro, Brazil, the destination of the Portuguese passengers.

They were in the middle of a huge ocean on a full ship with a porthole in their cabin just above sea level. Managing to get up for lunch, Bill went swimming and Dick went back to bed. The usual afternoon and evening entertainment on board consisted of tea, cards, dinner, and bingo or a movie, but that night, there was a dance scheduled for first and second class. The music transmitted just fine, but their fellow steerage class cohorts, the Portuguese émigrés, were content to sit and think. Therefore, they had to be content with reading and sipping their tainted brandy.

The next day was very athletic for them as they swam in the pool several times in twenty-four hours. In the morning, they went up to the second class pool and sunned until lunchtime and, after lunch, went back for a swim and some more sun. The sun was hot, but the breeze was cool, and when they started to burn, they moved into the comfortable shade. They both stayed on deck until teatime, which gave them enough sunburn to feel drowsy, but not feel much pain. Teatime meant flagons of lemon tea served with a small selection of meats, cookies, bread, and salt fish. The snack that tea afforded sent Bill back for a nap under a lifeboat, while Dick caught a few winks in his bunk until supper.

After dinner, all their table companions retired to the lounge for coffee and cards until the movie. Dinner was usually some variation on salt cod or pork with a vegetable. Bill had seen the film, so he left early. Dick suffered it to the bitter end. A dance was thrown for third class that night. Two buffet tables were set up with ham and beef sandwiches and some powerful red wine. Five glasses of that stuff packed a wallop. The dance was a bust, for the émigrés didn't know how to cope with a live orchestra, so they sat and stared, guzzling as much wine as they could.

When it was over at midnight, Dick went to the forward deck and found Bill taking in the moonlight and tropical air. They decided to go swimming again and went down to the cabin and put their swimsuits on underneath their pants, then went up to the first class pool, which they had to themselves for an hour's swim. They even climbed up to the deck above and jumped into the pool from the railing. Before jumping the nearly fifteen feet, they would wait for the ship to roll the water over to their side, giving the greatest amount of cushion to break the fall. The water and the breeze were warm, and after an hour of their horsing around, they were out and called it a day, taking showers to wash off the salt. They then gratefully hit the "pearly whites."

The day marked the halfway point for the trip, 900 miles from Venezuela. Bits of seaweed had started to appear in the water, and flying fish were shooting away from the bows. They didn't shoot up in the air, but rather skimmed along just over the surface of the water for 30 to 40 feet before plopping back in.

After lunch, they got into their trunks and swam, sunbathed, and played ping-pong until teatime. Their mild sunburns made them sleepy, so after tea, they grabbed forty winks before supper and played rummy until it was time for the 9:00 movie. Toward the end of the show, the ship gave an especially sharp roll that had everyone hanging onto their seats.

The island of St. Lucia passed them on the right the next afternoon around lunch, and an hour later, St. Vincent on the left. They knew at that point, they were in the Lesser Antilles, even though it still looked like the Atlantic. According to the map, they were sure to pass some small islands close to the Venezuelan coast by that evening. The sun took its toll on Dick. He was cooked like a lobster, especially his nose. Bill was faring all right, but still looked rather rosy.

CHAPTER 30 VENEZUELA

January 23, 1959

You must not judge people by their country. In South America, it is always wise to judge people by their attitude.—Paul Theroux

BEFORE DOCKING AT LA Guaira, they changed some money into bolivars. Instead of being stamped with the denomination, the coins stated the weight of silver they contained, which was five grams for one bolivar. One bolivar was worth approximately thirty cents. They amused themselves after lunch by diving for some pesetas on the bottom of the pool.

Just ten miles from La Guaira, they watched the sun come up over the mountains as the ship approached a man-made port with jetties enclosing an inner harbor. They watched as the ship was tied up. Their transit visas didn't come until after breakfast, and then they had to walk from the dock, through a terminal building, across a viaduct, and over some railroad tracks before standing on South American soil. A line of taxis stood waiting to take them into La Guaira, but they decided to walk into town to catch one instead for a cheaper ride to Caracas.

It was hot before they left town, but as they traveled uphill, it cooled off. The taxi dropped them off at the Plaza O'Leary in the Silencio District, at the east end of Avenida Bolivar. The road to Caracas was a nine-mile long, six-lane highway that cost seventy million dollars in construction and went from sea level to 3,400 feet. Riding through two tunnels, one for nearly a mile they wanted to get to the Plaza Venezuela and then start walking down side streets that roughly paralleled the Avenida Bolivar. Running into their shipboard tablemate who spoke Spanish, they proceeded to catch one bus after

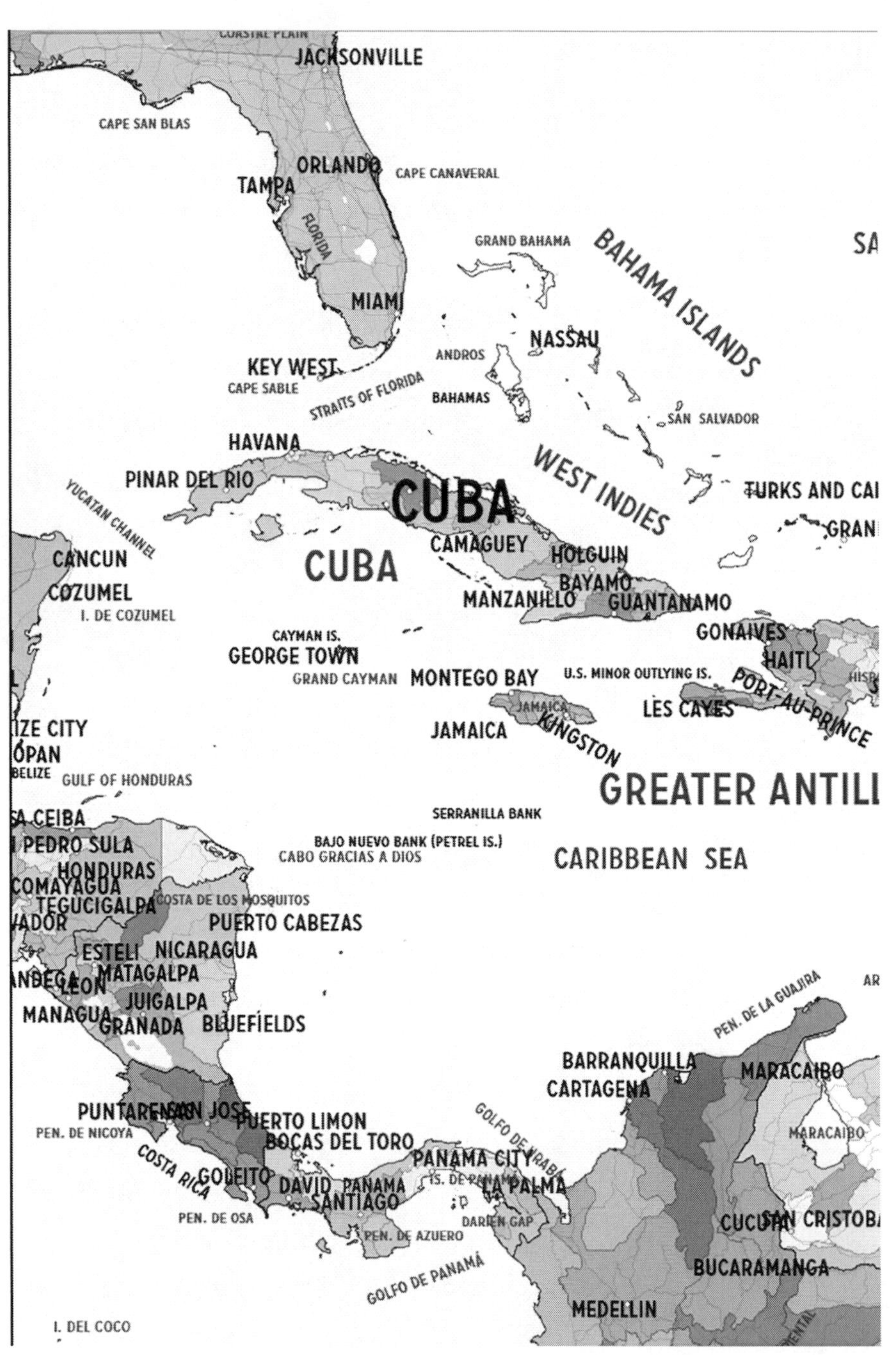

JACKSONVILLE
CAPE SAN BLAS
ORLANDO
CAPE CANAVERAL
TAMPA
FLORIDA
GRAND BAHAMA
BAHAMA ISLANDS
MIAMI
NASSAU
ANDROS
KEY WEST
CAPE SABLE
STRAITS OF FLORIDA
BAHAMAS
SAN SALVADOR
HAVANA
WEST INDIES
PINAR DEL RIO
YUCATAN CHANNEL
CUBA
TURKS AND CAI
CAMAGUEY
HOLGUIN
CANCUN
CUBA
BAYAMO
COZUMEL
MANZANILLO
GUANTANAMO
I. DE COZUMEL
CAYMAN IS.
GONAIVES
GEORGE TOWN
HAITI
GRAND CAYMAN
MONTEGO BAY
U.S. MINOR OUTLYING IS.
PORT-AU-PRINCE
JAMAICA
LES CAYES
JAMAICA
KINGSTON
GULF OF HONDURAS
GREATER ANTILL
SERRANILLA BANK
BAJO NUEVO BANK (PETREL IS.)
CABO GRACIAS A DIOS
CARIBBEAN SEA
HONDURAS
COMAYAGUA
TEGUCIGALPA
COSTA DE LOS MOSQUITOS
PUERTO CABEZAS
ESTELI
NICARAGUA
MATAGALPA
LEON
JUIGALPA
PEN. DE LA GUAJIRA
MANAGUA
GRANADA
BLUEFIELDS
BARRANQUILLA
CARTAGENA
MARACAIBO
SAN JOSE
PUERTO LIMON
MARACAIBO
PEN. DE NICOYA
BOCAS DEL TORO
GOLFO DE URABA
COSTA RICA
PANAMA CITY
GOLFITO
DAVID
PANAMA
LA PALMA
SANTIAGO
PEN. DE OSA
DARIEN GAP
CUCUTA
PEN. DE AZUERO
BUCARAMANGA
GOLFO DE PANAMÁ
MEDELLIN
I. DEL COCO

RGASSO SEA
COS IS.
D TURK
DOMINICAN REP.
NIOLA
ANTO DOMINGO
PUERTO RICO
SAN JUAN
PUERTO RICO
BRITISH VIRGIN IS.
VIRGIN IS.
U.S. VIRGIN IS.
ANGUILLA
ST-MARTIN
SINT MAARTEN
ST-BARTHÉLEMY
BARBUDA
ANTIGUA AND BARB.
SAINT JOHN'S
ANTIGUA
BASSETERRE
ST. KITTS AND NEVIS
MONTSERRAT
BASSE-TERRE
GUADELOUPE
LES
LESSER ANTILLES
DOMINICA
ROSEAU
DOMINICA
FORT-DE-FRANCE
MARTINIQUE
CASTRIES
SAINT LUCIA
SAINT LUCIA
SAINT VINCENT
BARBADOS
KINGSTOWN
BRIDGETOWN
GRENADA
SAINT GEORGE'S
GRENADA
TRINIDAD AND TOBAGO
TOBAGO
ARUBA
UBA
CURAÇAO
CURAAO
MARGARITA
PORT-OF-SPAIN
TRINIDAD
VALENCIA
BARQUISIMETO
CARACAS
BARCELONA
BOCA GRANDE
CIUDAD GUAYANA
AL
VENEZUELA
LLANOS
GUIANA HIGHLANDS
SALTO ANGEL
GUYANA
GEORGETOWN
SURINAME
PARAMARIBO

another and traveled out to the northern side of the city, then back into the center of things and the Hotel Tamanaco, which had been pictured in *Life* magazine. Round and round they went, finally reaching the Plaza Venezuela, which they had unwittingly passed on the first bus ride. After a walk up the hill, they caught the *teleferico,* or cable car, that took them 4,000 feet up Avila Mountain, overlooking Caracas, they had to climb another 3,000 feet to overlook the harbor.

The cable car ascended vertically for several thousand feet, then crossed a deep chasm. At that point, the cable was unsupported horizontally for a bit and made a deep dip before beginning the ascent again. The higher they climbed, the more mountains they could see on the other side of Caracas Valley. Near the top, they ran into clouds and disembarked in a fairly heavy rain. In about ten minutes, the weather changed from hot and humid to cool and rainy. Until the clouds cleared away, they were lost in the mist.

An interim stop sported a café and restaurant and connected with another cable line that took them to the Hotel Humboldt, up even higher. There was also another cable line that took passengers down the other side of Avila Mountain.

They spent about an hour viewing the city of Caracas, that looked more like an architect's mock-up of a city, then took the cable car back down. The experience was as good as an airplane ride. For some inexplicable reason, the cable car stopped as it passed over the chasm, and for a few minutes, they enjoyed the sensation of rising and falling as the cable flexed and oscillated. As they descended, the cool air in the car condensed when they hit the warm layer and sprinkled them lightly. After disembarking the *teleferico,* they walked down to the Avenida Urdeneta and back toward the Silencio District on the other side of Avenida Bolivar.

It was a holiday in Caracas, celebrating the first anniversary of ousting the last dictator. Gen. Perez Jimenez was booted out of office in 1957 by a large-scale riot. He had ruthlessly suppressed all criticism of his regime, forcing his opponents into hiding or exile. His secret police carried out mass jailing and tortured political prisoners. When the national election was held in 1957, the general had incarcerated all opposition leaders, stuffed the ballot boxes, and won the election, which resulted in a general strike and riot, where his police killed over 300 people. Jimenez had to flee the country after nine years of authoritarian rule.[1]

All the shops were closed, and Fidel Castro was in town to make an appearance late that afternoon and give a speech. The main avenues were lined with people so thick that when the crowd moved, one had to move too or risk being knocked over and trampled. Cars were driving up and down, honking their horns, and people were leaning out of the vehicles shouting. The cars were bedecked with flags and dragging chunks of scrap iron and tin cans, blowing their horns furiously. They walked a mile down Urdaneta until they came to the president's palace, Miraflores, where the crowd was thickest. Castro still hadn't showed, so they headed for the Plaza O'Leary, a few blocks away. There was a vast crowd facing a balcony all decked out with a huge Venezuelan flag, microphones, loudspeakers all over, and a hammer-and-sickle insignia stuck on a pillar underneath the balcony.

They listened to a couple of speakers warm up the crowd with some very jingoistic speeches, but still no Castro. They finally took off, catching a taxi back to La Guaira, not wanting to get left in the land of revolutions. A lot of people hollered and waved at Dick, because his wispy beard resembled Castro's, so he wondered if he would get mobbed when they reached Havana. Maybe the Caraquenos thought Dick was one of Castro's *barbudos*, his bearded revolutionaries.

Back on board ship, their cabin was nice and cool. After dinner, they went back ashore to unload their few remaining bolivars on a couple of beers. Across the dock from the *Santa Maria* was an American ship, the *Alcoa Cavalier.* They went aboard and talked to the assistant purser and third officer for an hour before re-boarding their own ship. Late that night, the ship sailed for Curacao, in the Netherlands Antilles, about 200 miles to the west.

CHAPTER 31 CURACAO, NETHERLANDS ANTILLES

JANUARY 24–26, 1959

Travel is the frivolous part of serious lives, and the serious part of frivolous ones.—Anne Sophie Swetchine

THE *Santa Maria* WAS ALREADY MOORED alongside an oil dock in St. Anna Bay by the time they woke up. They had to cool their heels for a while before disembarking until the local police cleared the ship. The basin they were in was the Schottegat—for the refinery and oil docks ringing it. There was a floating bridge across the bay, but when ships were moving in and out of the harbor, they floated the whole thing over next to the bank for ships to ingress. Two free ferries then took people back and forth across the bay. They had to take the ferry for a five-minute ride to Handelskade, which was one of Willemstad's main streets, and bought some guilders at a bank. They set out along the narrow streets to poke into shops, get a beer, and buy some toiletries. The guilder was worth fifty-three American cents.

Downtown Curacao traffic.

A brief, hard rainstorm bogged them down in their quest for postcards, but when it blew over, they took some pictures of the floating fruit and vegetable market bordering the De Ruyterkade. Composed of small boats tied up nose first, the market was lined with counters and awnings made of flour sacks on the sidewalks. Each boat had stalks of bananas hanging from the running gear, plus boxes of oranges, mangos, papayas, and other fruits on display.

Some of the advertising literature mentioned free samples of Curacao liqueur, so Bill hunted for the place where Senior's liqueur was bottled and had glasses poured. The basic ingredient is the peel of the Curacao orange, which is small and has sour-tasting pulp. The liqueur is white, slightly syrupy, and sweet to the taste, but not cloying. Its distinctive flavor made it melt and flow around the tongue instead of biting it. From *Senior's,* they wandered up and down narrow streets with high buildings on either side. The height of the buildings cut off the sunlight and made the streets seem cooler.

Most of the people seemed to speak English, but the local dialect was *Papiamentu,* a Creole language derived from African languages and either Portuguese or Spanish, with influences from Amerindian languages, English, and Dutch. Spoken on the Dutch ABC islands of Aruba, Bonaire, and Curacao, there is a second dialect of this spoken called *Papiamento,* to distinguish it from the other. Curacao in Papiamentu is called *pais korso.*[1]

Everyone in Willemstad looked well fed and content, which reflected on Dutch management of affairs. The predominant color of the buildings was an ocher yellow, which was very tolerable in direct sunlight, because it cut down on the glare. Most of the roofs were made of a red tile, and some houses had faded to a pale red, reminiscent of frescoes seen in Pompeii. Rambling along, they saw a synagogue built in 1732, which was said to be the oldest synagogue in the western hemisphere. They split up and Bill crossed a drawbridge over the Waaigat to the Scharloo district, where the American Consulate was located in a house that Teddy Roosevelt once lived in. Dick headed out in Handelskade past the Government House and the Water Fort, dating from Napoleonic times, to the Hotel Curacao, which was on the ocean. The hotel had a swimming pool set above ground, with glass ports in the side.

Close to lunchtime, Dick walked back toward the ship over the pontoon bridge known as "Queen Emma." Hot and sweaty by the time he got back, his guilders were all but gone. Bill came dragging up the gangplank a few minutes later in the same shape. By the time the ship got turned around in the Schottegat and they were in open seas again, it was later in the day. They took pictures of the city from the sundeck. Some forty miles from Curacao, they passed the island of Aruba off the port bow about ten miles away, which also had a refinery. The rest of the Netherlands Antilles was made up of three small islands south of Puerto Rico: Saba, St. Maarten, and St. Eustatius. An ever-changing group of islands under various rule, the Netherlands Antilles was originally discovered by the Spanish in 1499, passed into British hands, and the Dutch West Indies Company finally took possession in 1816. Working with power through the ranks of the company, Peter Stuyvesant became Curacao's governor in 1643. Stuyvesant later gained fame with his leadership of New Amsterdam in the 1660s on the mainland (now New York City).

Curacao used to be the center of the slave trade in the Caribbean and was the hardest hit when slavery was abolished in 1863. The economy of Dutch colonial islands was restored after the Second World War by the construction of refineries that processed and stored newly discovered Venezuelan oil.[2]

Downtown Curacao harbor in the rain.

In 1986, Aruba seceded from the Netherlands Antilles to become a constituent country of the Kingdom of the Netherlands. In 2010, the Netherlands Antilles was dissolved as a political entity, and Curacao and St. Maarten joined Aruba as autonomous countries within the Kingdom of the Netherlands, and St. Eustatius became an autonomous special municipality under the same umbrella.[3]

Throughout Europe and the Caribbean, they'd been in some hot and stuffy churches, but on Sunday morning, however, they hit the breeziest by far. Mass was held aft on B Deck in the open air, and there was a fairly strong, warm starboard wind. They couldn't hear a thing coming from the altar, yet the open sea and air made an excellent church.

Since leaving Caracas, the ship was comparatively empty. They ate dinner at the second sitting, and their table of four was isolated on one side of the dining room. One of their table mates, Benjamin, a waiter from New York City was on his way to Florida to follow his trade in Miami, via Spain, where he went for the "girls." He had a blurred, blue German concentration camp number tattooed on his upper left forearm he'd received at Auschwitz, the German name for the concentration camp in Oswiecim, Poland, where from 1939 until 1945, German occupiers murdered over 1.6 million people, principally Jews. Post-war statistics state that 65,000 prisoners survived when the camps were liberated.[4]

Benny was responsible for getting his tablemates kicked out of eating with their fellow class of passengers, because he insisted on wearing his yarmulke at dinner. This pissed off the Catholic Portuguese and Spanish passengers, who insisted that no head covering be worn at meals. Bill, Dick, and Karol elected to stay with him, even though they were relegated to the second sitting, where there were fewer diners. They were sequestered off in a corner of the dining room, but at that point, Benny refused to eat the ship's food, insisting, "It wasn't kosher." So, at all their stopovers, he cornered the market in canned fish like King Hakkon sardines, etc . . . For breakfast, lunch, and dinner, it was oily, canned fish or something he'd scrounged in port. Whether it was kosher or not, they didn't know, or maybe he just wanted to irritate the Catholics.

Their other table mate, Karol, was a Czech. He was a naturalized American citizen working in Munich, West Germany, going to the United States to comply with some immigration law. He was only going to stay in the United States for four days, then fly back to Europe. He was an intelligent, well-spoken person who deflected all questions about his occupation, but was otherwise a good companion for the trip. He would talk about anything except himself.

There were quite a few Cubans on board the *Santa Maria* as well, so they anticipated that the ship's passengers would number even less after Havana.

Sunday evening, they sighted Kingston, Jamaica, in the dusk, with its lights scintillating out to sea. After supper and coffee, they were opposite the first point of land on its western coast. A few minutes later, one of the more beautiful sights of the entire trip unfolded. The moon came up behind a cloud and broke into the clear when it was well up in the heavens, bathing the sea and the island in a strong light. The moonlight on the water extended back to the island, and the diffused light outlined the high silhouette of the coastline. Everyone on deck stopped talking as the transformation took place. The moon was full and round, and the shadows on its surface were sharply defined. Sometime in the middle of their moon watching, the movie *Aida* started on B Deck, and the music *Triumphal March* added a last touch to the scene of awesome beauty. It was a rare moment in which all five senses came to light: the moon and Jamaica to see, the sound of the waves and the music from *Aida* to hear, the breezes from land and sea to smell, the coolness of the air and water to touch, and they swore they could almost taste all those bananas and some of that Jamaican rum across the water.

Dick prepared another bottle ready to go over the side but waited until clearing the Jamaican coast by about sixty miles. They'd spent a very peaceful day on board, the effect of which was heightened by two consecutive days ashore. They were about 750 miles from Havana and 1,000 miles from Port Everglades, Florida. That meant they had over three quarters of the trip under their belt.

That day was their last, peaceful, uninterrupted time at sea and a very lazy one. The hours ran together and melted away. They read on deck, took a swim after lunch, each at separate times. The sunset was fantastic, seeming to be broken into three parts all across the western horizon. It gradually winked out one stage at a time, but not before they beheld some unique chromatic variations of orange.

The clouds didn't seem to reflect light, but to glow furiously, as if with some inner fire. All that afternoon, they'd been seeing ships sailing southward, which indicated they were in a major shipping route. Later that evening, they compared very faint lights that had been visible closer to the Cuban shoreline to one barely visible on a land line further north that seemed very low and distant. Havana beckoned, and they looked forward to a day of looking over the Castro regime.

CHAPTER 32 HAVANA, CUBA

JANUARY 27–28, 1959

Don't tell me how educated you are, tell me how much you have traveled.
—Mohammed

THE SHIP WAS TIED TO THE HAVANA DOCK. The sun was bright and hot when they picked up their landing cards and left with their table mate, Karol. The dock was about five blocks from the center of town, and they wandered through a bunch of narrow streets. On the way, an F. W. Woolworth beckoned, and they ordered an honest-to-God breakfast of orange juice, scrambled eggs, ham, buttered toast, and coffee. The café even had a case full of apple and cherry pie, so they knew they were getting close to home.

The MS Santa Maria docked at the quay in Havana Harbor.

Dock officials monitoring who can exit and enter the Santa Maria.

Lots of bushy-looking characters, Castro's *barbudos,* were walking around in fatigue uniforms with pistols and rifles.[1] Some had tremendous beards that made them look like members of a sect that used to preach on the corners in Tacoma. Dick didn't get nearly as many comments on his Castro-like beard as he did in Caracas. All the members of Castro's army seemed polite and easy to get along with, and none seemed to be as officious as one would expect.

Three weeks earlier, before they landed in Havana, Fulgencio Batista, the dictator abdicated as Fidel Castro's July 26 Movement forces lead an urban and rural-based guerilla uprising against the regime. Che Guevara commanded the rebels at the Battle of Santa Clara on New Year's Day, defeating Batista's army. Batista made a local judge the provisional President of Cuba, then decamped for the Dominican Republic, eventually finding refuge in Salazar's Portugal.[2]

While they walked the streets of Havana, *barbudos* mingled in the crowds, and wailing women and their children crowded the municipal building looking for their husbands and sons. Across the harbor entrance to Havana, La Cabana, an eighteenth century fortress, was on guard. Che Guevara headquartered there and prison tribunals were under way. Between January 2 and June 12, 1959, he oversaw the trials and executions of war criminals, political prisoners, traitors, *chivatos* (informants), and former members of Batista's secret police. Che, a medical doctor and revolutionary, had the last say.[3] *Time* magazine noted him, a dedicated Marxist-Communist, as "one of the hundred most influential people of the twentieth century." [4]

At the tourist office, they got a map of Havana and set off down the main street toward Morro Castle, on the other side of the harbor entrance. Walking down the street, they had to discourage a lot of hustlers who wanted to show them around the town and take them to places for the best time you ever had in your life, "Meester." They kept looking for signs of recent combat, like bullet marks on buildings, but didn't see any at all. They did, however, see more good-looking women than they had seen in a long time. They took a swing across a wide plaza that fronted the presidential palace and then followed the oceanfront west toward the more modern part of town, where the Havana Hilton was located. This was where the rebels bedded down for a couple of days gratis, in $30-a-day suites.

Cuban money was easy to figure out, because it was worth the same as American money, except there were twenty and forty cent coins. When they got in the vicinity of the Hilton, Bill and Karol took off in that direction, and Dick circled back toward town and the ship. Wearing his Portuguese pants, Dick observed that they felt like they were made from a horse blanket in that heat and humidity. Exploring small side streets, he had a few beers and mailed some postcards. He had missed tea and made a quick trip to grab a couple of chocolate bars. He also bought a pineapple for twenty cents!

Bill and Karol went to the Hilton and walked around, looking for the entrance, which they eventually found beneath a marquee sporting a Picasso-like mural. Ten or more of Castro's *barbudos* lounged around the driveway, and some were having their pictures taken by a photographer. Others were just taking the air. They decided to crash the joint and hurried past the doorman, who looked very tropical and important in his pith helmet and whites. Inside, they were told Fidel was sleeping, as he had just arrived that morning by plane from Caracas, so they didn't bother him for an interview. They settled for his picture from a photography shop inside the lobby, with him postured in a *forward men* pose, his mouth open in a rebel yell and his Tommy gun thrust into the air.

Across the street and behind the capitol building, they had lunch in a park, then took a guy up on his offer to show them the Vinetera distillery. Upon arriving, they were treated to a banana daiquiri and various other liquors, which all tasted wonderful and cooled them down after having been out in the sun for so long.

Karol enjoyed bargains, so he and Bill took an eight-cent bus tour of Havana, which took them to the other side of Havana Bay through the outskirts of the city and back again, covering about fifteen miles. It was an interesting side trip. When the bus driver slammed on the brakes to avoid a car, Bill was thrown into a *barbudo,* knocking him off balance and his M-1 rifle to the ground. Reeking of rum, the Cuban soldier was in fatigues and had Catholic holy medals pinned on his chest like they were decorations. From the bus window, they observed small children running around sans clothes. The obvious poverty of the neighborhoods stood out. After the bus ride, they toured the Pateros Cigar Factory and then headed back to the ship.

• JUL 79

Dick talking to a local by El Capitolio, Havana's capitol building.

BACK AT SEA

THE FINAL STRETCH APPROACHING, they had only 240 miles to go. They sailed away from Havana's docks, and Bill had the last roll of film in the camera and was clicking away. Dick alternately jumped into the pool and watched Havana recede into the distance. In preparation for their departure from the ship, they went through the business of tipping their table steward, waiter, and cabin steward. Everyone seemed happy with the pittance they bestowed.

It was time to go through all their stuff, weeding out the dead weight. They threw one last bottle overboard with a note to contact them. Bill left the rat gray pants he'd bought in Italy and a pullover he picked up in Barcelona, because neither fit well. The cabin steward had three kids living outside Lisbon, so they figured that was where the stuff ended up. After everything was packed, they still had to get rid of some remaining pesetas and escudos. They naturally thought they could drink them up, but after about four bottles of Dutch beer, they gave up and changed the remainder into dollars and hit the sack.

The steward came by and beat on their door bright and early the next morning. It was the first time he'd ever done that, so they assumed he was afraid they would miss the stop. The ship was docking at Port Everglades, while en route to Brazil.

Their first glimpse of the United States consisted of a modernistic Customs and Immigration Building, a big blacktop parking lot, plus some early-bird arrivals who were meeting people on the boat. After coffee and rolls, Bill started his paperwork for disembarking by getting clearance forms from the U.S. Public Health Service agent. After all those months abroad, his vaccination certificate was finally needed. He was clear to go ashore after negotiating with Immigration.

Everything in hand, they traipsed down the gangplank, stopped briefly at Customs, and passed from the gloomy confines of officialdom out into the hot, steamy Florida morning. They had arrived! But where were they? A fellow running a candy counter gave them the lay of the land—twenty-five miles north of Miami and three miles from the closest town, Fort Lauderdale.

CHAPTER 33 USA

JANUARY 28–MAY 16, 1959

Shod with wings is the horse of him who rides on a spring day the road that leads to home.—Bai Juyi

TAKING A CAB INTO TOWN, the three of them, Karol included, piled into a 1959 Olds—as big as a boxcar—and purred into the bus station at Ft. Lauderdale, where they connected immediately with a bus to Miami. The bus passed all sorts of causeways, stopped at Miami Beach, where they said good-bye to Karol, then went on a short ride across MacArthur Causeway.

They were in Miami. The bus let them off at Biscayne Blvd, the main north-south highway. At first, everything seemed rather glaring and blatant. There were signs everywhere and people talking all at once. Even though they could understand the language, it all impeded their senses after the quietness of the sea voyage. Gastronomically speaking, they got off on the right foot with a delicious lunch, including their first taste of ice cream and milk in months. They had acquired one extra piece of luggage, a box which contained two bottles of rum and a bottle of Cream de Cacao.

After lunch, they started making tracks to Key West, Florida, by walking down the boulevard a couple of blocks hitchhiking. A fellow offered a ride as far as the University of Miami campus. There they had to sweat it out for an hour and a half in the sun before moving again. Their umbrellas came in handy as sunshades. A lot of people driving by seemed to think they were amusing, but none gave them a ride, so they hitchhiked to the edge of the city, with one more ride taking them to Homestead, where they alighted in a tropical

SASKATOON
CALGARY
REGINA
COLUMBIA MTS.
WINNIPEG
VANCOUVER
VICTORIA
SEATTLE
CASCADE RANGE
COLUMBIA PLAT.
FARGO
PORTLAND
NORTH AMERICA
MINNEAPOLIS
ROCKY MOUNTAINS
BOISE
GREAT PLAINS
OMAHA
CENTRAL LOW
SALT LAKE CITY
GREAT BASIN
DENVER
KANSAS CITY
SACRAMENTO
UNITED STATES
SAN FRANCISCO
SAN JOSE
FRESNO
LAS VEGAS
ALBUQUERQUE
OKLAHOMA CITY
PHOENIX
SAN DIEGO
DALLAS
TIJUANA
MEXICALI
TUCSON
EL PASO
CIUDAD JUAREZ
AUSTIN
HOUSTON
SAN ANTONIO
HERMOSILLO
CHIHUAHUA
BAJA CALIFORNIA
ALTI-PLANICIE MEXICANA
GOLFO DE CALIFORNIA
TORREON
MONTERREY
MATAMOROS
CULIACAN
MEXICO
GULF OF MEXICO
LA PAZ
SAN LUIS POTOSI
TAMPICO
AGUASCALIENTES
LEON
GUADALAJARA
QUERETARO
MORELIA
TOLUCA
MEXICO CITY
PUEBLA
VERACRUZ
CAMPECHE
VILLAHERMOSA

MOOSONEE
LES LAURENTIDES
THUNDER BAY
CANADIAN SHIELD
GREAT LAKES
CHICOUTIMI
ST. LAWRENCE RIVER
GULF OF ST. LAWRENCE
ISLAND OF NEWFOUNDLAND
STRAIT OF BELLE ISLE
CAPE BAULD
QUÉBEC
SUDBURY
FREDERICTON
MIQUELON
ST. PIERRE AND MIQUELON
OTTAWA
MONTRÉAL
CHARLOTTETOWN
SAINT JOHN
BRAS D'OR LAKE
HALIFAX
SABLE I.
TORONTO
MILWAUKEE
BUFFALO
GULF OF MAINE
CAPE SABLE
DETROIT
BOSTON
CAPE COD
CHICAGO
PROVIDENCE
HARTFORD
MASSACHUSETTS BAY
CLEVELAND
LONG ISLAND SOUND
PITTSBURGH
NEW YORK
INDIANAPOLIS
COLUMBUS
PHILADELPHIA
CINCINNATI
BALTIMORE
DELAWARE BAY
WASHINGTON, D.C.
CAPE MAY
LOUISVILLE
APPALACHIAN MTS.
CHESAPEAKE BAY
VIRGINIA BEACH
ALBEMARLE SOUND
NASHVILLE
CHARLOTTE
PIEDMONT
CAPE HATTERAS
PAMLICO SOUND
BIRMINGHAM
ATLANTA
CAPE FEAR
BERMUDA ISLANDS
HAMILTON
SEA ISLANDS
COASTAL PLAIN
JACKSONVILLE
CAPE SAN BLAS
ORLANDO
CAPE CANAVERAL
TAMPA
SARGASSO SEA
GRAND BAHAMA
BAHAMA ISLANDS
MIAMI
NASSAU
KEY WEST
CAPE SABLE
STRAITS OF FLORIDA
ANDROS
BAHAMAS
SAN SALVADOR
HAVANA
WEST INDIES
PINAR DEL RIO
TURKS AND CAICOS IS.
CUBA
GRAND TURK
CANCUN
CAMAGUEY
HOLGUIN
MERIDA
PEN. DE YUCATÁN
COZUMEL
I. DE COZUMEL
BAYAMO
MANZANILLO
GUANTANAMO
GONAIVES
DOMINICAN REP.
CAYMAN IS.
GEORGE TOWN
GRAND CAYMAN
MONTEGO BAY
U.S. MINOR OUTLYING IS.
PUERTO RICO
BRITISH VIRGIN IS.
SAN JUAN
CHETUMAL
LES CAYES

downpour. They took shelter under a covered freight platform of the Florida East Coast Railroad. When the rain stopped, they got back to thumb-waggling, and after one short hop, a fellow took them for a long ride to Marathon, only forty-three miles from Key West. Thinking it would be hard to get a ride at night, they took the bus from there the rest of the way. From the dock to there, the 170 miles took nine hours! Their average speed was nineteen mph. Incredible. Carrying their bags up and down the main street, they ended up in a hotel across from the bus station.

Since leaving Puyallup on August 19, 1958, they had traveled for 163 days, so they figured spending two nights and a day in Key West, a sleepy little burg that didn't have much going on they could see, wouldn't hurt. They viewed the southernmost house in the United States and visited a movie set where some exterior scenes were being filmed—supposedly of a Filipino village—for *Operation Petticoat*. Two nights and a day was nearly too much.

When they returned to Miami, they took a comfortable room there outside the hustle and bustle of downtown and spent some time reading, going to movies, and swimming at Miami Beach. The water was warm, but the beach was crowded with Easterners who talked through their noses. To their Western ears, the northeastern accents made them feel like they were in another strange country. The "g's" and "r's" at the end of a word were dropped, or *here* became *hea*. The *o* sounded like *aw* as in *dawg*. It reminded them of Damon Runyon's take on Brooklynese: "toity poiple boids sittin' onna coib, boipin' an' choipin' an' oitin' doity woims . . ."[1]

Sitting around the beach, they were enlisted to dance in the sand with the vacationing New Yorkers. Not only dance, they had to sing too. No lying on their butts soaking up the rays:

Hava nagila, hava nagila, ... *Let's rejoice, Let's rejoice*
Hava nagila ve-nesmeha, ... *Let's rejoice and be happy*
Hava neranenah .... *Let's sing*
Hava neranenah .... *Let's sing*
Uru, uru ahim!.......................... *Awake, awake, brothers!*
Uru ahim e-lev sameah, ... *Awake brothers with a happy heart!*
Be-lev sameah .... *With a happy heart.*[2]

After a couple of rounds of that, hand-holding, and dancing in the sand in the hot sun, they packed it in. They enjoyed the exercise and the rhythm of the lyrics, but had no idea what it meant. It certainly roused them from their sun-induced somnolence.

They started hitchhiking again to Houston, but it proved impossible to get a ride. After fruitless hours of thumbing, they bought a 1950 Mercury from a used car lot about twenty miles north of Miami. For fifty dollars, they thought they would get their money's worth if they could simply make it to Galveston some 1,300 miles away, but the thing only ran for about seventy miles and then died in the middle of the Everglades outside of Tampa. It started to overheat in the middle of nowhere about fifteen miles from the nearest civilization, and they spent the night in the car on the side of a swamp. In the morning, Dick scooped water from the swamp with one of the hubcaps and filled the radiator, and they traveled on a couple of more miles until a tire blew. Of course, there was no spare in the trunk, so they hitched into town, bought a used tire, had it mounted to a rim, and caught a ride back. With that repair, they made it into town, but the car was red hot. When Dick replaced the broken radiator hose, they thought they had it made and took off again, but about half a mile out of town, a front tire blew out. They turned around and limped back to the first service station they could find. Luckily, a buyer came along and gave twenty-five dollars for the piece of junk. It had cost them $35 to cover those few miles, not counting the price of that ruined piece of metal!

Their luck at hitchhiking changed, however, and they made it to Tampa without any trouble. While there, they saw some of

Bill musing over his $50 purchase of a1950 Mercury; our escape carriage.

the Gasparilla celebration before taking the bus north to Perry. Gasparilla is Tampa's blowout celebration in commemoration of Jose Gaspar, joyous pirate. He was among the last of the buccaneers who terrorized the coastal waters of Florida in the late eighteenth century, serving as a lieutenant in the Royal Spanish Navy for five years until 1783, when he and fellow mutineers seized command of a Spanish sloop-of-war and began a life of piracy. His journal recites he burned thirty-six ships during twelve years as an outlaw of the sea.[3]

When waiting in the bus station, a Border Patrol officer stopped them and wanted to see their identification. He was looking for foreign sailors who had jumped ship. Apparently, they got quite a few deserters in Tampa.

The bus ride to Perry was uneventful, but they stopped to find an acquaintance of Dick's he'd met in the army, a chemist for Proctor & Gamble. They never found him, so they stayed overnight and then hit the road thumbing again. They got lucky—a Cuban who was going to Los Angeles picked them up and asked them to go all the way with him. They stuck to their original plan, though, and told him they were getting off in Houston, Texas.

He diverted into New Orleans in the wee hours before dawn, the day after Mardi Gras was over. The streets in the French Quarter were almost deserted. The gutters were literally piled high with empty beer cans—thousands of them. All the bars had set up sidewalk stands and dispensed beer at fifty cents a can. They didn't tarry long, arriving in Houston by the next evening, where they parted company with their driver and caught a bus to Galveston.

In Galveston, they moved into the Phi Chi Medical Fraternity house, because they had a spare room to rent and they started to look for jobs. Dick checked with the local newspaper where he had formerly worked, but they didn't have any immediate openings. For about a week and a half, that was the story for the both of them. Finally, the paper had a change of heart and Dick started working there again. Bill got a job with an outfit that serviced commercial and marine refrigeration and air conditioners. After he had been with them for a while, they gave him a truck and made him a straw boss with a helper. The truck gave them wheels to get around in during the evenings. Their shifts prevented them from seeing much of each other, however, except on Sundays. Their schedules kept them busy, but as the weather got warmer, they both did a lot of swimming in the pool at Phi Chi and in the gulf.

The barmaid in Judy's Bar greeted Bill as "Ranger," a nickname she gave him when she first met him, thinking he was a Texas Ranger. This was the local watering hole closest to Phi Chi, and they were there often enough. On April 2, Bill turned twenty-one and, to celebrate, bought a round of drinks for the house at Judy's. When the barmaid inquired the reason for the generosity, she about pole-axed Bill, since the drinking age was his newly acquired number.

The time spent in Galveston passed quickly. They had planned to leave June 1, but Bill got laid off his job when a contract was completed, so that furnished the excuse to leave two weeks early. On the night Bill told Dick he'd been laid off, they decided to pack up. Bill started throwing their gear into two piles—one pile was being shipped to Puyallup, and the other they were taking with them. Dick finished his last shift at the paper, giving them about four hours notice that he was quitting.

The next morning, they cashed all their checks, shipped the boxes to Washington, and said their good-byes before leaving with a friend of theirs, Scott Cohen. Scott was headed for a weekend in Mexico and agreed to drive them down to Laredo. At Judy's, they sat down and counted out their money, figuring that $687 ought to see them to Mexico City before heading back home to Washington State. They had spent almost three and a half months in Texas and decided that Galveston had been a pleasant interlude, staying in one place for more than one night. But they were definitely eager to hit the road again.

All the loose ends were tied up in good fashion, and they were out of Galveston by midday. The countryside was flat and green going west-southwest for about 150 miles, but after they passed through a town called George West, the character of the land started to change to gentle rolling hills with sagebrush and cactus. The air was much drier, and up ahead, they could see heat lightning flashes. Just a few miles out of George West, a light plane circled overhead, then landed on the highway and pulled into a ranch. Lightning continued to flash around them. They pulled into Laredo, headed for the Greyhound bus station to change into long pants and stow their bags, stopped at a hotel to leave their cash in a safe, and then headed over the bridge to Nuevo Laredo on the Mexican side.

CHAPTER 34 MEXICO

MAY 17–30, 1959

Stop worrying about the potholes in the road and celebrate the journey.
—Fitzhugh Mullan

THE FIRST THING ON THEIR MINDS was food, and after looking around, they found an open-air restaurant on a side street in Nuevo Laredo. Dick and Bill ate beef in a dark red, spicy hot sauce and Scott had a sheep's head. The skull was split down the middle and the brains were fried in the skull over a brazier. Scott sat there content and ate the brains and eyes with gusto. It gave the brothers a twinge watching him. They washed all the food down with good Mexican beer costing only two pesos a bottle.

The exchange rate was twelve pesos, fifty centavos to the U.S. dollar. A peso was worth about eight cents. Scott and Bill got haircuts and Dick, a shave. Everything was *en plein* air—sitting in a barber chair out in the open while the world paraded past. After their shearing, they felt better and decided to explore the *distrito*. They drove down and parked the car on a side street and started tramping around, drinking a beer here and there until they couldn't hold any more. It was getting late, well past midnight, so they decided to split up and meet at the car in the afternoon. Bill wandered around and ended up sleeping in the car. He woke up later to find a kid's skinny arm reaching through the partly opened window trying to snake his wallet.

They didn't know where Scott went, but Dick rented a room behind a bar, took a shower, and went to sleep before dawn. Bill and Scott found Dick after sunrise and went for breakfast. Afterward, they drove out to the airport and found out they needed twenty-seven dollars for a one-way ticket to Mexico City—far too expensive.

They got a hotel room on the plaza and took it easy for a while over brandy and Coke. Mexican brandy is sweet with very little bouquet and goes well with Coke. Scott had to get going back to Galveston, so the three of them went out and ate a dinner of lamb that was spitted and roasted over a bed of coals. They crossed back over the Rio Grande to Laredo and said good-bye to Scott. Only it wasn't good-bye, they'd go on to stay in contact and meet up through the years.

Dick went down to the district in Nuevo Laredo again and started drinking tequila. Lick the back of your hand to moisten it, sprinkle salt on it, lick off the salt, down the tequila, and suck on a lemon—it goes down like greased lightning. He was feeling his oats when he got in an argument in a bar and the bartender called the cops, who hauled him off to the local hoosegow. The cops told Dick that he would have to wait for the chief. After fifteen minutes, he didn't show up and the cops started talking about "coffee." Dick quickly got the idea and gave them eighty pesos for "coffee." They gave him his pocketknife back, which one of the cops was admiring, and they all parted friends. It was an amiable interlude, but if he had been obtuse enough to insist on seeing the chief or had demanded his "legal rights," he could have rotted in their cell.

They connected with the train to Mexico City at 6:10 p.m. For the first time, they were traveling first class, since it only cost $8.50 each for the 700-mile journey from Nuevo Laredo. The train was quite modern, with a few of the coaches made in Switzerland. A Mexican Army officer asked Dick why he was so tall. His snappy retort in Spanish was, "Hecho con leche."

The first 180 miles to Monterrey was across flat country, but they could see mountains in the distance. Out of Monterrey, they started to climb, swerving back and forth around sharp curves, crossing the Madre Oriental Mountains. It was a long train, and at times, they could see the engine higher up the slope, higher than the caboose. The diesel up front never eased off all the way to Saltillo, another sixty miles away. Somewhere in between, the engine stopped for some reason on a steep grade, then took off again. They climbed over 3,000 feet and it became noticeably cooler the higher they went.

There was a full moon, which threw all the shadows of the rocks into sharp relief. Stopping in Saltillo, they stretched their legs on the platform. There had been plenty of fresh air because all the coaches' windows were open, and they had their heads out to catch a breeze. When they weren't doing that, they would climb up on top of the coach with some of the other passengers and hang on to the roof. The conductor had a laissez faire attitude and didn't chase anybody back down. They climbed from 438 feet in Nuevo Laredo to 7,349 feet in Mexico City.

The closer they got to Mexico City, the more populous the areas became and the stops more frequent. All around were high hills with blue sky in the distance and green vegetation. They ate their last meal on the train at 6:00, and the only air-conditioning they encountered was in the dining room, where they damn near froze. They kept looking for the lights of the city, and when they did finally see them, they were not too impressive because of the flat terrain. The train slowed as it passed through the railroad yards and stopped and backed into the Buenavista Station, ten blocks from downtown. It was 8:00 p.m. on Tuesday, May 19.

MEXICO CITY

A CAB TOOK THEM TO THE REGIS HOTEL on Avenida Juarez. The room was fifty pesos or just over four dollars a day. The hotel was located in Mexico City's business district, where all the big banks and fancy restaurants were located, so it was pretty dead there at night.

They buried their heads under the pillows as long as they could and rolled out midday to have breakfast—bacon and eggs—at Sanborn's across the street. Their next quest was to find motor scooter rentals someplace in town; that led them to a Greyhound travel agent at the end of the Paseo de la Reforma. The agent was a young kid who attended high school in San Francisco and spoke good English. He gave all kinds of scoop on how to get around in the city, how far away certain places were, how much it cost, and how long it took to get there. They left him to catch a bus to the Reforma and the Parq Chapultepec, where the Castillo de Chapultepec was located. The castle sat on a hill about 200 feet above the Parq. As they toured, they discovered that Emperor Maximilian I made it his official residence in 1866. They viewed his elaborate coach of state, the display of his watch, his wife, Empress Carlotta's opera slippers, and a lot of other relics from Mexico's early history. Emperor Maximilian I ruled Mexico under the auspices of the French and Napoleon III from 1864 until the French retreated. Maximilian attempted to hold out with his Mexican loyalists, but was overcome by the Republican forces of Benito Juarez, ending the era of the Second Mexican Empire.[1]

On the train, they had passed through the town of Queretaro, where Maximilian was executed in 1867 after he was captured while trying to escape through Republican lines. From the castle, they could see the snow-clad peaks of Popocatepetl at 17,749 feet and Iztaccihuatl, at 17,159 feet to the northeast. During his conquest of Mexico in the 1500s, Hernan Cortes used sulfur taken from the edges of these volcanoes to make gunpowder when his supplies ran low.[2]

One local myth about the volcanoes is about Popocatepetl ("the smoking mountain") and Iztaccihuatl ("white woman" in Nahuatl, sometimes called the Mujer Dormida "sleeping woman" in Spanish), which relates to Popocatepetl as the warrior and Iztaccihuatl as the princess. Iztaccihuatl's father sent *Popo* to war in Oaxaca, promising him his daughter as his wife, if he returned, which the father presumed he would not. *Iztacci's* father told her that her lover was killed in battle and died grief stricken. When *Popo* returned and discovered the death of his lover, he committed suicide by plunging a knife through his heart. God covered them with snow and made them into mountains.[3]

After dinner, they went in search of some nightlife and found between twenty and thirty mariachi bands milling about on the Plaza Garibaldi, behind the Museo De Belles Artes on Avenida Santa Maria de Redonda. The bars and clubs in that area were doing good business. The mariachi bands were playing requests from individuals for five pesos a number, so they plunged into their pockets to hear them play *Perfidia*. Each band was made up of four or five musicians. The dominant instrument was the trumpet, and the usual combination was one trumpet, two violins, and a guitar. The roving bands played the traditional music of Mexico, which made them a prominent tourist attraction. They finished the evening with a bowl of soup and a bottle of beer at a *loncheria*.

After a late breakfast, they walked down to the Zocalo, known as the Plaza de la Constitucion, then on to the Museo Nacional of Anthropology. In from the main entrance across the courtyard was the huge basaltic stone commonly known as the "Aztec calendar," or Cuauhxicalli, which means "Eagle's Bowl." Unearthed at the Zocalo in 1790 and located at the end of the main business district, the calendar displayed a month of twenty days, a year of eighteen months, and was said to be more accurate than the European calendars of that period. When it was created in the Middle Ages, the European Georgian Calendar had not yet come into use.[4] A huge, twenty-five-ton piece of stone, it dominated the entrance and was the largest artifact in the museum. There were also relics from the Mixtec, Zapotec, Mayan, Toltec, and Tarascan cultures. The tour took just a short time, so they backtracked to the Zocalo for a peek inside the cathedral on the north side of the plaza.

The Zocalo cathedral, officially known as The Metropolitan Cathedral of the Assumption of Mary, was built on the original site of the earliest Christian church on the continent, dating from 1525. The cathedral was begun in 1573, finished in 1822. Its architect, Manuel Tolsa, designed it after the neoclassic style and adorned the interior with marble altars and statuary, gilded wood carvings, silver railings, and a plethora of paintings and tapestries.[5]

They took a bus ride out on Insurgentes Avenue to the University of Mexico. University City, eight miles south of Mexico City, is the home of the 450-year-old university. The campus was modernistic in the extreme, and many building were ornamented with mosaics by Diego Rivera. Covering 580 acres and accommodating 25,000 students, one of the campus's outstanding features was the stadium, designed to resemble the crater of a volcano. The library was unique as well, in that all four exterior walls were covered with vivid murals designed by the artist and architect Juan O'Gorman.

A leisurely stroll came next to the Greyhound travel agency just off the Reforma, and they talked to the girls there for a while before buying bus tickets to Guadalajara. Because they had a couple of hours to kill before the bus left, they took a cab back to the Zocalo and walked around in back of the cathedral to the Museum of Religious Treasures, where just a small part of what made up the treasury was on display. There were such items as a crystal chalice, several monstrances studded with emeralds and pearls, plus two statues of Jesus and Mary carved from ivory tusks. The statues had Asian features, because they were made in China. There were vestments encrusted with bullion and were rigid in their cases. It wasn't as magnificent as the treasury of St. Peter's in Rome, but all objects displayed had an immediate sense of history about them. After leaving the museum, they walked over to the corner and saw some excavated Aztec ruins. They took some photos of the ruins and a shot of the carving over a side door of the cathedral. Walking back into the cathedral again for another short look around, they found a crypt under the apse, where all the bishops or archbishops of Mexico City were buried, dating back to the time of the Conquistadores.

A few more quick pictures of the Belles Artes Palace and the Alameda were taken while buzzing about in a cab. After rushing to pack and leave, they hailed a cab and made it to the station just in time to catch the bus to Guadalajara. The first half of the trip was uncomfortable, because they didn't fit well in the small seats, and most of the trip took them over torturous roads, climbing over 10,000 feet.

The dinner break was the longest stop on the trip, and the food choices were not glamorous. They had to settle for eggs and beer. Several people got off at Morelia later that night, so they had the back end of the bus to themselves and managed to stretch out and get reasonably comfortable. A full moon came out and lit up the landscape, accentuating the cone-shaped hills, which suggested a geologically young countryside. Chugging past Lake Patzcuaro, they pulled into Zamora in the early morning hour, where they snacked on bananas, beer, and brandy before boarding again for the last 126 miles.

Their arrival in Guadalajara at dawn found them starved, so they ate breakfast at the bus station with a fellow from Zurich, Switzerland, who had been working on a ranch in Mexico for two years. He was on his way to California and then across the country to New York to take a ship back home. They left him at the station and started walking toward the city center looking for a hotel. After quite a bit of hiking and a few more inquiries, they discovered all the hotels were full. The last hotel clerk made some phone calls and found a vacancy for them near the bus station. They hailed a cab back and crashed into the beds about 8:30 in the morning.

It was late afternoon before they got going again. Guadalajara was warmer, because the altitude was about 5,200 feet. The second largest city in Mexico, with a population of 520,000, it was quite industrialized and in the throes of a modernization program. They wandered around, getting acquainted with the streets, and talked to a Belgian girl at a travel agency about going to Mazatlan, wondering, without asking, how she got from Belgium to Guadalajara. That evening, Dick went to a movie, after which he went to a restaurant and treated himself to an authentic Mexican dinner of *pollo asados,* or broiled chicken. Bill was looking at the nightlife of Guadalajara, discovering it was pretty well characterized by a place called LaCasaBlanca, a music and beer joint.

Up in time for noon Mass at the nearby brownstone church, the plain exterior masked the colorful interior, covered with frescoes and gilded carvings. They later headed out to take some pictures but were waylaid by a brief thunderstorm and had to hole up in a café until it passed. The rain cooled everything down, and they enjoyed the walk up the Avenida Independencia to Avenida Juarez, which brought them to the city center. After a bite to eat, they explored the cathedral, which dated back to 1571. The building was a hodge-podge of Byzantine, Greek, Gothic, and Arabic architecture. The twin spires on the roof were covered with yellow tiles. They took several pictures in the area of the cathedral and then found a concert which was about to begin in the municipal park at sundown. It was very pleasant to sit in the park and listen. At times, the cathedral bells chimed melodiously, blending in with the music. They went to separate movies after the concert, then met back at the hotel to go out for midnight supper. They weren't happy with the hotel, though, and were anxious to leave for Mazatlan the next day.

Their early start put them at the train station three hours before departure to Mazatlan. They caught a cab to the new, modern station, where the bus had left them on arrival. They thought that was the train station, but as it turned out, the train station was in another part of town. Catching another cab to the actual train station, they discovered it was in a remote area and had to kill three hours in a sweltering corrugated iron terminal.

Fortunately, the train's coach was somewhat air-conditioned. The train left more or less on time, and the yellow tiled spires of the old church were still visible a half hour later. Dining car prices were surprisingly low, and the food wasn't too bad. They read after supper, occasionally going back for a beer in the dining car. Bill happened to be sleeping when the train stopped at Tepic for twenty minutes after midnight. Dick noticed the fog had the smell of ocean about it. There was a detectable difference after the dry and undistinguished air of Guadalajara and Mexico City.

There were some tables set up in the cinders beside the track, where women were selling tacos and coffee heated on charcoal braziers. Under some of the tables were children asleep on the ground covered by coarse cloths, an indication of the abject poverty in Mexico, but it didn't appear to be nearly as bad as Portugal's. When Bill awoke, he joined Dick on the roof of the coach, and they rode through a particularly rugged section of countryside that, according to the early annals, all but daunted the first Jesuits and Franciscans—only recently had that rugged part of the country been spanned by railroad tracks.

The moon was out and the view was superb. There were very high green hills with deep cuts that wound back and forth, then gradually widened into a river bed. To get up on top of the coach, they opened a door, swung around the end of the coach, and climbed a ladder. Their footing was risky, as the top of the coach was dewy wet and the train was swaying around curves—comings and goings had to be carefully timed so as not to fall off at a curve or get brushed off while going through narrow cuts. They finally came down off their perch for a few hours of sleep and arrived in Mazatlan early that morning.

There were some very aggressive cab drivers waiting when they got off the train, but they brushed them off and caught a bus into town, to the marketplace. From there, they headed in the general direction of the beach, stopping off for breakfast and to check into a beachfront hotel, the Bel Mar. There was a swimming pool, but it was so heavily chlorinated they preferred to go across the street to the ocean. The beach had fine, soft sand and good surf, and they swam and body-surfed in the breakers and played catch with empty coconut husks until they felt revived and also a bit pooped.

After showering and dressing, they ate and then lingered around reading until Bill fell asleep. Later, when Dick was dead tired and ready for bed, Bill was raring to go after eight hours' sleep, so he went out, exploring the nightlife of Mazatlan. There were loads of discos, bars, and clubs. The town had something for every party animal and night owl. The music was diverse, ranging from easy listening piano bars to ear-blasting, bass-driven music at the clubs and discos. And that was not to mention the mariachi and tambora bands.

A desultory day, they succumbed to being beach bums, cooking their heads in the sun on a long walk. Dick was knocked out by the heat, so they went for an ocean swim before he hit the pad. Bill sat on the beach a while longer. Dick woke after a short nap, walked downtown, and then took a cab to the Copacabana Night Club. Bill showed up there eventually and they watched the floor show. The women's costumes were flashy yellow, red, and blue as they swooped in unison as they performed their staccato shoe-pounding dance to flamenco music that made the floor reverberate. The male dancers in their black matador costumes did counterpoint maneuvers to the women in a breathtaking rhythmic mimic. Afterward, they walked all the way from the Copa to the hotel, managing to work off a head of beer. They stopped at a fly-specked *loncheria*, the kind everyone warned tourists to stay out of, and ate sandwiches.

The beach bum lifestyle stuck with them one more day. Mazatlan was, and is still, a beach town south of the border, and it had such an enervating effect on them that it took two days to recover by sitting on the front porch of the hotel, rocking with the rest of the tourists.

They were out of the hotel and down at the station five minutes before departure to Nogales early on the morning they left. The train had three Pullman class coaches at the rear, a diner, a "primera especial classe" coach, and the rest were second class. For eighteen hours, they slithered up the coast. Dick had bridged himself across two seats facing each other, trying to get some shut-eye. The time passed quickly, even though it was a long train ride. The countryside's landscape appeared flat and littered with scrub and cacti. Several large black birds with reddish heads and white bills were seen—Turkey vultures. There were many little communities spread along the way, some completely isolated with stick fences and mud huts. Many were the homes of the innumerable section gangs they passed.

Their night was spent attempting to sleep curled up on the tiny seats. Fortunately, the crying children either went to sleep or got off. Breakfast was good the following morning. They looked out the dining car window as the train took the last, long pull up and over the steep Sierra Madre Occidental hills before arriving in Nogales. The disembarking point was downtown, close to the border. From there, they had to investigate bus schedules on the U.S. side. Since, they didn't know when they could continue their journey through the southwest, they checked their bags on the Mexican side and walked over the border to buy tickets on a Greyhound bus that left that morning for Tucson. After taking care of business, they crossed back into Mexico and shopped around awhile, spending their last pesos on Mexican gin that they toted across the border.

CHAPTER 35 EPILOGUE

MAY 31, 1959

Long voyages, great lies.
—Italian Proverb

THEY BUSED to Phoenix, Arizona, Blythe, Indio, Riverside, and Los Angeles, California, and then on to San Francisco—over sixty hours, only dozing on the way. In San Francisco, they found a room on Geary St. and crashed hard and heavy. They spent a week in the city visiting their mother's brother and their father's sister. A friend from school, Dick Ingalls, and his wife, Marge, put them up at their home in Burlingame. The Ingalls toured them around the bay area, picnicking at the ocean, taking in all the tourist sites. It was also the occasion where Dick picked up the sobriquet "godfather" to the Ingall's new daughter, Cynthia Rose. But after a week of visiting, sightseeing, and lounging, it was time to hit the road. The Ingalls took them to the train station, and their dad met them at the Union Station in Tacoma, Washington. The pilgrims had returned.

AFTERWORD:

THE *Arosa Kulm* WAS LAUNCHED IN 1919 and began life with many different shipping companies and assignments. She had accommodations for first class and tourist dormitories. The ship was designed to move large numbers of passengers at reasonable rates. It was used as an immigrant ship, for student travel, and transport for troops.

Known originally as the *Contigny*, subsequent names under other owners were: *American Banker, Ville d'Anvers, City of Athens, Protea,* and lastly, *Arosa Kulm*.

Three months after they left the ship, it was seized in Plymouth, England, as well as her sister ships, when the Arosa Line went bankrupt to the tune of $8.5 million in December 1958. Put up for auction, Belgium scrappers paid $150,000 and towed her to Bruges, Belgium, for dismantling.[1]

The *Santa Maria* launched in 1953, worked the colonial trade to Portuguese Africa, Angola, Mozambique, and Brazil. A notable event in her career was her hijacking on January 22, 1961. Captain Henrique Galvao, a Portuguese Army officer and politician and his team of twenty-four Portuguese and Spanish rebels, operating from a base in Venezuela, decided to attack the ship to protest the dictatorship of Franco in Spain and Salazar in Portugal.

A huge air-sea search for the liner was mounted by U.S. and British ships and planes. After eleven days, she was surrounded by four U.S. destroyers and surrendered and docked off Recife, Brazil. Galvao received political asylum in Brazil in exchange for the release of the 900 passengers and crew. In the taking of the ship, one ship's officer was killed and another wounded. Galvao went on to write a book:

Santa Maria: My Crusade for Portugal. In 1973, the Santa Maria took her last cruise to Taiwan, where she was scrapped.[2]

Over the next several years, Bill and Dick received messages from finders of their bottles thrown overboard. One, from Wales in Great Britain, came in five years after they returned home. A bit of wisdom: If ever ship-wrecked, don't bet your nickel on this bottle trick for a rescue.

REFERENCES:

Chapter 1. CROSS COUNTRY

1. Sputnik. October 27, 2012 from http://en.wikipedia.org/wiki/Sputnik-1# Before_the_launch.

Chapter 2. THE EAST COAST

1. Washington Monument. October 27, 2012 from http://en.wikipedia.org/wiki/Washington_ Monument
2. Pickett's Charge at the Battle of Gettysburg. June 20, 2012 from http://the historytrekker.com/travel.photography/mid-atlantic,pickett's_charge_at_the_battle_of_gettysburg.
3. Pickett's Charge. June 20, 2012, from http://en.wikipedia.org/wiki/Pickett's_Charge.
4. Bowery, near Houston St. (n.d.) from http://nymag.com/nymetro/realestate/neighborhoods/maps/10117/.

Chapter 3. AT SEA—THE NORTH ATLANTIC

1. A Day with a New York Harbor Ship Pilot. (n.d.) June 20, 2012, from http://sites-google.com/a/mercantilemarine.org/mercantile-marine/burns-phillip-new/february-news-2/a-day-in-the-life-New York.
2. Seven Man-made Wonders. August 28, 2012, from http://www.bbc.uk/england/sevenwonders/southwest/bishop_rock-mm/index.shtml.
3. Merry England. Oct 27, 2012, from http://en/wikipedia.org/wiki/Merry_England.

Chapter 4. ENGLAND

1. Southampton. August 28, 2012, from http://en.wikipedia.org/wiki/Southampton_England.
2. Rosetta Stone. October 27, 2012, from http://wikipedia.org/wiki/Rosetta_Stone.
3. Magna Carta. October 27, 2012, from http://www.brittanica.com/ebchecked/topic/356831/Magna_Carta.
4. What are the Elgin Marbles? www.britishmuseum.org/explore/highlights/rticless/w/what_are_the_elgin_marbles.aspx.
5. Anglo-Saxon Chronicles. October 27, 2012, from http://en.wikipedia.org/wiki/Anglo-saxon _Chronicle.
6. Bede. October 27, 2012, from http://en.wikipedia.org/wiki/Bede.
7. Taylor & Francis Online. October 27, 2012, from www.tandfonline.com/doilpdf/10.1080/030856950085911967.
8. The Blitz. October 27, 2012, from http://en.wikipedia.org/wiki/The_Blitz.
9. London Bridge. October 27, 2012, from http://en.wikipedia.org/wiki/London_bridge.
10. Great Fire of London. May 9, 20-14, from http://en/wikipedia.org/Great_Fire_of _London
11. Sir Walter Raleigh to Lady Elizabeth Raleigh. October 27, 2012, from http://www.rjg016.com/thoughts/dust/dust.html.
12. The Koh-I-Noor. October 27, 2012, from http://famousdiamond.tripod.com/Koh-I-Noor diamond.html.
13. Tower Bridge in London. October 27, 2012, from http://famous wonders. com/tower-bridge_in_london.
14. Colonel Blimp. October 27, 2012, from http://en.wikipedia/wiki/Colonel_Blimp.

15. Bitter (beer). June 23, 2012, from http://en.wikipedia.org/wiki/Bitter_(beer).
16. Gretna Green. October 27, 2012, from http://en.wikipedia.org/wiki/Gretna_Green.

Chapter 5. SCOTLAND

1. Teddy Boy. Man 31, 2012, from http://en.wikipedia.org/wiki/Teddy_Boy.
2. Scotland Licensing laws. http://en.wikipedia.org/wiki/alcohol_licensing_laws_of_the_United_Kingdom_#licensing_law_in_Scotland.

Chapter 6. IRELAND

1. Oliver Cromwell. October 27, 2012, from http://www.en.wikipedia.org/wiki/Cromwell.
2. Irish Travellers. June 24, 2012, from http://en.wickipedia,.org/wiki/Irish_Travellers.
3. Ibid. Irish Travellers.
4. Queen Maeve's Tomb. June 25, 2012, from http://www.rootsweb.ancestry.com/-irlsli/legend3.html.
5. Dublin. October 27, 2012, from http://en.wikipedia.org/wiki/Dublin.
6. Not a Sheep. October 27, 2012, from http://www.not a sheep may be a goat.blogspot.com/murder-of-Lord_Mount_Batten_end_comments.html.
7. Assassination. October 27, 2012, from http://en.wikipedia.org/wiki/Louis_Mountbatten,_1st_Earl_Mountbatten_of_Burma

Chapter 7. BACK TO SCOTLAND

1. Mons Meg. October 27, 2012, from http://en.wikipedia.org/wiki/mons_meg.
2. Edmund Hillary. October 27, 2012, from http://www./en.wickipedia.org/wiki/Edmund_Hillary.

Chapter 8. A PASS THROUGH ENGLAND AGAIN

1. Holy Trinity Micklegate, York. October 27, 2012, from http://holytrinityyork.org.
2. York Mystery Plays. June 27, 2012, from http://en.wikipedia.org/wiki/york_mystery_plays.
3. The UK Passenger Ship Fleet of 1967. October 26, 2012, from http://www.simplonpcco.uk/GB_Pass_A.html.

Chapter 9. HOLLAND

1. Rotterdam Blitz. October 27, 2012, from http://en.wikipedia.org/wiki/Rotterdam_Blitz.

Chapter 10. BELGIUM

1. Atomium. October 27, 2012, from http://en.wikipedia.org/wiki/Atomium.

Chapter 11. WEST GERMANY

1. Battle of Aachen. June 28, 2012, from http://en.wikipedia.org/wiki/Battle_of_Aachen.

Chapter 12. BELGIUM AGAIN

1. Chicken Life Cycle. September 25, 2012, from http://answers.yahoo.com.
2. Walloon Language. June 28, 2012, from http://en.wikipedia.org;wiki/Walloon_language.

Chapter 13. LUXEMBOURG

1. Luxembourg. June 28, 2012, http://en.wikipedia.org/wiki/Luxembourg.

Chapter 14. PARIS, FRANCE

1. Gargoyles and Chimera. July 3, 2012, from http://www.notredamdeparis.fr/spip.php?article 467.
2. Quartier Pigalle. October 11, 2012, from http://en.wikipedia.org.wiki/Quartier_Pigalle.

Chapter 15. LUXEMBOURG, SAARLAND, AND WEST GERMANY

1. Saarland. July 3, 2012, from http://en.wikipedia.org/wiki/Saarland.

Chapter 17. PRINCIPALITY OF LIECHTENSTEIN AND AUSTRIA

1. Liechtenstein. July 5, 2012, from http://en.wikipedia.org/wiki/Liechtenstein.

Chapter 18. NORTHERN ITALY

1. St Mark's Campanile. July 6, 2012, from http://en.wikipedia.org/wiki/St_Marks_Campanile.

2. Ibid. St. Mark's Campanile.

Chapter 19. YUGOSLAVIA

1. Diocletian's Palace. December 9, 2012, from http://en.wikipedia.org/wiki/Diocletian's_Palace.
2. Yugoslavia. January 6, 2012, from http://en.wikipedia.org/wiki/Yugoslavia.
3. Ibid. Yugoslavia.
4. Yugoslav Front. December 9, 2012, from http://en.wikipedia.org/wiki/Yugoslav_Front.
5. Josip Broz Tito. December 11, 2011, from http://en.wikipedia.org/wiki/Josip_Broz_Tito.
6. Yugoslavia: Pre-Slav History. December 9, 2012, from http://historymedren.about.com/library/text/bltxtyugo2.htm.
7. Flashback to Kosovo's War. December 9, 2012, from http://news.bbc.co.uk/2/hi/europe/5165042.stm.
8. Ibid. Yugoslavia.

Chapter 20. GREECE

1. Retsina. December 11, 2012, from http://en.wikipedia.org/wiki/retsina.
2. Eleusinian Mysteries. December 11, 2012, from http://www.Britannica.com/EBchecked/topic/184459/Eleusinian_mysteries.
3. Ibid. Eleusinian Mysteries.
4. Eleusinian Mysteries. December 11, 2012, from http://en.wikipedia.org/wiki/Eleusinian_Mysteries.
5. Elgin Marbles. December 11, 2012, from http://en/wikipedia.org/wiki/Elgin_Marbles.
6. The Caryatids of the Erechtheion. July 9, 2013, from http://

penelope.uchicago.edu/-grout/encylcopaedia_romana/imperialiafora/augustus/erechtheion.
7. The Trial of Socrates. http://law2.umkc.edu/faculty/projects/ftrials/socrates/socratesacount.html.
8. Corinth Canal. July 19, 2012, from http://en.wikipedia.org/wiki/Corinth_Canal.
9. Greece in the Second World War. July 19, 2012, from http://www.historyof Greece.com/worldwarII.htm.
10. Enver Hoxha. May 2, 2012, from http://en.wikipedia.org.wiki/Enver_Hoxha.
11. Bunkers in Albania. December 11, 2012, from http://en.wikipedia.org/wiki/Bunkers_in_Albania.

Chapter 21. WELCOME TO SOUTHERN ITALY

1. Pompeii. July 27, 2012, from http://en.wikipedia.org/wiki/Pompeii.
2. Erotic Art in Pompeii and Herculaneum. July 27, 2012, from http://en.wikipedia.org/wiki/erotic_art_in_Pompeii_and_Herculaneum.
3. Ancient Pompeii's Society and Social structure. July 27, 2012, from http://www.mariamilani.com/ancient_rome/Ancient_Pompeii%20society.htm.
4. The Trash Crisis in Naples, Italy. July 30, 2012, from http://www.simplified healthinsurance.com/travel/2912/03/15/the-trash-crisis- in-naples-italy.
5. The Camorra Never Sleeps. July 30, 2012, from http://www.vanity.fair.com/culture/2012/05/naples-mob-paolo-di-lauro-italy.
6. Ibid. The Camorra Never Sleeps.
7. Ibid. The Camorra never Seeps.

8. Tannins. October 17, 2012, from http://www.wineanorak.com/tannins.htm.
9. Roman Aqueducts. July 31, 2012, from http://www.unrv.com/culture/roman-aqueducts.php.

Chapter 22. ROME TO VENTIMIGLIA.

1. St. Peter's Basilica. August 2, 2012, from http://en.wikipedia.org/wiki/St._Peter's_Basilica.
2. Famous Relics Associated with Jesus Christ. December 11, 2012, from http://www.smashinglist.com/famous-relics-jesus-christ.
3. What's Inside Rome's Ancient Catacombs? August 3, 2012, from http://science.nationalgeographic.com/science/archaeology/rome-catacombs.
4. The Da Vinci Code. December 11, 2012, from http://en.wikipedia.org/wiki/The_Da_Vinci_Code.
5. The Christian Catacombs of Rome—Symbols. August 3, 2012, from http://www.catacombe.roma.it/en/simbologia.php.
6. The Christian Catacombs of Rome—Origins. August 3, 2012, from http://www.catacombe.roma.it/en.origini.php.

Chapter 23. THE PRINCIPALITY OF MONACO AND RETURN TO FRANCE

1. Monte Carlo. August 5, 2012, from http://en.wikipedia.org/wiki/Monte_Carlo.
2. Vin de Pays des Pyrenees-Orientales Wine. August 5, 2012, from, http://www. wine-searcher.com/regions-vin+de+pays+des+Pyrenees-orientales.

Chapter 25. BALEARIC ISLANDS AND THE MAINLAND

1. Palma, Majorca. December 11, 2012, from http://en.wikipedia.org/wiki/Palma_Majorca.
2. Francisco Franco, biography: August 8, 2012, from http://www.biography.com/people/francisco-franco-9300766.
3. Civil Guard, (Spain). August 8, 2012, from http://en.wikipedia.org/wiki/Civil_Guard_(Spain).
4. Palma de Mallorca Cathedral. October 22, 2012, from http://www.northsouthguides.com/mallorca_cathedral.html.
5. The Windmills of Mallorca. October 22, 2014, from http://www.firstmallorca.com/en/windmills
6. USS Ault (DD-698). February 8, 2012, from http://en.wikipedia.org/wiki/USS Ault_(DD-698).

Chapter 26. GIBRALTAR AND TANGIERS, MOROCCO

1. Gibraltar. May 11, 2012, from http://en.wikipedia.org/wiki/Girbraltar.
2. Pompius Mela. May 11, 2012, from http://www.encyclopedia.com/topicPompius_Mela.aspx.
3. Barbary Macaques in Gibraltar. May 11, 2012, from http://en.wikipedia.org/wiki/Barbary_Macaques_in_Gibraltar.
4. Ibid. Gibraltar.
5. Tangier. December 13, 2012, from http://www.britannica.com/EBchecked/topic/582513/Tangier/259477/History.

Chapter 27. SPAIN AGAIN

1. Battle of Trafalgar. May 11, 2012, from http://en.wikipedia.org/wiki/Battle_of_Trafalgar.

2. Miguel de Cervantes. August 19, 2012, from http://en.wikipedia.org/wiki/Miguel_de_Cervantes.

Chapter 28. PORTUGAL

1. Moped. July 5, 2012, from http://en.wikipedia.org.wiki/Moped.
2. History of Portugal. May 25, 2013, from http://en.wikipedia.org/wiki/History_ of_Portugal.
3. Belem Tower. December 13, 2012, from http://en.wikipedia.org/wiki/Bel%C3% A9m-Tower.
4. Old Cathedral of Coimbra. August 29, 2012, from http://en.wikipedia.org/wiki/Old_Cathedral_of_Coimbra.
5. Viagem em Portugal/Coimbra-Coimbra University. September 2, 2012, from http://www.portugalvacances.com/portuguese/circuit12_b.php.
6. Antonio de Oliveira Salazar. September 2, 2012, from http://en.wikipedia.org/wiki/AntC3%B3nio_de_Oliveira_Salazar.
7. Ibid. Antonio de Oliveira Salazar.
8. Cristo-Rei. December 13, 2012. from http://en.wikipedia.org/wiki/Cristo-Rei.

Chapter 29. AT SEA—MID-ATLANTIC

1. Solera. September 6, 2012, from http://en.wikipedia.org/wiki/Solera.

Chapter 30. VENEZUELA

1. History, The Perez Jimenez Regime. September 8m 2012, from http://www.countriesquest.com/south_america/venezuela/history/the_perez_jimenez_regime.

Chapter 31. CURACAO, NETHERLANDS ANTILLES

1. Papiamento. September 8, 2012, from http://en.wikipedia.org/wiki/Papiamento.
2. Economy of the Netherlands Antilles. December 23, 2012, from http://en.wikipedia.org/wiki/Economy_of_the_Netherlands_Antilles.
3. Dutch Antilles Dissolves as Two New Countries Created. September 9, 2012, from http://www.reuters.com/article/2010/10.10us-caribbean-islands-idUSTRE69913j20101010.
4. Auschwitz Concentration Camp. December 23, 2012, from http://en.wikipedia.org/wiki/Auschwitz_concentration_camp.

Chapter 32. HAVANA, CUBA

1. Barbudos. September 9, 2012. from http://en.wikipedia.org/wiki/Barbudos.
2. January 1959. January 16, 2013, from http://en.wikipedia.org/wiki/January_1959.
3. La Cabana. January 16, 2013, from http://en.wikipedia.org/wiki/La_Cabana.
4. Che Guevara. January 16, 2013, from http://en.wikipedia.org/wiki/Che_Guevara.

Chapter 33. USA

1. Preface to the 4th Edition: (Damon Runyon "The Lemon Drop Kid," 1931, Random House.
2. Hava Nagila. from http://en.wikipedia.org/wiki/Hava Nagila.
3. History of Gasparilla—The Legend. September 13, 2012, from http://gasparillapiratefest.com/history.shtml.

Chapter 34. MEXICO

1. Maxmilian I of Mexico from http://en.wikipedia.org/wiki/Maxmilian_I_of_Mexico.
2. Hernan Cortes from http://en.wikipedia.org/wiki.Hernan_Cortes.
3. The Legend of the Volcanoes Popocatepetl and Iztaccohuatl. July 18, 2014, from File:///C:Users/Owner/AppData/Local/Temp/2UD3JWV5.htm.
3. Aztec Calendar Stone from http://www.aztec-histouy.com/aztec-calendar-stone.html.
4. Zocalo. from http://en.wikipedia.org/wiki/Zocalo.

AFTERWORD

1. Arosa Kulm History from (http://www.swiss-ships.ch/schiffe-ausland/arosa_line/arosa-kulm-HOER/arosa-kulm-HOER-history-en-htm).
2. Portugal's Santa Maria from (http://www.oceancruisenews.com/bm4.htm).